An Exceptional Exceptional Child

Jane Schoenfeld

Copyright © 2013 Jane Schoenfeld. All rights reserved.
ISBN: 978-1-304-13050-1

For Anna and Alan without whom this book could not have been written – with thanks to all the doctors, nurses, therapists, teachers and very good friends who helped make Anna what she is today

Table of Contents

The Beginning	1
The In-Between Months	15
The Full Repair (1988)	20
The Growing Toddler	27
A Tune-Up (1990)	38
Nursery School	42
Yet More Heart Surgery (?) (1991)	47
Back to Nursery School	50
Grades K-2	67
A Brain Tumor (1996)	90
Third Grade	101
Shunt Failure (Winter Break 1996)	104
Back to Third Grade	109
Fourth Grade	113
The Brain Tumor Revisited (1998)	120
Fifth Grade	128
Sixth Grade	137
The Last (we hope) Heart Surgery (2000)	153
Seventh Grade	160
Scoliosis (2001)	169
Eighth Grade	187
Shunt Failure Again (Winter Break 2002)	198

Back to Eighth Grade	208
High School	222
Settling In	223
The Way It Went	228
Medical Situation	228
Therapy and Other Interventions	235
Passions/Obsessions	250
Growing Up	258
The Social Butterfly	271
Academics	286
Anxiety	307
Graduation	326
What Next?	333
Lessons Learned	334
Glossary	350
Cardiology Terms	350
Tuberous Sclerosis Terms	352
General Medical Terms	353
Education Terms	354
Notes	356

A Young Patient

Baby turning blue
Blue like the ocean
Blue like my backpack
Needed surgery
Very scared people
F
Two days
Blalock Taussig shunt
One month, they
Put in another.
At 15 months
The permanent
Repair.
At three, they
Widened
The pulmonary artery.
At nine, they removed
A tumor.
At nine,
A shunt
At ten,
It failed
At eleven,
It failed
At fourteen,
Scoliosis surgery
At fifteen,
My shunt failed again.
For all the surgeries,
They made
Incisions.
Now I will have
No more surgeries.

--Anna Louise Schoenfeld, 10th grade

THE BEGINNING

Late December 1986, one month before Anna was born. I remember a van parked in front of our house, a woman tugging at something heavy inside, and a small wheelchair standing on the sidewalk. The woman emerged holding a boy too old to be carried and gently placed him in the wheelchair. "No," I thought, "that won't happen to me." Although, at 39, I was old for a first-time mother, I was healthy: I walked every day and I watched what I ate. The fear that had briefly shaken my confidence vanished. I fully expected to have a bright, articulate, academically successful child. I got one too, but not quite in the way I expected.

My pregnancy was been uneventful. I had no unusual symptoms, the amniocentesis and the sonograms appeared normal, and I continued to work conscientiously as ever at my university administrative job. It was late at night when the contractions began, so I couldn't sleep. But that didn't stop me: I had a project to finish. I rose early, breathed through the contractions and paced until the project came off the printer. Then I gave in. My labor was long and slow. After more than forty hours without much progress, the doctor recommended Pitocin, which did the trick, an epidural and then an episiotomy. Anna arrived right on time. She was a small, beautiful baby, weighing 6.5 pounds and measuring 19 inches in length, with a full head of shiny brown hair, big brown eyes that eagerly consumed the world, and, because of slightly blue feet, an Apgar score of seven. Many new mothers are ready to go home at that point, but I was not, and I gratefully agreed when my doctor suggested an extra day in the hospital. It was a good thing I did.

Shortly before we were to leave, our pediatrician walked in. She looked worried. "Where's your husband?" she asked. Alan was in the cafeteria, but that didn't stop her – she had something to say. "The baby's oxygen level isn't good," she began. I sat down on the bed. "It could be an infection or it could be cardiac," and then, gazing sadly at me, she continued, "I think it's probably cardiac, so we're going to transport her to Children's Hospital." My stomach churned. What could this mean? Alta Bates was a good hospital, but Anna needed more specialized care than it could provide. She was whisked into an incubator, loaded into an ambulance, and slowly driven away. No sirens, no horns. Just an unearthly silence. We trailed behind in our own car and we wondered.

We had to find out what was going on, so the cardiologist performed a catheterization almost as soon as we arrived. He inserted a catheter into a blood vessel in Anna's groin, guided it into her heart and its arteries, and injected an opaque dye. In this way, he was able to visualize the insides of her heart and arteries and get a clear idea of their structure. We had a conference when he finished. I remember the cardiologist, the social worker, and the nurses, the pillow offered for my sore bottom, and the conference table around which we all sat. No, this was not related to my father's recent heart attack. Yes, this was a congenital heart defect. No, I hadn't done anything wrong. I wasn't too old; it wasn't something I ate or drank; it wasn't my fault. How could it be?

Anna was born with two major heart defects, tetralogy of Fallot and pulmonary atresia. Tetralogy of Fallot is a standard, though complicated, heart defect, which, in Anna's case, included a ventricular septal defect (a large hole between the ventricles), transposition of the major arteries, left pulmonary stenosis (narrowing of the pulmonary artery), and ventricular enlargement. The ventricular septal defect and the transposition of the major arteries meant that oxygen-rich blood went to the lungs without going to the body and that oxygen-poor blood went back to the body without passing through the lungs. The pulmonary stenosis drastically restricted access to her left lung, and the right ventricle had become enlarged because of the extra work required by this anomalous structure. Anna also had another defect, pulmonary atresia, which meant she was missing a large part of the pulmonary artery. She looked fine at birth, except for slightly blue feet, because her body was still using the fetal circulatory system, sending blood through a valve called the patent ductus arteriosus. But the ductus generally closes down within seventy-two hours after birth. When Anna's ductus began to close down and her circulatory system failed to kick in, her oxygen level fell, and she started turning blue. Anna needed major heart surgery; she would not survive without it. As the doctors explained all this, we wondered what would have happened if the delivery had been straightforward and we'd been sent home right away. We were first-time parents with no idea of what a healthy baby looked like. We wondered whether we would have realized that something was drastically wrong and whether we would have gotten our new baby back to the hospital in time. We wondered whether she would have died. We wondered whether she would die now.

Open-heart surgery is a big deal, and, in 1987, it was too big a deal for newborns. So the doctors proposed a temporizing measure: they would implant a Blalock-Taussig shunt, which would establish an alternative route for Anna's blood and thus enable much of it to reach her lungs. The doctors could do the "full repair" when she was older and stronger. Only then would they close the septal defect, effectively (though not actually) reverse the transposed arteries, widen the existing pulmonary artery, and implant a conduit to stand in for the missing section of the pulmonary artery. Anna would be only partially oxygenated until then, but she would grow and develop normally. "Children," they assured us, "have lots of energy. They need it to acquire their large motor skills – to turn over, sit, walk, run and climb. These kids have only slightly less energy than others. They move a little more slowly and, when they get tired, they automatically squat down, which makes it easier for the blood to move through their bodies."

We sat around the conference table. The cardiologist talked and we listened. He was relaxed. He was optimistic. He knew she could be fixed, and we believed him. Less than twenty-four hours later, we were in the parents' waiting room sitting through our first big surgery. We sat numbly. Not understanding. We barely knew we were parents. It felt strange to say the words "our daughter." We knew only that somehow we were tied to this tiny broken being and that this tiny broken being had to be fixed.

Our lives stopped. But the world was still turning, and the business of the university rushed on. I had to let someone know. I had to withdraw from the office maelstrom to deal with my own. I called my boss's assistant. "I won't be in for a while," I said. I nearly choked as I tried to explain: "I had the baby and her heart's all messed up."

The surgery went well, and Anna's father, Alan, began his email saga shortly thereafter. Alan's an academic. Like many modern-day academics, he lives on email. Our friends and relatives needed to know what was going on and we certainly couldn't return all their calls. In fact, I didn't want to return any of them. But, for Alan, communication is key. He also wanted his colleagues to understand why he wasn't getting as much work done as he usually did. So, most days after he got home from visiting Anna, he would type out long detailed email notes, which he would send to anybody who wanted information. People clamored to be on his list and each report was eagerly and fearfully anticipated. On January 13, he sent out this note.

> The main piece of news is Anna. She had surgery today, and everything went very smoothly. For those who know the details, she had a "modified Blalock-Taussig shunt" – surgery that makes a connection between the heart and the pulmonary artery, allowing her blood to be oxygenated. If all goes well in recovery, this "patch" should last about four years or so. It allows her blood system "plumbing" to work, though not at full efficiency. She can grow with it, until she's about 4 or so – at which point her heart will have grown to the point where they can do a second operation, and permanent repair – making the plumbing the way it should be. Laura [a family friend with a Ph.D. in medical sociology] is familiar with the procedures, and is reassuring. She says that it's one of the best worked out neonatal cardiac procedures, that it's got a good track record, and that after the 2nd operation kids are pretty much normal. (After the 1st they tire easily, but there are no serious problems.) So, we're fairly optimistic… but taking life one day at a time. Thanks to friends like Laura giving us information and support, Noreen showing up at the hospital, and others showing up with dinners, we're doing pretty well….

But Alan was putting the best possible face on things, presenting a cheery front to the world. I remember when we first walked into the ICU. There she was, that tiny little thing, spread-eagled on a small, padded table with tubes attached to almost every part of her body. She was intubated because she couldn't breathe on her own, and she had at least four IVs, a couple of drains, wires protruding from her chest in case a pacemaker had to be installed, numerous leads attached to monitors and a bright red light taped to her finger. She was naked, though covered with a light blanket, and half of her abundant brown hair had been shaved for an IV. She lay there under the bright lights of the ICU, temporarily paralyzed to protect all her paraphernalia, in unnatural silence. That was when she got her name. The nurses insisted upon it; they didn't want to take care of Baby Girl Schoenfeld when they could be taking care of someone with a real name, a baby girl named Anna. "How do you want us to pronounce it?" they asked. I thought for a moment. When we named her Anna, we pronounced it the old way, the Russian way: Ahna. But we hadn't dared hope that the unusual pronunciation would stick to the California tongue. These nurses made it stick. And Anna, with her strong sense of self, has made it stick forever.

Alan, ever the scientist, learned to read all the monitors. I did too, but I wasn't as willing to risk a nurse's displeasure by studying the charts and records as intensively as he did. As the nurses got to know us and we learned the language, they began to welcome our interest. Some of them even thought Alan was a doctor. We began to feel that things were more or less under control. We thought there'd be no more surprises since we had the best doctors and we understood what was going on.

As Anna recovered and the shunt began to do its job, tubes were DC'd (discontinued). We celebrated each time a tube was removed, and Alan chronicled Anna's path toward normalcy. First, the ventilator came out; she was breathing on her own with a little extra oxygen on the side. And her "sats" (oxygen blood saturation levels) were good. Then came the pacemaker wires; her heart rhythms were good so she wouldn't need a pacemaker. Then the drains and various IVs.

But no recovery is straightforward. On January 18, Anna had a setback. Alan's email tells it best.

> Like the rest of us, Anna has her ups and downs. We're now back on the up phase after a downer. As of my last message, she was progressing rapidly; we hoped to have her de-tubed in the near future. Unfortunately, she caught a rather severe infection – pus in the incision, probably a staph bug floating around the hospital – and that meant lots of antibiotics, a worsened oxygenation rate, and other complications. Friday and Saturday weren't much fun. But the antibiotics seem to be doing their job, and she looks much better today. Once again, she seems on the mend.

She was all hooked up again, but her recovery continued. On January 24, Alan told this story.

> We have some very good news, and some other news.
>
> Anna has conquered her infection, and her recovery from surgery is now moving along quite well. Today was her best day since being admitted to Children's Hospital. Things were up and down over the past few days, when she was fighting the infection. But

within the past 24 hours she's been weaned from her respirator, and had all of her IV tubes pulled. That means that her "fuel intake" can once again be oral – milk as Mother Nature intended plus daily doses of digoxin (a form of digitalis, to strengthen ventricular function). Best of all, it means that (although she's still attached to a couple of monitors, which make for electronic spaghetti) we can pick her up and hold her. It's been a week since we could do that, and it's wonderful.

The other news is that the data are now in from her blood flow tests. Her shunt (which connects the aorta to the right-hand side of the pulmonary artery) is working well. The right lung, which is near the shunt, is getting a good blood supply; the left lung about half as much. This is good enough to have her come home, get fattened up, grow, and be healthy for a while. But some time during the coming year – anywhere from two to twelve months from now, and her body will tell us when – Anna will have to return to the hospital for a second shunt. That one will be on the left side, to get more blood flow into the left lung. The cardiologist tells us the second operation is easier, with speedier recovery, than the first. Then we wait until she's four or five, when she gets the operation that makes her "plumbing" look like everybody else's.

P.S. I don't care if I am biased; she really is cute.

Once again she was slowly de-tubed, and we celebrated. Monitor leads were kept on until the doctors were sure she was functioning well and only the little red light that monitored her sats or oxygen saturation levels still burned. At last, she was transferred to the "floor," to a regular room with a crib and only one roommate. But there was a hitch. She wasn't doing quite as well as expected. A previous CT scan of her brain had shown a slight anomaly and one cardiologist decided to repeat the scan, to get more information. We waited in the cafeteria, drinking cup after cup of terrible coffee and wondering what this could mean. Having to deal with a heart defect was bad enough. We weren't sure we could handle having a child who also had developmental disabilities. But the radiologist's report was good. There didn't seem to be a problem, and soon she would be going home. Many years later, we wondered what exactly it was that the cardiologist had seen and whether knowing early on what we found out when Anna was older would have changed our lives.

January 28th dawned bright and sunny: Anna was coming home. We gave our dog one last sniff of her tee-shirt so he would know to expect her, anchored our car seat in the car for the second time, and tucked a precious pink outfit into our backpack. If we had been singers, we would have sung all the way to the hospital, but we weren't and so we could only beam. We parked, signed in and went up to her room, but she wasn't there. Where was she? Had she gone for a test? A stroll? Suddenly, a young nurse burst into the room crying. "I'm sorry," she wailed. "I'm so sorry." The cardiologist had been playing with her when she turned deathly pale and was rushed back into the ICU. Well, at least she'd chosen her playmate wisely.

The ICU was humming as usual, Anna was once again all hooked up, and the cardiologist wasn't quite sure what had happened. Either the infection she'd had earlier had flared up again or her pulmonary artery was shutting down under stress. After a course of antibiotics to handle any infection, the doctors decided a second Blalock-Taussig shunt was necessary. As Alan said in his email note,

> One bit of uncertainty has been settled. We knew that she'd need a second shunt some time this coming year. We now know when: Monday. We've probably told you that this operation is less serious than the first: it's a "backup," since her main oxygen system is already in place. Success rates are high; there's more tolerance in terms of blood flow; and there's more "insurance" in that she already has a functional system, and is a month old. Plus, we have every confidence in the medical team.
>
> Standard recovery time is two weeks: a week in ICU followed by a week on the floor. Then we get to take her home, and since she'll have had both operations, we won't have to worry about the possibility of running back to the hospital at some unspecified time during the year.

Monday morning found us once again in the parents' waiting room. The surgery was expected to take four hours, and we were prepared for the wait. We had newspapers, books and more food than anyone could reasonably expect to eat. But we were tired, so tired. We settled ourselves in and took the first call from the operating room: they had made the incision and were just beginning the procedure. An hour and a half later, the phone rang again. They were done! The surgery had gone very well. Here's Alan's report:

> Anna returned to the ICU about 4:45, where she was once again hooked up to all her support apparatus: monitors, IVs, respirator. A complete tech junkie by

now, I could happily read all the monitors, check the report on her blood gases (pH about 7.4, which is where it should be), read off her oxygen saturation levels (in the high 90s and occasionally hitting 100 – bingo!), and all that. All's going well. The O_2 sats (which measure the amount of oxygen getting to the periphery, fingers and toes – that's the test she failed last week, indicating that the second operation was necessary) indicate that she's oxygenating much better; 100's as high as it goes. Switching from tech junkie to speaking as a clinician, I can report simply that she looks better. We could see the color returning to her face over the couple of hours after surgery. Even though she'd been through one hell of an ordeal, by 7 PM she looked better than she had prior to the operation.

Anna's recovery was pretty straightforward after that. She came off the respirator quickly; wires and tubes were removed; and three days later she was moved into an ordinary room. Our schedule remained the same. We had only one car, so Alan would drop me off every weekday in the morning. Then he'd hustle off to work till about 5:00, pick up dinner somewhere so we wouldn't have to eat the hospital food, and sit with Anna and me till 10:00 or 11:00. He and I would then go home for a good night's sleep.

But that wasn't good enough for the nurse cardiologist. She, who'd never had children, wanted us to learn "what it was like to be parents." As if we hadn't been learning all along. Or maybe she wanted us to learn what it was like to be normal parents. At any rate, we modified our schedule at her request and the alternating night watch began. The rooms were set up so that one parent could stay with each child. They had window seats that fit some parents (like me) but not others (like Alan). Taller parents could be accommodated by a foldout chair, which could, if you were bone tired, be surprisingly comfortable. Sheets, pillows and blankets were available, and the staff usually "didn't see" parents using patient bathrooms. What made the accommodations even more comfortable was that, since there'd been a case of chicken pox in the ICU, all kids moved out of the ICU had to be isolated. We settled happily into the isolation suite, a large private room with a double set of doors, which were superb sound insulators. We had privacy, we had quiet, Anna was doing great, AND she didn't get chicken pox.

By February 17, she was doing fine, though she didn't have much energy, and she was a skinny little thing. She weighed in at less than six pounds, almost a pound below her birth weight. To make matters worse, she wasn't eating much. Since the nurses had to measure her intake, I was dutifully pumping milk and feeding it to her in a bottle. I started out with a manual pump but soon realized that was just too difficult. It went much faster when the hospital lent me an electric pump, but I felt like a mechanized cow. And so I sat, several times a day, listening to music and gazing at Anna's first ever picture as I pumped away, cried floods of tears, and told myself how important the breast milk was for Anna. But she wasn't drinking a lot, and the doctors began to worry. They wouldn't let her go home until she'd gained some weight, and she was drinking only 20 cc's or two thirds of an ounce at a time. True, she was working her way up and finally reached the enormous amount of 60 cc's or two ounces. But that still wasn't enough and the doctors began to talk gavage. "Gavage" is what French farmers do to the geese whose livers they're fattening up for *pâté de foie gras*. You take a long thin tube, insert it through the esophagus into the stomach, and pour in the food product. The doctors wanted to train Alan and me in the procedure, and I really tried to learn. But the first mistake made by every novice is inserting the tube into the windpipe, instead of into the esophagus. It's obvious when that mistake has been made because the patient begins to choke. So you pull out the tube and try again. Alan did fine. But this was no job for the squeamish and that was me. After my first attempt, I made a decision: there would be no gavage. I would merely feed Anna little bits of milk as often as possible, even if I had to wake her to do it. And so I did. I set the alarm for two-hour intervals. Our baby didn't wake us up screaming with hunger; I woke her up, but more often than not, I fed her as she slept.

Anna still wasn't gaining weight, but she was strong; her strength showed in her screams. She soon developed a reputation for feistiness, which spread throughout the hospital. Some nurses said you could even hear her in the cafeteria, which was two floors away from her room, and you always knew when there was a phlebotomist around. But the nurses told us not to worry. "It's the feisty ones who survive," they said.

Apparently, we had passed some kind of parenting test as well. On February 26, 1987, one month and sixteen days after Anna was born, the doctors sent us home. Of course, Alan reported the big event.

> I'm pleased to write that Anna Louise is home where she belongs. It's clear she adapts rapidly. Although she's only been here for a few hours, she pees, poops, feeds, and burps just like she did at the hospital! We are looking forward to the pleasures and rigors of normal parenthood. (As I understand it,

some law of conservation applies: as she develops sleep habits, gains weight, and makes sense of the world, I lose sleep, lose weight, and lose what little sense I have left. We'll see.)

This is, I hope, the last Anna update for quite a while. Since she's home and well, there's no need to broadcast ordinary parental gripes and grumbles. We expect the next n days to be a period of mutual adaptation. Depending on how that goes, we'll discover whether she'll be a test case for my theory that children should be living alone, and self-supporting, by the age of 18 (weeks, that is).

THE IN-BETWEEN MONTHS

So Anna came home, and I tried to nurse. Although she nursed well as a newborn, after that, her food came either through a tube or from a bottle. Now, babies know what they like. If they're used to the breast, they won't take the bottle, and if they're used to the bottle, they rarely switch back. I tried to nurse and she screamed; she wouldn't even close her mouth enough to latch on. Following a La Leche League recommendation, I taped a straw to my breast hoping the milk dribbling through it would convince her that "breast fed was best fed," but she was too smart for that. This girl wanted her bottle and wouldn't accept a weak substitute. It took her only a few days to convince me. Meanwhile, I continued to pump, fill bottles, wake her every two hours, and cry. The cardiologist could see that I was exhausted. "Two months worth of breast milk is enough," he said. "You made a valiant effort and you've given her all the immunity she needs. Go buy some formula and let your milk dry up." So much for any of the romantic earth-mother notions I had left.

At almost two months old, Anna was essentially where a newborn would have been. She couldn't hold her head up, she didn't smile and she was welded to her pacifier. Our normal life began. What was not normal was that I continued to wake her for feedings and worried constantly that she would "wake up dead." The cardiologist reassured me, but his reassurances were hard to believe. A six-year-old who'd had a pacemaker installed had just died without warning. Even though her condition was completely different from Anna's, I worried. I wouldn't go back to work and I, who had always been seriously addicted to reading, couldn't concentrate enough to read.

But things did normalize. One of the first things that happened was that Anna found her thumb. That meant she was no longer waking us up by screaming when the pacifier fell out of her mouth; her thumb took its place. Then, when she was four months old, my boss called asking if I would work on some projects at home and I agreed. At this point, I was feeding Anna every three hours. Since I was waking her up only once a night, I was getting a bit more sleep. She was also taking two two-hour naps a day. A new regimen began. When Anna was awake, I was all mommy. Then, as soon she went down for a nap, I would tear over to the computer and work madly until she woke up, when I would tear back to her room. This went on for three months, but it couldn't last. It was too much. When Anna was seven months old, I hired a temporary babysitter and began to work five hours a day, mostly at the office. When Anna was nine months old I hired a new babysitter, Bess, to work six hours a day. Bess stayed with us for exactly three years. She didn't live with us, but she came and went as if she did. With her experience raising a son and her deeply intuitive understanding of children, she taught me how to be a mother. She and some of our very good friends constituted the extended family who helped Anna grow.

And Anna grew. She gained weight, though so slowly that she weighed only ten pounds when she was a year old. We carried her in a front pack because she was so light, but she never snuggled into our chests. Instead, she insisted on facing outwards, her large brown eyes staring almost unblinking at the world around her. When we carried her without the pack, she refused the usual cuddly positions and preferred to be held facing forward, supported down the chest and between the legs by one parental arm. Vocalizations began early. Our best friends would often bring dinner and we'd sit for hours afterward talking while I swung Anna back and forth in my arms. One day, when she was about six months old, she'd obviously had enough. The grown-ups weren't the only ones allowed to talk. She wanted to be heard. As I swung her about, she let loose, and with her loudest non-scream ever, she took center stage and made her first extended speech: "GA, GA, GA, GA, GA."

She was still on center stage at eight months. She would happily open her mouth wide to accept puréed food. She'd grab the spoon as often as we'd let her and spray goo at anyone who came too near as she crammed it into her mouth, and she really wanted to hold her own bottle. It was clear she had a mind of her own. Her sense of humor was also beginning to show. She'd thrust her tongue out in a particularly juicy raspberry when she'd had enough food and she'd giggle. When she got tired of sitting in her chair she would begin to kick loudly and rhythmically, often knocking her plate right out of my hands and spreading the rest of the meal all over the kitchen counter. Socially, she appeared normal. She made eye contact, collapsed in giggles when we imitated her raspberries, and laughed whenever we did.

But major milestones like sitting up, crawling, walking and climbing came slowly. She couldn't sit upright until she was eleven months old. We were at a party for another girl who was just a few weeks older and who was already starting to walk, when I put Anna down on the floor, expecting to provide the usual support. She held the position on her own. At first, she looked around uncertainly, while everyone cheered, but then she beamed. Her gross motor skills were developing slowly because she didn't have the stamina other toddlers had;

she couldn't get up, fall down, and get up quite as often as they could. But she insisted on being active. She wanted to walk at fifteen months, even though she still wasn't crawling, and would grab the nearest furniture, pull herself up to standing and cling to it as she walked. She was happiest when we took her by the hands and walked her over to her dresser where she would rummage among her clothes, to her toy chest where she would stand holding the edge and pulling out toys, or to our night table where she would take careful inventory of its contents.

Anna's fine motor skills appeared to be less delayed, and she seemed to be on target cognitively. She began to brush her teeth, though not very effectively, at fifteen months. She would nest blocks if given them in the right order and sometimes even figure out the shapes in a shape sorter. One of her favorite activities was looking at books. She would turn the pages of *Pat the Bunny*, and, when we asked her to, she would "pat the bunny," "smell the flowers," "feel Daddy's scratchy face," and wave goodbye at the end. She also loved to feed herself; when I put frozen carrots, peas, bits of chicken and toast on her highchair tray, she'd pick them up and put them carefully into her mouth murmuring "umm's" of appreciation. Food she didn't like went on the floor. When she was done, she would pull off her bib, hiding her head in its folds and giggling, and, if I didn't get the message quickly enough, she'd start throwing food. She was also very interactive. She would flirt with Alan, saying "Hi, Daddy," whenever he came into the room, indicate what she wanted to eat by repeating the name of the food ("Do you want some toast," I'd ask. "Tote," she'd reply), and begin to eat whatever food was in front of her when asked if she was going to eat it. She also had a wide range of affirmative noises, and, by the time she was fifteen months old, a vocabulary of 150 words.

We made periodic trips to the hospital where the cardiology clinic monitored Anna's health with blood tests, X-rays, electrocardiograms (ECGs) and echocardiograms (echos). Anna didn't like these tests one bit. She screamed through the ECG; she screamed through the X-ray; and the doctors had to sedate her, so that she would lie still and quiet, to get the necessary echocardiogram readings. Making her fall asleep was nearly impossible. Tiny as she was, the doctors had to triple the dose to get her to close her eyes and she fought sleep even then.

THE FULL REPAIR (1988)

When Anna was a bit more than a year old, we had a cardiology visit that did not go well. The doctor didn't like the color of Anna's lips or her nail beds. Although we hadn't noticed how blue they'd gotten, the change was clear to him and he scheduled a catheterization to find out what was going on. The cath showed that Anna's heart was doing well, that the supporting vessels were holding up, and that she had only one ventricular septal defect (hole between the two ventricles). Unfortunately, it also showed that the left shunt was barely functioning because scar tissue was blocking its access to the subclavian artery and that she had an occlusion in the pulmonary artery. Luckily, she had grown strong enough for surgery.

The question was which surgery. The cardiologist described two options. The surgeon could simply disconnect the two shunts, insert a central shunt, and hold off on the full repair until Anna was stronger. This would increase the number of projected operations to five and delay the point at which she'd be fully oxygenated. Or he could do the full repair. The full repair would normalize her blood flow. It would include a Rastelli procedure, which would close the ventricular septal defect, effectively reverse the transposition of the arteries, excise some of the thickened ventricular muscle, and widen the existing pulmonary artery. An artificial blood vessel would also be inserted to replace the missing section of the pulmonary artery. Before the surgeon could even consider the full repair, however, he would have to reconstruct the occluded pulmonary artery. If the occlusion was large and reconstruction difficult, the full repair would have to be postponed. No one could predict the size of the occlusion. So, when Anna went into the operating room on April 14, 1988, no one knew which procedure would be performed.

Once more, we brought our baby in for testing. This time we both spent the night, and we both endured her howls of hunger. Babies don't understand that eating is not allowed before surgery. Babies don't understand surgery. Anna was wheeled into the operating room at 7:30 AM. We made our way into the parents' waiting room and, with pounding head, I lay down to try to make up some of my lost sleep. Alan, ever the mathematician, reeled off the statistics we'd gotten from the surgeon: "Downside risk on the artery-patch-plus-shunt is relatively low at 5-10%; downside risk on the full repair is 10-20%. These are much better odds than she faced the first time around." He didn't define "downside." And we waited, Alan with a latte in hand, while I could only stare at the foam. Three operations in fifteen months. Could anyone survive that?

It took more than an hour to prep Anna and put all of the IV lines and monitor leads in place. Then the medical team went to work. The surgeon saw that the occlusion in the pulmonary artery was pretty localized, did the necessary reconstruction, and then, since Anna's heart physiology was good, decided to do the full repair. The surgery went very well, as Alan indicated in his first email note.

> Anna was put on the heart-lung machine (on which she remained for 3 hours 10 minutes), and the major reconstruction began. That meant patching the hole between the ventricles, carving away some excess muscle tissue – which had thickened through overuse – angling the wall between the ventricles so that the arteries opened into the proper chambers, and building a connection from the newly self-contained

right ventricle to the pulmonary artery, thus giving the blood for the first time a direct path from heart to lungs. With her shunts disconnected, her aorta and newly self-contained left ventricle do what they're supposed to: the ventricle pumps the fully oxygenated blood returning from the lungs to the whole body via the aorta. In other words, she's somewhat irregularly shaped and with a few used parts, but her plumbing is just like everybody else's – and she'll be fully oxygenated.

After the surgery, Anna was wheeled into the ICU with all the usual paraphernalia. Since she was also fully sedated and temporarily paralyzed to make sure she didn't pull out any of her tubes and since we knew our energy was limited, we went home to sleep. We went back to the ICU early the next morning, and, with one fairly good night's sleep behind us, began our usual hospital routine: we both spent our days at the hospital reading Anna's charts, watching her monitors, and chatting with hospital staff. Then, after dinner, usually brought in by a friend, one of us would leave to go home, take care of the dog and sleep. Alan would also do email. His next email described the course of Anna's recovery.

> As I mentioned in my last report, the idea for the first 2 days was to keep Anna immobile, and let her body recover its strength. She returned from surgery looking better color-wise – the blue was gone – but she was pale as a ghost, since (a) she needed blood, and (b) what blood she did have was devoted to restoring internal organs. The expected course of recovery was:
>
> -She'd pink up a bit.

-She'd run a fever.

-She'd plump up with edema, a consequence of the pounding her capillaries took on the heart/lung machine.

Well, she's been true to form.

Her lips are a much better pink, and her color overall is now pretty good. Pinch your finger and watch it recover its natural color. The time it takes is a measure of your circulatory effectiveness. She'd been pretty slow, but now she recovers her color about as fast as we do.

Over the 1st 36 hours she ran a fever of 38.6 C (that's 101.5 F), but she's down to 37 (or 98.6 F) – flat normal.

She now looks like a little Anna helium balloon – but that will soon change.

For the first 48 hours she was flat out with a combination of muscle relaxants and tranquilizers. They've now stopped the muscle relaxant to let her move around a little bit – this will help with the edema, as will the diuretics – and as she gets stronger the tranqs will be curtailed as well.

The event of greatest importance is a non-event: the 48 hours after surgery are the most critical, so she's past another milestone. (5-7 days is the next, after which it's generally considered that you're home free from the surgery.)

As for the rest, it's a waiting game and a numbers game, watching the minor adjustments indicating she's making progress. Inveterate dial watchers and report readers like us note that her heart rate has gone down from the mid-170's to the mid-140's (that's good), even though the dosage of her dobutamine (which strengthens ventricular function) has been decreased; that her blood pressure has stabilized in the right range; that her PO_2 and oxygen saturation readings have remained high despite the fact that her respirator has been moved down from 40 breaths/minute at 80% oxygen to 28 breaths/minute at 55% oxygen; and so on. The details are meaningful for us, but probably irrelevant for everyone else; the substance is that things are on course, and everything proceeding smoothly. Anna began the first of the series of tube removals today, when her surgical drainage tubes were taken out. As she gets better she'll be weaned off the respirator and the various IV's will be removed.

But no recovery is straightforward. The next day found her depressingly inflated with fluid in her lungs and a slightly elevated temperature. The doctors feared pneumonia, but once they took her off the paralyzing drug, and she was able to more around a bit, she began to get rid of the fluid, and the fever abated.

Recovery then proceeded more smoothly. Since this was Anna's third surgery, we had become experts and could chart her recovery simply by watching for tube removals. She was "digitized": that is, her digoxin, a medicine which strengthens heart function, was given in two doses, rather than continuously, in preparation for home oral administration. Both of her IV heart medicines were DC'd (discontinued) and the associated IV lines removed. The pacemaker wires that had been inserted in case the surgery affected the heart's conductive system were found to be unnecessary and removed. Her tranquilizers were then cut back to prepare her for extubation, when the respirator would be removed and she'd have to breathe on her own. The weaning process began. In weaning, the number of breaths per minute and the percentage of oxygen provided are both gradually decreased until it appears that the patient will be able to breathe on her own. Anna was extubated four days after the surgery. Once extubated, she was able to start getting some real nourishment and the old Anna began to make herself heard. She screamed whenever she saw the respiratory therapist, that nasty lady who banged her on the back to loosen any fluid that might be building up in the lungs. She screamed and thrashed about when she saw the phlebotomist. Blood tests, which had been so easy before since the IV site precluded the need for "sticks," became wrestling matches. She also went back to turning pages on cue when she and Alan read "I'm a little teapot" together. But she didn't talk. This girl, who'd babbled non-stop as an infant and who'd been spouting single words before she went into the hospital, stopped talking completely.

Maybe there'd been an "incident" like a minor stroke during the surgery, maybe the heart-lung machine was somehow responsible, or maybe she was just mad. We'll never know, but we do know that extended periods on the heart-lung machine can affect brain function. The heart-lung machine, which allows a surgeon to stop the heart so that surgical procedures can be performed, is currently essential for many open-heart procedures. It siphons unoxygenated blood from the upper heart chambers, pumps the blood through an oxygenator, and then sends it back into the body bypassing the heart. Unfortunately, it can also cause strokes or trigger inflammation, damaging organs and organ systems. That's why surgeons try to minimize its use. We also know that surgery, anesthesia and pain medication can affect brain function. The question is how long these effects last. Some doctors think that the effects of the anesthetics used for the surgery and for post-operative pain management wear off within a day. Others think that patients don't recover full awareness, mental acuity, or short-term memory for much longer. Some doctors believe the effects of major anesthesia are transient, while others say they are long-term. But all surgeries have unintended side effects. At the very least, according to one of Anna's surgeons, "each surgery knocks off a few IQ points."

Finally, when all Anna's tubes had been removed, she was moved into an ordinary room. The doctors felt that she needed a quiet atmosphere more than continual monitoring. And they were right. For the first time in a week and a half, Alan's silly behavior made her laugh. And she went back to "reading" her favorite books. But she was still psychologically fragile: she had a hard time going to sleep, slept very lightly, and would often startle awake and look around for reassurance. We went home on April 28, only eleven days after we went in.

The Growing Toddler

After the full repair, Anna's personality changed; her sunny disposition turned dark. She became clingy, wouldn't let me out of her sight, and was afraid of other adults. Leaving her with a babysitter, even Bess, was hair raising because she would scream when the babysitter appeared, scream as we left the house, and scream as we drove off in the car. For a time, she would even scream when Alan tried to hold her. Crowds of people were intolerable. We avoided festivals and even the local produce store with its long lines and clanging cash registers. Strangers, frenetic activity, and mechanical or loud noises terrified her because she couldn't filter sensory input and ignore things that didn't matter. She probably felt, as her neuropsychologist later said, like she was at the center of a 3-D movie, like she was being bombarded by objects flying in from all directions and by sounds echoing chaotically. So she closed in upon herself. She clung to her bottle and pacifier with a strange intensity, and, for months, instead of playing with toys and using her whole body to explore the environment, she mainly used her mouth. She chewed on everything, even dog hair and rug fuzz. Although she gradually became more active once again, she continued to put things in her mouth for many years.

She regressed. Her fine motor skills and focus deteriorated; she couldn't turn pages or stack plastic cups as well as she could before the surgery. The 150 words that had constituted her vocabulary disappeared; nouns she'd labeled weeks before no longer had names. It wasn't until a full month later that words started coming back, and they weren't the words she'd known before. But then, after two weeks of ramping up, the verbal onslaught began. She started with nouns. There were fruits of all kinds, some vegetables, medications (called "meds"), animal sounds, animals (our dog was a "buppy"), favored destinations like the "part" (the park), and even a few prepositions, like "up" and "down." At seventeen months, she could name some pictures in books, identify body parts and distinguish between "your hair" and "Daddy's hair." By nineteen months, she could count from one to ten. She loved to "fweel" (swing) and would ask for a "horsie ride" or to go "way up." She would even add "pease" (for please) upon request. She loved her "bobbie" and crawled around the house with it hanging from her lips. But most of the words she'd learned before the surgery didn't reappear until several months later. By August 1988, four months after the surgery, when she was nineteen months old, she was making two and three word combinations. She would say "don't bite me" to the dog, announce "I drop spoon" with a giggle as she was about to do so, and admonish herself "Oh, Anna, be careful." She loved her dolls and insisted on naming each one. The soft hand-made doll, which she received from the hospital's child-life specialist and immediately covered with band-aids, was named Doe-Doe (probably a variation of doll). Another doll became Umm-Umm.

By November 1988, when Anna was 22 months old, her language development seemed to go slightly off course. She was uttering full sentences, but most of these sentences were not original; they were repetitions of things she'd heard other people say. "Don't draw on the wall," she'd say while heading toward the wall with a crayon. "Don't play with the scotch tape," as she twisted it into knots. "Don't play with Daddy's disks," as she grabbed for the floppies. She was two people, one always telling the other what to do or rather, what not to do. By December, at 23 months, she seemed to know the present progressive tense ("she is talking") and was beginning to use the past. But she would often refer to herself as "she" and didn't use the first person possessive, preferring to replace it with her own name as in "Anna's pants." She used questions as statements. If she wanted a glass of milk, for example, she would ask "Does Anna want a glass of milk?" or she'd look at us and say "Does Anna wanna go to the park?" She would reverse her subjects, as if she hadn't quite figured out who the subject was, saying "do you wanna swing?" when she meant "I wanna swing," and she appeared to be merely repeating questions she'd been asked at some point. In a video shot at the age of two years and three months, Alan swings her until he's had enough and the following dialogue ensues.

Anna: Anna's a swinging girl.

Alan: Yes, Anna's a swinging girl, but this is the last time.

Anna: This is the last time. Do you wanna swing, bunny?

[She puts the stuffed bunny in the basket and goes over to the toy garage.]

Anna: You want me to open it?

Alan: [Opens the garage.]

Anna: [Takes out a small plastic car, which she brings over to the basket. But the dog barks, startling her, and she puts the car back in the garage. Then she puts her doll in the basket.]

Anna: Are you ready? [Swings the basket.]

This video highlights her anomalous language usage. The reference to herself as "Anna" lasted through most of preschool, and the phrase, "Anna is a swinging girl," is just one example of a frequently used structure, which was unfortunately reinforced by the adults around her—she was also "a walking girl" and "a jumping girl." The question "You want me to open it?" was intended in her usual way to mean "Would you please open it?"

The video shows her obsession with swinging; when Alan tires of swinging her, she wants to swing the bunny, the car and the doll. Her favorite destination was the park across the street. There, I would push her until my arms ached since she'd refuse to do anything else for more than a few minutes. Her favorite toy was a small plastic swing that she was always taking apart and putting back together, and she would frequently use it to swing smaller objects.

Despite these differences, Anna behaved in many ways like a typical two year old. She would talk to her dolls non-stop, push them in the stroller and pretend to bathe them, putting shampoo on their heads, and rinsing them off with a plastic container. She'd complain, "Wanna give Doe-Doe a *real* bath," and then she would pretend to dry Doe-Doe's hair with a towel. Seeing this, our good friend Sally made a small version of the quilt that she had previously given Anna. She thought Anna would use it to extend her repertoire and put some of her dolls to bed, but she was wrong. Anna dissolved in tears the moment she saw it. We wondered whether she thought we had shrunk the original and showed her we hadn't, but she refused to use it.

She would play interactive games like Peekaboo and repeat "Peekaboo, I see you" as she covered her face with her hands. She would also play a slightly more complex version in which she would pull a blanket off her head or lift the crib bumper so we could see her when we asked where she was. She'd come to us whenever we called, and she wanted to be just like Daddy. Alan often worked at the computer with Anna perched on his lap. One day, as she sat there, looking down at his fingers, she glanced to the right at their reflection in the mirror, saw herself sitting in front of the computer, just like her dad, sat up straight and began to pound the keyboard. "Anna's typing! Anna's typing!" she cried.

Alan and I are readers, and we wanted Anna to be one too. We wanted reading to be one of the joys of her life. So we read to her everyday. One day, when she was nineteen months old, Alan was reading her one of her favorite books, *Chicken Soup with Rice,* and his throat caught. Anna finished the line he was reading. So began a game we played for a long time. "Jack and Jill went up the _____," Alan would say turning the pages of a book, and she would quickly chime in "hill." "To fetch a pail of _____," he'd continue, she'd cry "waya," and she'd finish off the other two lines as well. We read poems like "Mary Had a Little Lamb," "Patty Cake," "Twinkle, Twinkle, Little Star," and books like *Chicken Soup with Rice* and *Goodnight Moon* in this way. By the time Anna was three, she had memorized entire books and managed to convince some of our friends that she knew how to read. But the pictures in the books were another matter. It was never clear that she understood the relationship between them and the reality. To her, the apple in the picture book was not a two-dimensional representation of a real apple. It was something entirely different, and the fact that both objects were called "apple" was merely a curious coincidence. The chicken in the picture book was definitely not the same as the chicken at the Little Farm we visited in Tilden Park; it was two dimensional, differently colored, not fuzzy, and it didn't move.

As the surgery receded into the past, Anna's sunny disposition gradually returned, although her fear of crowds persisted. When she felt comfortable, she would talk non-stop, frequently interspersing babble with lines from nursery rhymes. And she picked up some very bad language. By February 1989, at 25 months, she was telling complete, though formulaic, stories. I recorded the following two in her scrapbook.

The Airplane

We got in the car and we drove to the airport. We got in the airplane and we went up in the sky. Then we got off the airplane.

The Museum

First, we got in the car. Then, we drove to the train station. Then, we went down the stairs and we got on the train. We rode on the train. It was dark in the tunnel. Then we got off the train. We walked up the stairs. We went to the museum and we saw the statues. We saw Giacometti. There was a statue of a man pointing. There was a big woman. There was a statue of a doggie. There was a statue of a man with a big nose.

Both stories were, of course, entirely true.

When she was about two and a quarter, she began to play with words. She made her first joke saying "we walked up the diaper," and she called me "Mommy Mom." Other jokes soon followed: a "diaper" became a "ciaper;" a "shirt" became a "yirt;" and she insisted laughingly that "we went to the rain station and got on the rain." Words themselves could make her laugh: "itch," "vacuum," and "violence" brought on gleeful gales. Her sense of mischief also emerged. She would turn off the light when asked, then, amid giggles, turn it on almost immediately.

She loved to move and wouldn't sit still unless constrained by a seat belt. Even when she was constrained, the belt couldn't always hold her. One day, as I pushed her up the street in her stroller, she managed to wriggle out of the seat belt and topple over onto the sidewalk. She landed on her head, and a large blue egg rose on her forehead as I carried her home. Luckily, that was the extent of the damage. Another day, she toppled off the couch and, when her eyes rolled back in her head for a moment, I thought that was the end. But no, the girl was indestructible. Then, when she was seventeen months old, she began to crawl. It was a strange, one-sided crawl in which she used her left knee and her right foot, but, by the age of eighteen months, she moved fast enough to scare the dog. She hadn't learned to crawl before the surgery probably because she hadn't been sufficiently oxygenated.

She could stand supported by one finger at seventeen months and much preferred standing and being walked around to sitting. She walked for the first time "by 'self," as she put it, on August 22, 1988 when she was nineteen months old. The first time she really walked was a full month later. Her babysitter Bess (or "Ba" as Anna called her) was sitting on one of our two living room couches, Alan was on the couch across the room, and I was on a chair against a third wall. Anna pushed herself up off the floor, as she'd been doing for a few weeks, and, at Bess's urging, propelled herself across the room and fell into her arms. Then the game began: "Come on, Anna, come here," I cried and she eagerly pulled herself away from Bess and toddled over to me. Then it was Alan's turn. Back and forth she went among us, with an irrepressible grin spread across her face. This was living. This was ecstasy. Things couldn't get any better. It was five months after the full repair, she was fully oxygenated, and she finally had enough stamina to walk like the grown-ups.

Approximately two months later, she was motoring around on her own. She would walk all over the house, bottle dangling, open doors, close doors, and generally get into things. One day, she locked me in the closet, but Alan knew I was there and she let me out as soon as he asked her to. She would push her stroller through the house, crawl up the two steps to our bedroom, and climb onto the couch so that she could look out the window. She would try to get out of her crib and ended up falling so many times that we had to get her a "grown-up bed."

When she was 2 years and 3 months old, she began to take charge of the house. She hated the television, the stereo, and the radio and would turn them off as soon as she heard them. At first, we were at a loss to explain this behavior. But then we remembered. The hospital is full of electronic sounds: IVs beeping, monitors wailing, announcements echoing, and televisions blaring. Televisions were everywhere and bed-ridden children lay for hours with their eyes glued to the set. We couldn't stand the continual noise and found the programs irritating. Although we had to live with the IVs, monitors, and announcements, we could shut off the TVs, and, wherever we were, we did. Anna's TV was undoubtedly the only unused one in the entire hospital. But then, we would leave her bedside for a moment, to use the restroom or get some coffee, and when we returned, the TV was blaring away. Perhaps the nurses didn't realize we were there and thought she needed to hear the sound of the human voice. Perhaps they were trying to make her feel as though she had company. In any case, it was clear that Anna associated electronic sounds with the hospital and wasn't going to let them in the house.

By the time Anna was three, she had it all together and was loving it. She chattered constantly, though her language was often echolalic. She accepted (or rejected) commands using exactly the same words we did. When, in a video, we admonish her not to squash her stuffed pig, she replies echoing our words: "Don't squash Piggy." Responses to questions followed the same pattern. When, in the video, she puts some change down her nightgown, she and Alan have the following exchange:

> Alan: Did you put the change down your nightgown?
>
> Anna: Did you put the change down your nightgown?

This response was not simply echolalic, though, because it had communicative intent; it was clear from her giggles and her facial expression that she meant that putting the change down her nightgown was exactly what she was doing. When asked a question that called for a more complex response, she often failed to properly reverse the subject and object pronouns. She and Alan have the following exchange in the video.

> Alan: What am I holding?
>
> Anna: I am holding the camera.

Alan: What am I doing?

Anna: I'm taking a picture of you.

She would repeat herself endlessly and did not always respond verbally to direct questions, though she would often respond to requests by doing what was requested. She also had an atypical, strangely staccato–yet melodic–intonation, and her pronunciation was generally quite clear.

Anna seemed to be delayed in her social development too. She didn't play with other children, even in parallel, but she did seem to empathize with them when they cried. She would stop whatever she was doing, stare sadly at the child, and sometimes, even walk over. One day, she went even further: walking over to a crying boy, she placed one hand on his chest and the other on his back. She then stood quite still looking sadly at him. It was as if she had located his grief in the place where she had been hurt the most.

In other ways, Anna seemed to be developing normally. She still enjoyed playing with words and continued to make jokes. "It's not a hossil," she would say over and over; "it's a fossil." She loved to make rhythmic noises: she'd play with coins, throwing them into piles and laughing at the sounds they made, and she'd whoop repeatedly into the microphone of her tape recorder glorying in the sounds of her amplified voice. She toilet trained herself with almost no intervention on our part, kept dry at night, and would independently follow the entire bathroom routine: pushing the stool over to the toilet, climbing up, doing her business, climbing down, pushing the stool over to the sink, climbing up and washing her hands. She was a bundle of energy, jumping and wriggling, but she knew that she had to sit quietly when Alan put her "way up" on top of the bookcase. She could put molded puzzles together and loved her alphabet puzzle, which had a cut-out space, or "bed" as she called it, for each letter. She could even name some of the letters, and she knew some of the colors.

Anna spent the first part of her third year working on gross motor skills. Her obsession with swinging intensified. By the time she was three and half, she could climb onto a regular swing, stand on it, and twist it around while lying on her tummy. She could also climb into a baby swing and balance one foot in, one foot out while waiting for the swing to stop moving so she could get in properly. She could spin the merry-go-round and hang swinging from its bars. Through all this, she remained joyous and interactive, following commands even those as complex as "don't get off until the swing slows down," and "can you turn around and get into the swing the other way." But her language development seemed stalled and her pronominal confusion persisted. In a video taken at that time, she telegraphs her intention to make the swing go sideways even as she is still on the merry-go-round. She waits for the merry-go-round to slow down while intoning "she was going side to side." Then, when it stops, she gets off, hops on the swing, and begins to make it go sideways, saying "she was going side to side" all the while.

A TUNE-UP (1990)

After the big fix in 1988, Anna visited the cardiology clinic for periodic check-ups. The routine was straightforward. Before seeing the cardiologist Anna would get an X-ray, an ECG, and an echocardiogram. These tests, along with clinical observations and a "listen," allowed the cardiologist to monitor her progress.

Over the two years following Anna's major heart repair, it became clear that there were still problems. The echocardiograms didn't indicate any blood flow to the left lung. This wasn't a great surprise, for we had known that the left pulmonary artery was so poorly developed that it had very little capacity. We'd hoped that blood flow would make the artery grow, but it didn't. Of greater concern was the right-hand side, Anna's "good" side. The echocardiograms showed that blood flow to the right lung was only about 60% of what it should have been and that her heart was working very hard to pump blood to her body. That meant that something – perhaps scar tissue, a clot, or failure of the artery to grow – was impeding blood flow.

The cardiologist needed more information but was reluctant to do a catheterization because it was invasive and Anna had already been through so much. Instead, he wanted to send us to UC San Francisco for a cardiac MRI and he wanted that MRI read by a specialist he called "the father of cardiac MRIs." Although he knew our insurance company would object, he was resolute. "I'll tell them the only alternative is a cath," he said. "That'd cost another $8,000, so it should convince them." A cardiac MRI, which produces beautifully detailed 3-D pictures of internal organs, provides more information than any other non-invasive test. It requires the patient to lie absolutely still inside a narrow closed tube for (in this case) more than an hour, something no three-year-old kid is going to do willingly. The day that Anna went for the MRI was no fun. There were long waits. The sedative Anna was given was injected into a leg muscle, and the shot was painful. It took a long time to take effect, and Anna was very unhappy until she finally succumbed to the anesthetic; she was also uncomfortable for some time afterwards. But by the time evening rolled around, she was asking to "be an upside down swinging girl" and Alan could only ignore his tiredness and oblige. The MRI indicated there were obstructions impeding blood flow to both lungs, although more blood was flowing through the right pulmonary artery than through the left, and that both arteries needed to be widened. A catheterization that was performed shortly thereafter confirmed that diagnosis, and surgery was scheduled for August 8, 1990.

The next two weeks flew by, with all of us trying to follow our normal schedule. Anna, of course, had no idea of what was coming up. Alan typed madly on his computer trying to clean off his desk in time for our "brief vacation." I went to work, as usual, trying to pretend that life had not changed, and Bess, our part-time babysitter, mooned around the house every day even after I'd come home.

On August 7, we trudged over to the hospital for testing and an essentially sleepless night. The floor of the Monitored Care Unit, where we laid our foam pads, was not the best place to sleep. The beeping IVs, the bright lights, the chattering nurses, our bouncing daughter, and our own anxieties kept us going until late into the night.

The next morning, we kissed Anna good-bye, and she confidently marched into the surgical suite holding the hand of her old friend the anesthesiologist. Once more, we headed to the parents' waiting room and lay down on the couches not knowing how long a day this would be. It turned out to be one of the shorter ones. The doctors found that the conduit filling in for the missing part of the pulmonary artery was open and fully functional, so nothing had to be done there, but blood flow through the right and left-hand branches was insufficient and the left pulmonary artery was still too small to send much blood to the left lung. They decided to widen and patch both branches in hopes that the resulting increased blood flow would stimulate growth, especially in the left-hand branch. The entire procedure took less than three hours. As soon as we got the surgeon's report, we high-tailed it over the ICU where we watched the team wheel her in and hook her up to all her appliances.

Anna's first day post-op was pretty slow, since she had a lot of residual anesthetic in her system and was in considerable pain from the surgery. But she wasn't too logy to be angry and was she ever! She was especially angry because the respirator made it impossible to talk and, for her, talking is like breathing. The respirator was gone by evening, though, and she could make her displeasure clear. "Wanna go home," she yelled over and over. The doctors could only smile. Three days after the surgery, she was her old sweet (and loud) self, many of the tubes had come out, she had taken a few halting steps and, she was ready to move to a less closely monitored room. Six days later, we were home. After checking out the house, having a long conversation with the dog, who was thrilled to see us all, Anna climbed into bed and announced in a tired voice, "It's a nice bed." Indeed it was.

Everyone agreed that her recovery was spectacular, but there were still reasons for concern. She had a pneumothorax, an accumulation of air in the lung cavity, which had shrunk but not disappeared, and a blood perfusion test showed less circulation to the left lung than the cardiologist would have liked. But five weeks later, she was fully healed and ready to "be an upside-down swinging girl" once again. She was ready to move on to the next phase: at 3.9 years old, she was headed for Dandelion Cooperative Nursery School.

Nursery School

Dandelion accepts kids starting at 2.9 years of age. But at 2.9 years, Anna wasn't ready for school, even two mornings a week. She was now 3.9 years old, so we decided to take the plunge. She appeared much younger than her chronological age. She didn't relate to other children. Her attention span was minuscule: she rarely sat still or focused on any one activity for very long, unless an adult was holding her. She didn't play with many of her toys or even seem to care about them. When I bought her a wooden dollhouse, she ignored it except to randomly pile in the furniture. She was willing to abandon her fancy pink tricycle a few blocks from our house when she grew tired of riding. Her language was still different from other children's. Although her vocabulary was large, she seemed to have difficulty determining the subjects of her sentences and rarely used the word "I." She had several very loud tantrums every day. When she got hurt, even if it was only a small "owie," she would take to her bed screaming and push away anyone who tried to comfort her. Alan and I soon learned that touching her when she was hurt would only make her scream louder, and we began to keep our distance. One day after she fell flat on her face, another mother stared at me in horror as I stood there letting her scream.

On the first day of nursery school, I was prepared for separation anxiety. My child development books said that the introduction to school could be traumatic. I took a week off from work expecting to bring Anna in and gradually extricate myself. I stayed only an hour. Anna didn't need me; she was used to being abandoned—abandoned to hospitals, abandoned to surgery, on her own with no one to defend her. I, however, was at loose ends.

Accustomed to thinking about her, worrying about her, night and day, I didn't know what to do with myself. So I went grocery shopping!

Since Dandelion required parent participation, I spent one morning in ten there leading activities and helping with snack. During the first year, Anna acted just like she did at home. On cold days, she would go to school, take off all her clothes and sit in front of the heater. She loved the feeling of the hot air blowing on her naked body and saw no reason to deprive herself of that sensation. Her conversations consisted of questions she'd heard elsewhere, and she repeated herself constantly. During activity time, she wandered from one thing to another barely stopping to even start a project. She would arrive at a table where the other kids were painting, sit down, and watch the supervising adult set her up with paper and paints. She would even take the first steps dipping her brush in the paint and applying it to the paper, but then she would take off. The teachers tried very hard, as did the participating parents, but no one could get her to focus on any one thing, except the heater, for very long.

Part of the reason focusing was so difficult was that Anna was constantly trying to keep track of everything; she had no way of filtering out irrelevancies. A teacher described her behavior during story-time. Anna would sit among the children, rarely looking at the teacher, and constantly turning – left, right and all the way around. Although she didn't seem to be paying attention, she could always answer a few of the questions posed by the teacher. She could also tell you that one child had just leaned over and whispered something to his neighbor and that another had just picked up a pencil from the floor. We wondered how much of this hyperawareness stemmed from anxiety and the need to guard against surprises and how much was neurologically based.

But then, despite her continuing hyperawareness, she started to branch out. She found a toy that she really liked – a small version of the merry-go-round she used in the park, which held only one child – and she spun obsessively. When she wasn't spinning, she was watching the other children, especially those who were crying. She was very active, would watch fascinated as the other kids climbed on the dome or in the tree, and then she would try, with adult help, to do it herself. "Anna's trying to do it," she'd exclaim. She also learned to how to smell. Until well after her fourth birthday, she thought smelling meant blowing her breath out through her nose, and no explanation or exaggerated inhalation could convince her otherwise. But then it clicked and she was astounded. A completely new world had opened up to her; walks became smelling sprees and flowers, aromatic intoxicants. When we later wondered at the intensity of her response, a neuropsychologist noted that smells are based in the limbic system and form the earliest memories. Since Anna's earliest memories were so painful, she might have blocked her sense of smell to avoid them.

Despite these signs of progress, I always came home depressed after participating at Dandelion. The other kids were doing projects. The other kids were playing games. The other kids were learning to draw and even starting to form letters. The other kids were telling long, complicated stories. And the other kids were making friends. Anna was just wandering around doing nothing, interacting with no one except the adults who held her still. She rarely looked anyone in the eye and she didn't like hugs. And she would do some very unusual things. One day, when I was chatting with another mother at the end of the school day, Anna disappeared. We frantically combed the school premises, but one of the teachers had a different idea. She ran out the door towards our house and found Anna heading down a major street after having already crossed another. Horns were honking. People had stopped in their tracks, and drivers on the first major street she had crossed were sitting shaking their heads. At least she'd been going in the right direction. Another day, I walked into the kitchen. There, I saw her balanced giggling on the windowsill – stark naked with the window wide open. Luckily, she had good balance.

Anna also developed a number of obsessions, some of which lasted well into elementary school. The first was band-aids; she had to have several whenever she got hurt, no matter how slight the injury, and a band-aid could often stop her tears. She couldn't stand to get her hands dirty – whether with mud, paint, or magic marker – and when she did, even if it was only a single mark, she would scrub them until they were completely clean. And face painting terrified her. There were more positive obsessions too, obsessions that seemed to make her happy: swinging, which preceded her Dandelion years, and water fountains. She adored water fountains, would stand staring at the decorative ones, and would insist on drinking from every bubbler and water cooler she saw. Most of the time, we could accommodate this obsession, but there was hell to pay when we couldn't. A visit to the cardiology clinic became much more difficult when sedation was scheduled because she was not allowed to drink, and running to catch a plane was nearly impossible because of all the water fountains we passed.

By the middle of Anna's first year at Dandelion, I'd stopped reading child development books. They depressed me almost as much as my participation days. Although Anna was making a number of the developmental strides they described, she was making them at different times and in qualitatively different ways. Her language development was atypical, her fine motor skills poor, her attention span minimal, her imaginative play limited, and she wasn't progressing socially. But since Anna was our only child, we knew little about child development, and cardiologists had not yet established any links between developmental delays and cardiac anomalies. So we didn't realize how different she really was. We didn't want to either. At a support group meeting for parents of cardiac kids, when some of the parents described their children's learning differences, I vigorously denied that Anna had any.

Yet More Heart Surgery? (1991)

After the 1990 repair, we had settled back into the routine of periodic check-ups at the cardiology clinic. Every few months the doctors would monitor Anna's progress, using some combination of X-rays, ECGs, echocardiograms, and clinical observations. Anna's right lung and the pathway to it were in good shape. The 1990 operation had cleared the route from the conduit to the right pulmonary artery, and blood flow seemed good. Blood flow to the left, however, had never been good despite efforts made in 1988 and 1990 to widen the left pulmonary artery, increase blood flow and stimulate growth.

The cardiologist wanted to find out how much blood was actually flowing through the left pulmonary artery. So he scheduled a perfusion scan in which a small amount of radioactive dye is injected into the blood stream. If the whole system is working well, traces of the dye appear in both pulmonary arteries and both lungs. There are no traces where there's no circulation, and only some where the circulation is impeded. Unfortunately, this test requires an IV, and Anna, with her tiny veins, was a "tough stick." The first attempt to insert the needle failed. Anna began to cry. The second attempt only made her scream. By the third attempt, she was hysterical, her arms and legs flailing, so they brought in two strong men to hold her down. Tears burned my eyes as the fourth and fifth sticks missed their mark. We were ready to stop. But then the hospital's best phlebotomist came to the rescue, and the procedure began.

The scan showed that there was virtually no blood flowing to the left lung. Even though Anna was doing well, the doctors would have preferred to see some blood flow for a number of reasons. First of all, the second lung serves as backup in cases of pneumonia or a collapsed lung. In addition, two functioning pulmonary arteries balance the circulatory system and help make sure the heart muscle pumps efficiently. With only one pulmonary artery open, the heart works harder and could wear itself out faster. We were afraid that it was time for surgery #5.

Since the doctors had been unsuccessful in their attempts to open the left pulmonary artery, this time, they were hoping to create a new pathway to Anna's left lung by replacing a portion of the artery with Gore-Tex tubing. The tubing wouldn't grow and would have to be replaced when Anna was bigger. But they wouldn't be able to do this unless the left pulmonary artery had a section large enough to serve as a base. They decided to do a catheterization to find out what they could before the surgery.

The cath was performed on April 26, 1991, and the cardiologist found that the pressures in Anna's heart chambers were excellent: they were, in fact, about what they'd be if she had two functioning lungs! The right pulmonary artery was wide open, and the right lung was functioning well. This explained why she had enough energy to run circles around us. The left lung, however, was not functioning, probably because the entire left pulmonary artery was too narrow, and since there appeared to be no section wide enough to anchor a patch, a successful surgical intervention seemed unlikely. A few weeks later, Anna had an MRI, which confirmed this diagnosis. But the cardiologist still wanted to try. Ever the optimist, he thought there was a chance the surgeon could open the left pulmonary artery enough to allow some blood flow to the left lung. "How great a chance?" Alan asked. Anna was doing well, and we weren't convinced that another major intervention was worth the toll it would take. He continued to press the cardiologist; he acknowledged the importance of having two functional lungs, but he made it clear that another surgery would have a serious psychological impact. And what if the surgery was unsuccessful? The cardiologist backed off. He agreed that four operations in four years was enough, and he assured us that Anna could do quite well on just one lung. "After all," he said, "tuberculosis treatment used to involve lung resections." "And, if we wait," he added, "heart-lung transplants could become the norm." There would be no surgery, and Anna would get the break she needed to live a normal life.

BACK TO николаNURSERY SCHOOL

Our lives really were becoming more normal, and we had established routines that worked. The mornings were Alan's responsibility; I got up early and headed off to work, while Alan woke Anna, gave her breakfast, and took her to school. Since I worked only part-time, I would pick her up at 2:00 and we'd spend the afternoons together doing errands, playing games, and walking the dog. Although she wasn't ready to read, she loved to listen to stories, and we spent many an hour reading and re-reading stories like *Good Dog Carl.* Then it was dinnertime. Alan and I both love to cook. But since cooking everyday can be a drag, we have always alternated – very strictly. So it was that the days Alan cooked, he would play games with Anna or read to her while I cleaned up, and on the days I cooked, it was the reverse. Anna thrived. But she wanted more. She saw how much we loved to cook, and she wanted to cook too. So I pulled a stool up to the counter and together, we sifted flour, broke eggs, stirred in sugar and chocolate chips and made her favorite – chocolate chip cookies. Her favorite dinner food was pasta, which Alan often made from scratch using a food processor to mix the dough and a hand-cranked pasta machine to roll it out and cut it. Anna was right there with him and soon she was rolling and cutting the pasta like an expert.

But preschool wasn't going quite as well. At the end of her first year of preschool, two months after the traumatic lung perfusion scan, the teachers approached me. Something was wrong: Anna was too different from the other children. As older parents of an only child, we had no idea how different she really was. We had to look into it, the teachers said; we had to take her in for an assessment. Alan and I were devastated. We could deal with multiple surgeries. We could put our heads down and charge through health problems as long as they could be fixed. But how could we, with our high-level, academic expectations, deal with a child who was not developing the way she should?

On July 9, 1991, we took Anna to the Child Development Center at Oakland's Children's Hospital. The report we received summarized the doctors' findings.

> Anna is an appealing 4 year 6 month old child with complex congenital heart disease necessitating surgical intervention.... In this testing, Anna presented as a likable, highly distractible and often perseverative youngster. Developmental assessment, at this time, suggests that Anna's nonverbal problem skills are consistent with that of a 3 to 3-1/2 year old child. One word expressive language abilities are somewhat less developed and at approximately the 2.11 year level.[1]

The doctors recommended play therapy and provided a list of neuropsychologists who specialized in chronically ill children. That's how we met Dr. W. She was a straight talking New Yorker and we clicked immediately. Anna started seeing her weekly soon after the assessment and continued to see her, though less frequently, for many years. Dr. W. immediately and permanently corrected some of Anna's anomalous pronunciations like her Bostonian "R" and gradually weeded out the misused interrogative: "Do you wanna swing?" became "I wanna swing," for example. The doctors also recommended a brain MRI, which was not performed. Enough was enough.

Anna was 4.9 when she started her second year at Dandelion, and she continued to develop. Her coordination improved: she could run short distances; jump on a trampoline; speed along on a stationary bike using either one or two feet, even though she was too short to sit on the seat; and climb up onto the climbing structure and drop into the sand. "Look at me! Look at me!" she'd cry. But she didn't yet alternate feet as she walked down the stairs, and she did everything slowly and deliberately. Her gross motor skills improved even more as the year progressed. Toward the end of the school year, when she was almost 5 ½, she could climb trees, grunting as she went; slide down a pole; do a summersault on a horizontal bar; and even jump from the daredevil height of four steps.

Her attention span increased slightly, and she was able to sit still long enough to complete simple projects. She became more interactive, started asking adults for help, and would ask "what?" or "where?" when appropriate. But she didn't always respond as we would have liked. In a video shot in November 1991, she found a golf ball and had the following exchange with Alan.

Anna:	That's a ball.
Alan:	It's a golf ball. It's heavy. Don't throw it.
Anna:	[Throws the ball]
Alan:	Anna, you just hit me in the arm with that.
Anna:	That's a ball.

Even though she was almost five years old, she did not yet understand the need for apologies.

Her conversations were also becoming more interactive. But she felt most comfortable when following a script, so she would often slide into one, even when none was appropriate, and she would have difficulty extricating herself. The following conversation took place one day as she was climbing a tree. She was 5.5 years old.

Anna:	[With no preface] My dog is big. How big?
	That big [making the appropriate gesture]
Alan:	[Mishearing her] It's not your dog in the tree? Who's in the tree?
Anna:	[Trying to stay within the script] That big. Me.
Alan:	Oh it's you. OK.
Anna:	[Still trying to stay within the script] That big. [making a tiny gesture]
Alan:	[Accepting her need to stay within the script] How big is Dorcque? (our dog)
Anna:	[Making a more expansive gesture] That big.
Alan:	That's more like it.
Anna:	How big is Tegan's dog? [She tries inappropriately to branch out, not understanding that Alan doesn't know Tegan's dog.]
Alan:	I don't know. How big is Odie's cage?
Anna:	This big. [With an appropriate gesture]

Alan: Yeah, he's got a big cage. What color is it?

Anna: [With a big grin] Blue.

She would repeat things over and over and make random statements. Walking around the park, she would say, "They were fixing the park," which they certainly had been. Other comments were less relevant to what she was doing: "Cinderella" she would blurt while navigating the climbing structure, or "stepsister." Once, when Alan tried to turn those random utterances into a conversation, we were confronted with how literal she really was.

Anna: Did the godmother go to the ball?

Alan: The godmother? What are you talking about? You can get down by yourself, and then, if you want, I'll give you some help on that ladder. Would you like that?

Anna: Yeah.

Alan: OK.

Anna: Where's my stepsister?

Alan: Your stepsister (who doesn't exist)? Cleaning the house, just like Cinderella. Your stepsisters are getting ready for the ball.

Anna: Where's Cinderella? In the house?

Alan: Uh huh. Are you a stepsister?

Anna: I'm not a stepsister.

Alan: Are you Cinderella?

Anna: I'm not Cinderella.

Alan: Who are you?

Anna: [Very clearly] Anna.

We still had to watch her carefully, for she could be gleefully and unstoppably disobedient. Once, when she persisted in vigorously shaking her head from side to side and Alan told her to stop, she kept on, chanting "Daddy told Anna to stop and Anna did NOT stop!" When visiting people's houses, she would go from room to room, picking up whatever interested her, no matter how inappropriate. One day, she marched into our friends' living room covered with the shaving cream she'd found in the bathroom.

Water play was her favorite activity, and she loved to turn faucets on and off, especially in the doctor's office. We put in a garden that year, she watered it faithfully, though none too gently, and would often fling the hose about gleefully watering everything in sight. She loved to play with bubbles and was adept at controlling their size whether by blowing or by waving about any one of a number of wands. And she was fascinated with the tide pool at the aquarium.

At school, she was very interested in what the other children were doing. She would crowd in upon them as she tried to see, but when asked if she would like to participate, she'd be very slow to answer. On pajama day at Dandelion, she watched as the other children cooked scrambled eggs, and the following dialogue ensued:

Teacher: Do you like scrambled eggs?

Anna: Are you gonna have?

Teacher: Are you gonna have scrambled eggs too?

Anna: Yeah.

Later, when she had finished eating and a parent asked her how her breakfast had been, Anna looked like she hadn't heard. She merely got up, left the table, and, unlike the other kids, had to be reminded to put her plate in the trash. She was, however, beginning to imitate some of the other children's games, putting on a tutu and dancing around or sorting through the plastic fruit, although she usually did it alone and for only a short time. Her imaginative play was becoming somewhat more elaborate, but it was still rigid and ritualistic, and it almost always centered around hospital and doctor visits. And, story time was still hard for her; she found it difficult to sit in a circle with other children and focus on the storyteller, so the teachers kept her in the group with the youngest children.

The problems she was having during story time stemmed from hyperawareness and her consequent lack of focus rather than from lack of interest. In fact, she loved stories so much that she began to tell some of her own. This story, which she dictated to me in April 1992, shows her preoccupation with rain, her tendency to repeat herself, and her growing desire for independence. The story's narration circles back on itself, muddying the actual sequence of events and suggesting that Anna did not, as yet, have a clear understanding of linearity. Betsy was her doll.

A Walk in the Rain by Ourselves

I'm going to take Betsy out in the rain, and we're going to wait for the green light and zup around the block. We're going to do that. We're going to wait first. Then we're going to wait and go past Dustin's by ourselves. We're going to go out the door. That's right. And I'm going to open the side door and get in. We're going out there to walk Bets.

Although her fine motor skills were poor, she was also interested in letter production and spelling. She would sit at the computer with the font turned up very large and type our license plate number, repeating "I typed my license plate," over and over. She would type "MOM," "DAD," all of our names, our dog's name, and her grandparents' names.

Anna was assessed by the school district at the age of 5 and a half. The psychologist observed that she "was good natured and cooperative throughout" the testing session, but that she "had a difficult time focusing and attending to structured tasks for a period of time."[2] She also noted Anna's reliance on questions as a primary form of communication and her tendency to ask and repeat questions to which she clearly knew the answer. She characterized Anna's play as rigid and ritualistic and noted Anna's difficulties with prepositions ("between" was a particularly difficult concept) and storytelling. She noted that the fine motor skills needed for grasping objects, fitting things together, and drawing were delayed, that Anna's pictures were rudimentary, and that Anna was clearly not ready to write. She also found Anna's general knowledge and comprehension scores scattered. Although Dr. W., Alan and I agreed with the general picture drawn by the psychologist, we felt that Anna's distractibility and the psychologist's inability to really connect with Anna inaccurately skewed the results of the testing. In addition, the psychologist had concluded the evaluation predictively, saying that the scores should be "viewed as approximates of her 'true' ability." We consequently wrote a letter to the assessors, part of which is excerpted here.

> What we want to stress are some themes that emerged consistently in our conversation about the draft report. As Lois noted in our conversation, Anna doesn't fit any of the standard profiles: her test scores are all over the map, defying simple classification. Some times during the formal or informal interactions Anna seemed to be performing at high levels; other times she was distracted and unfocused, and seemed to be performing at fairly low levels. Much of this was reflected in the test scores, which varied widely. After meeting with Dr. W. we have a much clearer understanding of the tests, what they reveal, and what they may be incapable of revealing at this point.
>
> As noted, Anna's skills and performance vary widely – for some specific reasons. Anyone who spends extensive time with her comes to see that what she knows, and what she is capable of revealing at any moment, can be very different. Although Anna is improving in this regard, she often lacks focus and is very easily distracted; if she is not attending at the moment she can seem unresponsive and/or cryptic. (Later on she may surprise you by mentioning things you didn't think she could have noticed at all.) In particular, as a legacy of her hospital experiences, Anna tends to withdraw in situations that she finds threatening, over-stimulating, or over-constraining. At such times what she knows is well hidden – buried under the layers of defenses – and she tests very poorly. That is particularly the case with tests such as the ones administered in the evaluation,

many of which have as a precondition the child's continued focus on the assessment task. Her very uneven performance is no surprise.

The reason this matters is that, when she is not attending, the test does not at all give an accurate assessment of what she knows or is capable of doing. Hence it is extremely important not to take the test scores as an indicator of potential: they merely indicate what she is capable of revealing, now, under testing circumstances. As we have discussed, Anna's cardiologist (Dr. C.H., head of cardiology at Oakland Children's hospital) says that "cardiac kids" tend to make significant progress during extended periods of health. Anna is in the midst of one, and if she continues healthy, we expect her to continue to make the kinds of significant strides she has been making this year.

The psychologist's report also confirmed Anna's eligibility for some special services, so Anna started receiving speech therapy for language processing, expressive social language, and social skills, and occupational therapy for gross and fine-motor skill deficits while still in preschool.

Although she was a January baby and would have been 5.9 years old when she started kindergarten, we knew she wasn't ready, so we kept her in Dandelion for an extra year. All that time, Anna was listening and watching. She learned to follow instructions, and she began to try playing with the other children. One day, when a few of the girls were dancing to "The Nutcracker Suite," she joined in for a few minutes, walking in circles and waving her hands around like a ballerina. She wasn't dancing to the music, as the other girls were, nor was she following their choreography, but she was clearly trying to participate in the dance. She was becoming more involved in art projects and beginning to accept the inevitability of getting her hands dirty: paint-covered hands became a common occurrence. And she was becoming much more interactive. Although I initiated and structured most of her play dates, she independently developed a relationship with a younger boy who had some speech delays, was thrilled to go visit him even if it was only to play in parallel, and talked about him a great deal. A video shot during the last quarter of her third year at Dandelion, when she was 6.2 years old, shows how much more interactive she had become and how her dirty-hand phobia had faded. The children are sitting around in a circle playing carefully with a small snake and Anna is fully involved. Not only is her attention riveted on the snake, but her contributions add to the discussion, and she makes frequent eye contact with the teacher. She rarely replies to the teacher's comments however. The scene goes like this.

Anna: I have a rubber snake.

Teacher: I didn't know you had a rubber snake. Is he bigger than this one?

Anna: Hold that snake? [Reaches for the snake.] Want the snake.

Teacher: [Hands her the snake.]

Anna: [Watches fascinated as it coils around her wrist.]

Teacher: [Touching Anna's skirt.] He probably loves this skirt, Anna.

Anna: He doesn't like being touched there. [Points to the snake's head and looks up at the teacher inquiringly.]

Teacher: On the head?

Anna: [Nods vigorously.]

Teacher: It's OK. You can touch him on the head.

Teacher: [Noticing that Anna has paint on her hands.] Look at Anna's hands. Anna has purple and blue hands.

Anna: [Giggles briefly while maintaining focus on the snake. Then puts the snake around her neck.]

Teacher: I'll get him so he goes around this way. You're a real snake charmer.

Anna: [Bouncing up and down with excitement, while maintaining her cross-legged posture with the snake dangling around her neck.] I saw a snake at the Academy of Science. [Then looks sideways at the camera.]

Her increased interactivity also enabled her to participate eagerly in storytelling games that used scripts and gestures. In "Who stole the cookie from the cookie jar," for example, she would sit attentively in the circle, clap her hands to the beat along with the other children, say her lines perfectly, and choose another child when it was her turn to do so. She knew that game so well that she would shout out the words and laugh when other children used silly voices. But she still wasn't comfortable listening to a story in a group setting.

Despite that, Anna still loved stories. She would listen eagerly as we read to her at home, and she tried to tell her own stories. This story, dictated in the fall of 1992, calls into question her understanding of story telling, although it does show an increased understanding of narrative linearity. It also indicates her ongoing preoccupation with nakedness (in the story even Dorcque, our dog, took off his clothes), reflects her difficulties with waiting her turn, and highlights her tendency to repeat herself. The use of Alan's name, instead of the more typical "Dad," and the reference to me as "Jane" and "Dorcque's mom" suggest the extent to which she was distancing herself from us at that time. It also shows how interested she was in her fellow students. Cara, Drew, Samantha, Johanna, and Gwen were all classmates.

> I saw an appointment when I didn't know. I saw Care Bears and they gobbled me. Then I went home for another bear to eat me. Happy birthday, my friend Anna, Love Cara. On January 10th. When I saw Johanna and Gwen, then they saw Drew and Samantha walking by behind them. They said, "You can't open the gate, Johanna, but you can try." Then Johanna opened the gate and Gwen said, "You can't open that." Then Johanna said, "Let's fly over the gate." And Gwen said, "yeah." And she did. And Johanna was flying over the gate and Gwen was. Then there was boats. Then Johanna and Gwen were waiting with me and Dorcque. Then Johanna and Gwen were waiting with me and Dorcque. Then Johanna went on a boat ride and the man put her on a boat. Then Johanna went. Then Jane said, "Get behind Gwen." Then Jane went away and Alan went away too. Then I liked them going away. Then Gwen went on a boat ride and the man put her in a boat and

he turned the boat switch and Gwen went. Then I was waiting. Then someone said, "Let's go outside." Then some said, "Get behind Anna, Dorcque" and went away. Then I was going on a boat ride and he put me in the boat and turned the boat switch then I went. Dorcque was waiting and waiting and waiting and waiting because I was going on a boat and I was in the water out of the boat swimming. And I was naked. I took off all my clothes. Then all of the kids were naked. Then Dorcque's mom said, "You have to wait till everybody gets out." Then everybody didn't get out. There are four in the water. Then Alan went away and then there were three so he could go in. And I was in too. And someone said, "Do you want to go in the water with Anna?" And Dorcque said, "yeah," and he took off all his clothes and did. Then he was jumping in and I was jumping in, and I was jumping in, and I was jumping in. And I saw Barney coming. Then Barney went home. Then I saw Barney coming again.

At home, life was complicated by Anna's intense desire to please, hyperawareness and a resulting lack of focus on what was important. One day, I was mowing the lawn with the garage door open. Since the garage led into the house and Alan wasn't home, I didn't want to leave my purse accessible. So I hid it away in the closet. Anna was playing in the back yard adjacent to the garage and had a clear view of the door. When I finished mowing, I forgot that I'd moved my purse and, after searching frantically, concluded that someone had entered the house through the garage and stolen it.

Jane: Did someone go into the garage?

Anna: Yes.

Jane:	[Knowing I couldn't ask her to describe the person, I resorted to multiple choice.] Was it a man or woman?
Anna:	A woman.
Jane:	Was she African American or white?
Anna:	African American.
Jane:	Was it a kid?
Anna:	No, a grown-up.
Jane:	Did you see her carrying my purse when she came out?
Anna:	Yes.
Jane:	Are you sure?
Anna:	Yes.

So I was right, I thought, and promptly went inside to call the DMV, my health insurance company, the airlines and all the credit card companies. I even talked to the police. Only after I'd finished did I find my purse hanging in the closet just where I'd left it. Anna couldn't separate what she thought I wanted to hear from reality.

Anna went to Dandelion for three years but did little else because new activities, with their minefield of unknown rules, made her very anxious. We tried a dance class and didn't make it through the first hour. When she was four years old, I took her to a low-key gymnastics class in which the kids used elementary gym equipment and sang songs. She started to scream immediately and demanded to go home. But this teacher was considerably more savvy than the dance teacher, and she knew what to do. First, she persuaded Anna to stay and watch. That worked.

Then she tried to coax Anna onto the equipment. That was harder, but the teacher was determined. For two whole classes, she carried Anna on her hip until Anna began to feel secure. Then slowly, activity by activity, she integrated Anna into the class. She knew that, for a kid like Anna, new activities required slow, carefully structured introductions.

Travel required the same sort of slow introduction. Anna couldn't fly at first because airplanes are pressurized only to eight thousand feet and her oxygenation level wasn't good enough. This changed after the full repair. We began with a visit to our parents, which went well because Anna was on familiar territory visiting people she loved. Other trips were harder because she could not tolerate the changes they involved. The most difficult was a conference in Quebec that we took her to when she was four; she loved the pool in our hotel and felt comfortable in the hotel room, but she felt very uncomfortable in the unfamiliar territory of the city. I bribed her with swim breaks so she would agree to go sightseeing, but she wouldn't stop screaming as I pushed her around in the stroller, and Alan could often hear us coming, blocks away.

The screaming began even before we left the house two years later while I was making hotel reservations in French. Hearing me speak another language terrified her, even though she loved languages and made up nonsense words by the dozen. But, at the age of six, she was a much better tourist than she had been earlier. When we finally got to France and she understood that speaking another language didn't change who I was, she begged to join in. She wanted to be heard just as she always did. So I provided her with the phrases she needed and, with her excellent French pronunciation and her enthusiasm for *soupe au pistou,* she charmed everyone she met. She was a willing sightseer too; she walked for miles without complaining and, at the Louvre, she jumped off every chair she could find.

GRADES K-2

At the end of Anna's third year at Dandelion, we knew she had to move on. We weren't convinced she was ready, but Anna was 6.9 years old and the Dandelion teachers had done all they could. The question was to where. We didn't want to put her in a special school or even in a special class because she has always learned best from the children around her, and we wanted her to learn typical, rather than atypical, behaviors. So, with the exception of elite academically oriented schools and Catholic schools, I looked at every regular school — public or private — that I could find. The more I saw, the more I realized that private schools did not have the resources to deal with Anna; they wouldn't be able to provide the speech, occupational therapy, or academic support for which she qualified, and, if we chose a private school, it would be difficult to get the school district to step in. In addition, many of the private schools were populated by white upper-class students and lacked the diversity that can breed tolerance of difference.

When I visited the classrooms, I found that public-school classrooms were consistently calmer and more structured than private-school classrooms, and the teachers were generally better. Chaotic classrooms would make it impossible for Anna to function productively. Inadequately trained teachers would not be able to help her grow or make her a real part of the class. I finally zeroed in on Jefferson Elementary School with its strong and supportive principal and a kindergarten teacher who sang her way through routines designed to integrate the children into the life of the school. It didn't hurt that our best friend, Anna's "second mother," taught second grade there. So although we lived directly across the street from another elementary school, we requested an intra-district transfer to Jefferson. Luckily for us, it was granted. The placement couldn't have been better. Anna was there for six years, and each one of her teachers helped her grow in different ways. They all appreciated her enthusiasm and her resilience, they handled her disruptive behaviors with humor and understanding, and they taught her to focus more effectively on her work. Best of all, they created a supportive school community, which Anna took with her to middle school. Her first middle-school teacher was surprised at how accepting the other kids were; they all knew Anna, appreciated her strengths, and tolerated her differences. She was part of the Jefferson-School community, which endured for many years.

Anna loved elementary school. In kindergarten, she was in room 105 along with two other children from Dandelion. But 105 did not stay in school. She and her friend Caitlin played 105 every time they saw each other, and Anna played it with her dolls. For that entire year and several years afterwards, we would frequently hear the 105 songs and the distinctive tones of the kindergarten teacher coming from her room. By the end of that school year, her conversation had become much more natural, partly because of the scripts she picked up in 105, partly because of her increased responsiveness, and partly due to her increased use of interactive words such as "yeah," "OK," and "uh huh." In a video shot in March, she and Alan pretend they're in the classroom.

> Alan: Tell us what you're going to share. Do you have something to share today, Anna?
>
> Anna: Well, yeah. These are my rocks that I found on a walk. [Said in a distinctive,

	sing-song tone often used by children sharing in class]
Alan:	Oh.
Anna:	And when I throw them, sometimes I catch them. Sometimes, they fall on the ground. After that, you have to say the magic words.
Alan:	Can you teach me the magic words?
Anna:	OK. [Claps her hands.] Do it.
Alan:	Claps.
Anna:	No, you have to do it. [Makes a gesture.] Point to me.
Alan:	What are the magic words? Wanna whisper them in my ear so I can say them?
Anna:	Uh huh. [Whispers in his ear.]
Alan:	OK. Would you like to finish sharing?
Anna:	Yeah.
Alan:	What do you have to share?
Anna:	This is my entanglement.
Alan:	What do you do with entanglement?
Anna:	Play with it.
Alan:	Wanna show me how?
Anna:	[Walking around.] I'm looking for a piece to pull.
Alan:	Ohhh. Can you pull it very far?

Anna: I'll try.

Anna then segues into the routine her teacher used for assigning jobs. She knows all the children's names in alphabetical order and the job assigned to each one. For those who don't have a job, she mimics the chant used by the teacher: "You don't have a job, but you will next week." When Alan asks her the teacher's job, she responds jokingly with that same chant. Then, when Alan goes through the class list and inevitably misses a name, she gets very angry, yells "NO" and vehemently makes the necessary correction.

Jefferson emphasized physical activity. The pogo ball introduced by her kindergarten teacher was an instant hit and, when we bought her one for her birthday, it became her favorite toy. When the school participated in a fundraising event for the Heart Association and held a jump-rope assembly, she worked very hard on perfecting her rope jumping skills. Her heart defect receded into the background. In first grade, she worked hard on the rings, determined to swing all the way across. It was almost an obsession, for every recess would find her swinging away. When she got good at it, she stopped and never touched a ring again.

Parent participation had been an intrinsic part of Dandelion's program, and we tried to maintain the tradition at Jefferson. Since my job responsibilities had increased, I could no longer reserve one day a week for the school, so I relegated my participation to occasional field trips and after-school committee work. But Alan had a more flexible work schedule, and partly because he specializes in mathematics education, he thought it would be interesting to help out in the classroom. So every week as Anna went from kindergarten to eighth grade, he spent an hour in her class helping the kids with math. This routine had many advantages. Anna loved having her dad in the classroom; it made her feel more secure and it gave her something special to share with the other kids. It gave us a clearer picture of Anna's classroom performance. It led to deeper relationships with the teachers and made them more willing to give Anna the extra support she needed. And it was fun for Alan. He often said that the hour he spent in Anna's classroom was his favorite part of the week.

Leaving Dandelion also brought other changes. In previous years, Anna had attended Dandelion's summer session, but this year, she was too grown up. Dr. W. suggested Camp Kee Tov, a large temple-affiliated day camp that didn't have a real site, except for the school bus in which it traveled. Every year, the campers played pretty much the same games, took the same trips, and sang the same songs, and of course, Anna became an expert. The sounds of 105 quickly gave way to camp songs with all the gestures. Kee Tov was large and it could be chaotic, but its well established routines were just what Anna needed; she always knew what to expect. She could feel secure because she knew the rules and these rules were not going to change. The counselors were a large group of funny, affectionate, teenagers. They pounced on Anna, carrying her about, and enveloping her with love. There was Dani who demanded real hugs instead of the weak, one-armed variety Anna was prone to giving and who later went on to work in special education. There was Dani's big bear of a brother Adam, who said he'd carry Anna's pack on the backpacking trip and even promised to carry her down the mountain to a doctor if a medical problem developed. Most of these kids came back every summer, so for ten whole summers

Anna got the consistency, acceptance, and affection she needed.

After kindergarten, academics began to play a larger role. Anna had eagerly anticipated homework and did it willingly and carefully at home under my close supervision until about the middle of second grade. She loved the idea of homework – and of giving it. In second grade, she developed and sent a math homework assignment to some of Alan's graduate students, who dutifully completed it and sent it back for a grade. She then happily graded their work. With structure and supervision, she did her work well. But at school, in a class of 30 children, she was not closely supervised and there were too many other things to pay attention to. Just like in story time at Dandelion, she knew everybody's business too well to focus on her own. The other problem was that she didn't always understand exactly what she was supposed to be doing; teachers' oral directions flew by too fast for her to grasp and her reading comprehension was too shaky to rely on. She certainly tried her best, but the work she produced was limited in scope. This became painfully clear to us at Back-to-School Nights, when we saw the reams of paper filled with detailed drawings or the long, complex stories displayed by the other kids. Anna's teachers complained that she finished in-class assignments almost as soon as they were given. They tried everything they could think of to slow her down, but the anxiety that fueled her haste was unrelenting. Anna was frequently too anxious to focus. When she did focus, the work she produced would often center on dying or hospitals. Despite these thematic preferences, her perspective was never maudlin; she was ever optimistic. Under the picture of a goldfish, for example, she wrote the following story: "He is dead swimming. He is just dead. He's gonna come up again from the gravel." She always tried to make her stories funny, and her main strategy, incongruity, as well as her thematic preference is illustrated in this story from second grade.

> One rainy day a dog was going to the dentist to get braces. A dolphin was in the water. The dolphin was drowning. The dog saved him and pulled him out. "Thank you," said the dolphin. The dolphin gave the dog flowers.
>
> The End.

Anna was different from the other children in other ways too. In first grade her attention was everywhere and only sporadically on her own work. She was easily distracted and would loudly refuse transitions or changes in plans or schedules. The school resource specialist recorded the following observations in the middle of Anna's first-grade year.

> Anna was observed briefly in her general education classroom. About one third of the class, including Anna, was doing seatwork while the remainder of the class was reading on the rug with the teacher. When the teacher mentioned that she was about to read a story Anna shouted, "No!" which was ignored by everyone. Anna faced the group on the rug, rather than her desktop, and appeared to be listening while mouthing marking pens. Her attention would shift briefly to her seatwork and then back to the rug group. When Anna noticed me across the room she stood up and asked, "Are you here for me?" When told no she went back to watching the group. When the OT came for Anna's scheduled time Anna

> transitioned quickly and easily from the class. However, when taken for her educational testing Anna would find the non-routine interruption generally not acceptable and would at first say no or refuse to come. When the examiner indicated that the departure was flexible Anna usually came quickly.[3]

She did learn the school routines, though, and by second grade, she fit in somewhat better. The school psychologist recorded these observations in her report.

> During a classroom observation, Anna appeared to be following the class schedule. Initially, she was at the sink mixing paint. She went to the teacher when called upon to get her work corrected, and lined up at the door with other classmates when directed to do so. In line, Anna played with one of her classmate's hair, and appeared to be interacting with this peer without too much difficulty. In the library, Anna was on the floor with her classmates. However, Anna had her head down on the floor versus sitting up like the rest of the class. She did not appear to be paying attention to the story being read. She fidgeted by tapping her teeth with her finger and picking her lip and nose.[4]

Anna saw the world differently, and she represented it differently. She didn't use conventional frames for drawing: a picture of a sunflower, for example, might focus on the bright gold center of the flower, rather than showing the flower as a whole, or a picture of a clown might focus on part of the clown's face or body and be otherwise incomplete. This perspective was most appreciated by the teachers who were themselves artists. But her expression of it was hampered by a need to finish each project as fast as she possibly could and by her significant deficiencies in fine motor skills. Writing was difficult: her handwriting, with its large, uneven, wobbly letters and its frequent letter reversals, was almost illegible. These deficiencies were described in an occupational therapy assessment on February 1, 1993, while Anna was still in preschool.

> Anna also demonstrates delays in writing and drawing skills. She is able to draw vertical and horizontal lines as well as circles, but initially wanted to trace the items. She did not draw angles lines, a cross or a square. She attempted to draw within lines, but could not do so. She is able to cut with scissors, but unable to cut along a line. Her drawing of a person consisted of only five parts and was not recognizable without verbal description from Anna.... Fine motor/perceptual skills are delayed approximately 2-2 ½ years.[5]

By second grade, the occupational therapist could say she had "made significant improvement."

> She is able to oppose each of her fingers and copy hand and finger movement with improved accuracy and efficiency. Anna has demonstrated good bilateral eye hand coordination with lacing and beading activities. She demonstrates a firm grip on her pencil during writing activities. Indeed she does hyperextend the IP joint of her thumb and holds the pencil vertically as opposed to obliquely. She demonstrates good wrist stability and the above tendencies do not affect the fluidity of her writing. . . Anna is able to cut straight lines, zig zags and curves with fairly good accuracy."[6]

But her fine motor skills were still about three years behind those of her peers.

Anna had a phenomenal memory: she could repeat long conversations, word for word. But she had difficulty processing verbal information – questions and directions, for example. They just went by too fast. Someone would ask her a question, she'd automatically answer "no," and then she would provide a more considered response. The "no" was a placeholder while she figured out what the answer should be. We think she was memorizing the questions without understanding them, playing them back until she understood, and only then answering. Her memory also shaped her conversations in other ways. Sometimes when she was asked a question, she'd give an answer that made perfect sense but that didn't quite fit either her experience or the situation. She was appropriating other people's responses to similar questions and could, when we thought to ask, always tell us whom she was imitating. She often sounded just like her teacher, and she picked up quite a few African-American locutions from her classmates. Her memory served as a valuable tool when on-the-spot processing was difficult. Instead of remaining silent while she made sense of a question, searched for the answer, and found a way to put that answer into words, she was able to produce an immediate response that seemed to fit. That was quite a labor saving device, but it made it difficult for others to know what she really thought.

Anna had another conversational labor saving device – scripts. She had certain questions she liked to ask people, especially when she didn't know what else to say. Many of them, like "what are you doing?" would be effective when the answer wasn't clear, but just plain silly when it was. Our friend Sally called the silly questions FDQs or Fairly Dumb Questions, and the moniker became a useful tool that even Anna used to correct herself. Anna loved babies and would always approach a parent to batter him or her with questions: "How old is the baby? What's the baby's name? Is he/she an only child? How many kids do you have? Does he/she have any brothers and sisters? How old are they?" These questions are engaging, especially when asked by a young child; they often got Anna involved in pleasant conversations. But she rarely listened to the answers and the conversations often turned into interrogations. We tried to take advantage of this tendency by teaching her scripts for specific predictable situations and modifying the ones she already had to make them more socially acceptable. Those scripts later served as the basis for more flexible conversations, but she never dropped them completely.

Despite her language-processing difficulties, Anna was unstoppably sociable. She would talk to anyone who struck her fancy, especially if they had children or dogs. When there was no one else to talk to, she'd talk to herself. Throughout elementary school, middle school and much of high school, when Anna lay in bed at night, there would often be two people in the room, not just one. Her imaginary conversational partner would ask her a question and she would answer it: "Anna, is your teacher nice?" she'd ask herself. "Yes," she would answer, "she's very nice." She would recapitulate the events of the day in the course of this dialog. In elementary school, she invented a number of imaginary friends and named them Rifka, Delilah and Violet after her literary heroines. These friends were subjected to multiple medical tests and operations, all of which she duly recorded on her calendar. They also traveled a great deal, just like her father. They stayed with us through middle school and even surfaced occasionally in high school.

Anna's sociability was both hampered and enhanced by an inability to see social cues. In doctors' waiting rooms, she would try to talk with everyone, irrespective of their demeanor. She didn't care if they were trying to read, if they were worried about their appointment, or if they answered her with unfriendly monosyllables. Only a sharp reprimand could discourage her. Sometimes people were annoyed, but most of the time she managed to turn a dreary waiting room into a friendly, supportive community. She brought in the sunshine. Once when she was four, she approached a homeless woman who was wearing a ratty old fur piece and began to stroke the fur. The woman smiled toothlessly. Another time, she asked a tough looking, leather-garbed biker his name. I was surprised to see him look down at her sweetly from his enormous height and answer with a smile. The two of them then had a very gentle conversation and I understood that my prejudice against bikers was at least partly unfounded. When she was about eight, I took her to the park so I could run around the track. Naturally, she had little interest in going round and round with me, so she dropped to the side to swing on some bars. After a short while, I noticed she had disappeared. A man had invited her up into the grove of trees to play Frisbee and she had gone with him! I didn't want to scare her, but I had to make it clear that she was not to do that again.

But her sociability was superficial. She distanced herself from us, calling us "Jane" and "Alan," rather than "mom" and "dad" when she was eight years old. Other people thought that was cute, that she was being independent, but we knew otherwise. She, like other children who have spent long periods of their babyhood in hospitals, was afraid to trust, afraid to love. She thought we hadn't cared enough, that we hadn't been in the hospital with her, perhaps because we'd done nothing to protect her from invasive hospital procedures or perhaps because our albums didn't have many hospital pictures of Alan and me. We had thoroughly documented her hospital stays, filling our albums with pictures of her, her medical apparatus and her nurses, so she believed what she didn't remember. Our presence at the hospital, however, wasn't as verifiable as hers since vanity had made me leave most of our pictures out. But I had not thrown them away, and they came in very useful. Anna and Dr. W. spent many therapeutic hours with these pictures. They looked at them over and over and they talked about them. These pictures helped convince Anna that we had indeed been there in the hospital with her and that we cared. But Anna wasn't the only one whose trust had to be restored. As surgery succeeded surgery with four operations in eight years and the aborted threat of another, Alan and I had to be convinced that Anna was not going to disappear. Of course, we had faith in the doctors and the technology they used, and, intellectually, we knew she'd survive. But we'd been blindsided too many times. Like other parents who had so often come so close to losing their child, we had to overcome our fear that our love would be wasted and our trust betrayed. We had to be convinced that she would live. Once we were, once we truly felt Anna's resilience, we could overcome the fear and love her fully, and we could help teach her to love.

Although Anna was fascinated with other children, she really didn't know how to play with them. Instead, she gravitated toward older women. First grade saw the beginning of a pattern of infatuations that was to last even beyond high school. She focused on Donna, the mother of one of her classmates, a pleasant, low-key woman who often spent her time hanging around in the playground or helping out in class. She clung to Donna, sitting close by in the playground, persistently asking to visit her home, and talking about her non-stop.

But Anna needed friends her own age, so, at Dr. W.'s suggestion, I worked hard to help her find some. I would invite any child who showed the slightest interest in her to our house. I would then have to structure the entire play date because Anna would never really play with the other child: we baked cookies; we played with shaving cream; we blew bubbles – anything to make sure the other child had a good enough time to keep coming back.

As part of this socialization process, when she was eight years old, I insisted on a birthday party. Her last party, held when she turned four, had been difficult; she had felt completely overwhelmed, hidden her face when her guests sang, and ended up falling down the back stairs. Since then, we had always celebrated her birthdays quietly with only adults present. This party was a stellar affair. We held it at the Lawrence Hall of Science in an animal workshop. It was very structured and Anna was in her element. While all the other girls held back, except to pet the furry little chinchilla and the guinea pig, Anna was fearless. She held a dove, a rat, several small snakes and a 20-pound anaconda, which wound itself around her shoulders, and she beamed. She hadn't learned the girlish fear of rats and reptiles; once again, the stereotypes did not apply.

Shortly after that, we invited Anna's newest friend Erika over. Erika was two months younger, but a year ahead in school. We had met her at a kindergarten open house when Anna was still in preschool. Anna remembered that she had had a band-aid on her nose and that she'd asked Erika's grandmother about it. Erika had speech deficits and some coordination issues. This was the first time I felt I didn't (or at least, couldn't) structure the play date. Erika wanted nothing to do with me; she took Anna into her room and closed the door, and they played alone for three hours. Much of their play was parallel, rather than truly interactive, but they were on their own. Erika became Anna's closest, and for about seven years, her only friend.

Anna's other relationships dropped off, although she was always intensely interested in ill children. First, there was Ruby. Ruby had a brain tumor. When Anna was in second grade, the doctors realized that Ruby's tumor was growing and a resection was scheduled to remove the tumor or at least reduce its size. Although Anna barely knew her, she worried the whole time Ruby was gone from school. She was afraid Ruby would die. She constantly asked her teachers for updates on Ruby's condition and even made her a card. Then she saw her at a school performance, wearing a sparkling gold scarf on her bald head. Seeing her from afar was all she could handle. My suggestion to say "hi" was met with a resounding "NO." Shortly after that, we met Rosy. Rosy had cystic fibrosis and often went into the hospital for treatments. Anna always knew when Rosy was in the hospital. She even went to visit her twice, although they were not friends and barely spoke during the visits.

As Anna got older, we tried to push her gently out into the world. We took her to movies, concerts and plays. I took her to her first movie when she was about 7. It was Disney's "Snow White and the Seven Dwarfs." She started to whimper almost immediately. I tried to talk her through it. After half an hour, it became too much. She started to scream, and we had to leave. When she was eight, I took her to see "The Little Princess." Since I was in the play in sixth grade and remembered it vividly, I told her the story in great detail before we went. But that barely helped. I spent the movie explaining what was going on and reassuring her that the princess was going to be fine. Her questions were continual. "Who's that?" "Is she rich yet?" And worst of all: "Is it done yet?" It was painfully clear that she understood very little and that she thought it was really somebody's dreadfully unhappy life unfolding before her eyes. We tried videos because the screen was smaller and the viewing situation, more controllable. She hated "Pollyanna" because the heroine fell out of a tree. She hated "Pippi Longstocking" because Pippi's father left her on her own and, to Anna's great dismay, Pippi played hooky from school. It wasn't until Anna was about 16 and had seen many videos at home that she truly began to enjoy going to movies. And even at the age of 19, the slightest violence in a movie, even a fistfight among children, terrified her.

She found live performances overwhelming and, if she didn't start screaming, would fall asleep. I took her to see a local production of "The Nutcracker" shortly before her seventh birthday. The music was too loud and screechy and she was terrified by the battle scenes, so we left at the first intermission. She was like a different child a year later, though, when her friend Rachel and some other acquaintances were performing. Captivated, she sat forward in her seat devouring the performers with her eyes, shifting around in her seat to get a better view, and intently following the story and the dancing. Tears welled up in my eyes at the change.

By now, we had accepted Anna's differences. We appreciated many of them and tried to deal with the others. But the difference that was the most difficult to deal with, and the most debilitating, was her anxiety. During her elementary-school years, new situations terrified her. In kindergarten, she encountered her first Halloween parade. The children all brought their costumes to school, put them on, and paraded around the schoolyard. I had made her a terrycloth bunny suit, complete with ears, but it was too much: I can still see her standing there all suited up, ears erect, with tears streaming down her face. On field trips she stuck close to the teacher for fear that she would miss something important or even be left behind. Although she was relatively comfortable with classroom structures, field trips were more complex. Anxiety was a natural result of her history; strange adults were always pushing her, prodding her, sticking needles into her, and worse. We, her parents, offered no protection. She had been ripped from the womb and thrown into hospital hell. For all she knew, it could happen again at any moment. And because of her over-sensitivity to stimulation and her fear of the unfamiliar, the world outside of her house, her school, and the wonderful day camp she went to every summer was terrifying. Her anxiety was exacerbated by familial tendencies. Her paternal grandmother had lived a life paralyzed by anxiety; her maternal grandfather obsessively controlled his fears; and tranquility had never been my strong suit. She also realized that the academic and social antes were going up. In third grade her schoolwork was getting more difficult and she was starting to realize how hard it was to make connections with other children. She was beginning to think, if only subconsciously, that she might just not measure up. Her tantrums increased.

At school, she *had* to be first. She couldn't wait on line. She couldn't wait anywhere, especially in doctors' offices, and would often scream loudly even when the waiting time was very short. But it wasn't just her lack of patience that concerned her first-grade teacher; it was her relentless egocentrism. For a long time, in fact, Anna had no theory of mind. She did not realize that other people had thoughts and feelings that were different from her own. She could not put herself into other people's shoes. Although she empathized when someone was hurt and would stare at crying children from afar and although seeing me cry would usually make her scream, she found less extreme situations incomprehensible. Her first-grade teacher told us that the wishes of other children held little meaning for her and that she'd go off on her own rather than accede to them. She couldn't be one minute late or absent for even one day, because she might miss something very important. Learning to take the school bus, which was an hour late the first day, was painful. I took it with her several times, and we assured her that the teachers wouldn't punish her if the bus was late, but the screaming continued. Certain songs sent her through the roof; in first grade, her teacher quickly shut off "Did You Ever See a Lassie" when the screaming began, and, even today, she can't listen to that song. We often wondered if her surgeons had been singing it as they worked.

After-school classes were a bust. I started with an African dance class. Anna's coordination was poor and the loud music and frenetic activity assaulted her senses. I gave up after several breakdowns. Since, however, she has a nice singing voice, I decided to try chorus. That didn't work either. It was as if she'd resolved to get through the school day and nothing more. As Dr. W. said, at the end of the school day, Anna was ready to "take off her girdle." I tried taking her to classes I thought might be therapeutic. A clowning workshop for young children run by a very sensitive and caring teacher sent her screaming from the room because she thought a pratfall was real and couldn't believe the fallen clown wasn't hurt. The one class she was willing to take was swimming, but she feared the water as much as she loved it, and group lessons were useless. She decided to abandon the effort when she got older and discovered she was often the only girl in the class.

Anna's anxiety increased in the last few months of second grade partly because homework was getting more difficult. She was always in such a hurry to get it done and so worried about getting it done right that our sessions would frequently degenerate into shouting matches. But there were other sources of anxiety. Her fear of illness increased. Even suggesting that she might have a tiny cold brought on floods of tears. Alan's frequent business trips got harder for her (and me) to bear, and sometimes only her nightly telephone conversation with him could calm her down. Her dependence on routines increased, and vacations were becoming more difficult again. She would start yelling "let's go" well before it was time and "no talk" when she felt we should be running out the door.

Anna did her best to control her anxiety, and she often succeeded. Her second-grade class performed a play for Chinese New Year. Right before the play, while the other kids jumped, yelled and roughhoused, she sat quietly holding herself together. She held herself together during the play too. Her teacher had paired her with another, very mature child who could help her steady herself, and together, they said their lines. Anna's hands were tightly clenched and her elbows bent at an odd angle, but she did her part perfectly. Then it was time for the dance. Anna ran out with the other kids, drum held high, a confident smile on her face. She could feel the music and play her part. Not just a vague participant, blindly doing the steps, she was really there. True, her timing was a bit off, and she had to monitor the other kids to make sure she was doing the right steps. But she was dancing along with her classmates.

Anna could control her anxiety when she had to, but that was not enough; she had to come up with a way to alleviate it. Routines were the answer, and she clung to them. She insisted that her teachers adhere to their agendas and loudly protested any changes. I had to pick her up from school exactly on time. If I arrived earlier, I couldn't let her see me because she'd get distracted, and if I was late, I could hear the screaming as I ran up the stairs. Every afternoon and weekend or holiday had to be carefully planned or she would get into trouble. She would sit on the sink with the faucet going full blast, spray shaving cream on the bathroom walls, or torture the dog. She would do the same things at other people's houses, not caring what any of us thought of her behavior. She refused to do anything new unless we could describe it in detail before we left: for each expedition, we had to clearly state where we were going, what we were doing, how long we would stay, when we would get home, and what we would do next. As long as things happened according to plan, Anna was fine. But variations could cause tantrums. When Anna was about 8 1/2, a trip to Marine World nearly ended in disaster because she momentarily lost sight of the friends she was with and started screaming. If her anxiety hadn't gotten the better of her, she could have found our friends inside the building from which she had just emerged. Instead, a kind woman thought she was really lost and took her to the Lost and Found at the other end of the park. I disrupted a retirement party by briefly disappearing while she and Alan were getting some Jello. Her screams resounded. These tantrums were exhausting for all of us; they made me feel like I had to tread gingerly, carefully planning out each part of the day, being as explicit as I could about these plans, and trying to avoid the little slipups that could bring the sky down around our heads.

Throughout it all, we worried about her health. We knew that the conduit, part of her pulmonary artery, would have to be replaced at some point. The cardiologist had thought it would last five to eight years because the small size necessitated by Anna's age at implantation meant it was too small to support a larger child and because artificial vessels tend to calcify more quickly than natural ones. It would probably have to be replaced when Anna was between six and ten years old. She started elementary school when she was 6 3/4. When she was 8 1/2, her ventricular pressures showed a slight increase; her heart was working harder than it had been. The cardiologist planned to take another look the following October, plot the graph of the pressure increases, and then decide whether more testing was necessary. He did his best to minimize the disruptions to our lives. But I worried; I worried when she was tired, when she was sick, and even when she didn't seem to be quite her usual self.

Anna's early elementary-school years were difficult: we were worried and she was anxious. But much of the time,

Anna was a very happy kid. She would dance around the house, laugh at her own jokes, and giggle when Alan teased her. She would stomp in puddles, roll in leaves, and when it rained, jump on the bed chanting in a high, melodious sing song, "It's raining outside." She was also becoming more affectionate; she would return our hugs, albeit somewhat offhandedly, and climb into our laps at every opportunity. The five-year break she'd had from surgery was beginning to pay off. By the time she was eight, we were enjoying domestic chores like folding clothes together, and she was getting more involved in cooking. Weekend mornings were special. Anna and Alan would conspire on breakfast and she would carefully follow his instructions, breaking the eggs they needed and gleefully tossing the shells into the sink just like he did. She became a perfect restaurant patron, amazing waiters as she chose *escargots* and blue cheese and amazing us by actually using a fork.

Reading was still an essential part of the bedtime ritual, although Anna couldn't read much herself. Every night, while one of us was cleaning up after dinner, the other one would sit reading with Anna on his/her lap. *Rain Talk* by Mary Serfozo was a favorite, and Anna was starting to like the books about Frances (*Bedtime for Frances* and *Bread and Jam for Frances* by Russell and Lillian Hoban). She loved children's poetry too for it appealed to her love of words and the silly sounds they could make. "Susie's Galoshes" by Rhoda W. Bacmeister was a favorite.

> Susie's galoshes
>
> Make splishes and sploshes
>
> And slooshes and sloshes,

As Susie steps slowly

Along in the slush.

But she refused to listen to fairy tales because the wicked witch was far too scary, and certain books like *Chicka Chick Boom Boom* by Bill Martin Jr., John Archambault, and Lois Ehlert turned her off completely because of the damage inflicted upon the poor letters as they fell from the tree. Then, she would only scream "NO." Later, when she was older, she would often explain how much she hated this kind of "damage."

Anna was feeling more comfortable. Despite her anxiety, she loved school and camp, and the routines we had established at home were bearing fruit. She was growing and changing. But then we were hit with another surprise.

A Brain Tumor (1996)

Second grade ended on June 14, 1996. Throughout that year, Anna's anxiety had been increasing. We thought it was because homework was getting harder, but we soon found out there was another reason as well. On the very last day of school, right before the good-bye party, Anna threw up in the classroom garbage can and complained that her head was hurting. We weren't alarmed since we, ourselves, had just been through a bout of gastroenteritis and since headaches ran in my family. Perhaps she had a virus or was growing up into migraines. We were scheduled to leave the next day for a vacation in Washington State, planning to visit good friends in Seattle and then to explore the Olympic Peninsula. So, despite our concern, we headed for the airport. Anna lay there next to us waiting for the plane, looking pale and thin, and we worried. She was no better when we arrived and only got worse as our departure for the Olympic Peninsula loomed. The doctors in Seattle diagnosed gastroenteritis twice, but we wanted our own doctors so we decided to skip the Olympic Peninsula and head for home. Anna got better slowly; her headaches seemed to be under control and she wasn't throwing up.

So we sent her to camp with a Motrin in her backpack, just in case. She made it through the first day and came home exhausted but happy. But that night, she woke up screaming; her head was hurting more than ever. We got through the night and the next day with Motrin and no idea what these episodes could mean. Then, Alan took her back to the doctor, where she threw up again. This had gone on too long. The doctor knew we had to find out what the problem was and ordered a brain MRI for the next day. Alan was taken aback. He was supposed to leave for South Africa, on a long-planned business trip, the next day. What should he do? Should he postpone the trip, he asked. The doctor looked at him seriously. "I would," she said.

The next day we headed for the imaging center where the MRIs are performed. We were greeted by one of the many anesthesiologists we knew from previous surgeries and catheterizations. Anna was sedated and slid headfirst into the machine. Even though she was fast asleep, we chose to sit in the room with her and listened, not knowing how much to worry, to the pounding of the machine. The procedure took a very long time. When it was over, the anesthesiologist took us both by the hand saying that he didn't usually work this way, that he usually left reporting to the radiologist, but that the results were too clear. Anna had a brain tumor the size of a large walnut. He couldn't believe it and neither could we. How could that walnut fit inside her head? How could one child have two, such completely unrelated major conditions? It was a testament to her will power and her strength that she had held off her symptoms until the end of the school year.

The anesthesiologist's instructions were clear. This was an emergency. We were to go straight to the hospital, where Anna would be seen by a neurosurgeon and would undoubtedly require immediate surgery. We were not to stop off at home; we were not to go out of our way to pick up anything we might need. Anna began to scream as we headed off in the car. We were numb, but at least we now understood what had been going on. Alan explained it in the first of his email notes to friends and family.

> The brain has its own circulatory system. . . . Under ordinary circumstances cerebrospinal fluid brings

nutrients to the brain and drains waste materials. There are four ventricles or fluid chambers in the brain. Anna's tumor, which was in the third ventricle, had obstructed the drainage pathway. This caused the brain's ventricles to distend and created extreme pressure. That pressure is what caused her headaches and nausea. Left unrelieved, it could rapidly cause her to die.

Anna was admitted directly to the ICU, for the doctors felt she had to be closely monitored until a tumor resection could be performed, and she was put on drugs to reduce some of the intracranial pressure. But the surgery couldn't be performed until the next day because of its length. So there we were with Anna screaming from hunger, as well as from fear, for she hadn't been allowed to eat the morning of the MRI. And we weren't prepared: because of the rush we had neither the "blankie" she'd had since she was born nor a single stuffed animal. The hospital chaplain, who knew us from previous surgeries, hurried to fill that gap: she gave Anna a huge dog to stand in for her live one and a hand-made quilt for her "blankie." That dog is still on her bed, although it's been eighteen years since the surgery.

Here's the story as Alan told it.

> Preparation for sedation began Friday at 6:40 AM, and Anna was sedated at 7. She was wheeled into the operating theater before 7:30. One- or two-sentence messages were relayed up to us by a nurse every few hours. We got a report at 10:30 that the doctors had reached the point where they could begin working on the tumor. At 12:30, a nurse called saying, "they are in the middle and she is stable." At 1:30, "they are closing up and she is stable; you can expect to hear

from the surgeon in an hour or more." At 3:45, we called down and were told they were just about to wheel Anna into the recovery room.

The surgeon came in to tell us about the operation. He told us that he thought he had been able to remove 75-80% of the tumor. He had tried to loosen more of it, but he didn't want to be too aggressive. The area of attachment was near regions of vital brain function, and a mistake could cause blindness, paralysis, or permanent memory loss.

Overall, the surgeon felt good about what he'd been able to accomplish. Today's post-op MRI confirmed that much of the tumor was gone, and the areas of swelling in the ventricles had receded. Anna is recovering well from the surgery, although she's exhausted – she's sleep-deprived and nutrition-deprived, since she'd only been allowed to eat one meal in the past 3 days (no food is allowed before any procedure that requires an anesthetic). We hope that now that all the major procedures are done for a while, she'll relax and recover.

We now get to wait, in order to find out a number of things. For the time being Anna has an external drain to get rid of excess cerebral fluid: a tube from inside her brain leads to a device that collects the excess fluid and lets the doctors see how much has drained. Over the next few days the excess fluid should drain out, taking with it some of the brain and tumor material broken loose by the surgery. It's ugly looking now, bloody too. The fluid should clear up as the brain heals. In the best of all possible worlds, the surgery will have opened up the drainage system. If the internal passageways are clear and begin to function as usual, then at some point the external drain will simply be removed. More likely, some form of shunt/drain will be necessary to get rid of excess fluid on an ongoing basis. We'll have to wait and see. The other thing we have to wait for is the biopsy, which will take a week or so to come back from the lab. That will say what kind of growth the tumor is. Knowing that will shape the course of treatment.

Alan's note didn't tell the whole story though. He did say how long the surgery was, but he didn't say how long it felt. Based on our previous experience, we expected it to be finished by early to mid-afternoon, so we waited patiently until then. But as it got later and we received only telegraphic updates, I began to pace. I couldn't focus on anything. I got more and more frantic. This was the operation that would finally do her in! When the surgeon finally arrived, I nearly fell into his arms.

As Alan said in his note, only 75-80% of the tumor could be removed because of its location and the possibility of damage to sensitive areas. The tumor's position also made access difficult. Of course, we were disappointed that the doctor hadn't been able to get the whole tumor. But relief won out; Anna seemed fine. The doctor received the pathology report a few days later. The wait would have seemed interminable, but we were focused on Anna and afraid to look even a few days ahead. The tumor was a sub-ependymal giant cell astrocytoma, a low-grade tumor that grows very slowly and that often stops growing after resection. Happily, there would be no chemotherapy and no radiation. Instead, tumor status would be monitored by periodic MRIs. Anna had her baseline MRI 24 hours after the surgery. It had to be done quickly because the brain usually begins to swell a few days after surgery. Since the hospital didn't have its own MRI machine at that time and the imaging center was less than a mile away, patients were loaded into an ambulance with many pounds of monitoring equipment. We went with her and watched open-mouthed as a female paramedic who barely reached my shoulder bent her knees and hefted the gurney into the body of the ambulance. The trip went smoothly and the MRI confirmed the neurosurgeon's assessment.

Anna recovered pretty well. There were the standard ups and downs, of course. And the ICU was... the ICU. To the uninitiated the sight of all the tubes and monitors, including the external drain tube attached to Anna's head, could be disturbing. But being confronted by post-op "plumbing" was nothing new to us, and we were used to gauging recovery by the sequence of post-op de-tubing. We waited impatiently for the fluid inside the external drain to clear up and the external drain to be removed. But the fluid did not clear up and the amount of cerebrospinal-fluid drainage did not decrease; the external drain continued to collect about 2.5 times the normal amount. So the surgeon decided to implant a ventriculoperitoneal (VP) shunt in Anna's brain. The shunt consists of 3 parts: a pressure-sensitive valve, which controls the amount of cerebrospinal fluid drained, and two catheters. One of the catheters is threaded into the brain. Excess fluid drains from the brain through the pressure-sensitive valve into the abdominal area, where it's absorbed by the body. Since the catheter is coiled in the abdominal cavity and uncoils as the child grows, it rarely gets too short for a growing child.

For the surgeon the shunt implantation was business as usual: the procedure is much less risky than tumor resections. But it wasn't business as usual for Anna or for us. Several hours after the operation, we noticed that one eye was quite swollen. Since the swelling decreased when we changed her position, our concerns diminished. After the anesthetic wore off, however, we had something else to worry about. Anna – our happy, bubbly girl – was completely uncommunicative. She wouldn't say a word, wouldn't look at anyone who spoke to her, and just stared off into space. Her vital signs (blood pressure, heart rate, temperature, and so on) were about right, but the old Anna just wasn't there. It didn't seem as if *any* Anna was there; she lay in bed passively, not responding to anything. We were terrified. Had she had a stroke? Was something wrong with her eyes? Was she gone forever? We begged her to blink in response to our questions. At long last she did, once; then the vacant stare returned, for hours. The physical recovery continued. Anna got stronger and had some tubes removed. We took her for walks in a wheelchair trailing an IV pole behind us. We went through the hospital garden, trying to interest her in the flowers and babbling on about their beautiful colors. But she remained uncommunicative. The doctors said they'd never seen a reaction like this, but they were sure that she would come around. Their reassurances sounded hollow.

But she did come around, somewhat, after she was moved out of the ICU into a regular room. Thirty-six hours after the shunt implantation, she woke up whining, eyes averted, still fairly withdrawn and listless. Her balance was way off. When we moved her to a wheelchair, we had to hold on tightly – she'd have fallen right out if she hadn't been belted in. Even when she began to communicate, it was mostly to refuse food.

Jane: Do you want to go home?"

Anna: Yah.

Jane: You have to have some food or they won't let you go home. Have a little broth.

Anna: No.

It took a visit from Dr. W. and her beloved second-grade teacher to bring back her laughter.

Just like when she was a baby, eating was another matter, and just like when she was a baby, she couldn't go home until she ate. We tried everything: broth, popsicles, Jello. But she refused. In desperation, we asked her whether she'd eat a grilled cheese sandwich and French fries – her favorite foods after chocolate and chips. "Yah," she replied, somewhat unenthusiastically. The nurses were reluctant; you have to tolerate a liquid diet before you'll get a solid one. But the neurosurgeon who was doing rounds and who looked like he enjoyed his food agreed: "Get that girl a grilled cheese sandwich," he bellowed. The nurse set out a mountain of French fries. They vanished immediately, and we knew we were going home.

Anna went home after 12 days in the hospital with a bag of pills: Dilantin to prevent seizures, Decadron to reduce brain swelling, and Ranitidine to soothe the stomach irritation caused by the other two drugs. Decadron is a steroid, which increases appetite, a welcome change, and irritability, an unwelcome one. It also made her face and stomach look temporarily like two bowling balls connected by pipe cleaners. There were still many uncertainties. Her balance was off, she listed to one side as she walked, and she ran the risk of shunt failure. Shunts fail when their drain tubes clog or when the implantation site gets infected. Although infection is more likely during the first few weeks after surgery, shunts can fail at any time. The long-term prognosis was unclear. How likely was the remaining portion of the tumor to grow? How fast? Would more surgeries be required? We had lots of questions, but few answers. Our questions would be answered during the next visit to the neurosurgeon and in the months that followed. Anna was quickly weaned off the Decadron and Ranitidine, but stayed on the Dilantin for some months. The Decadron had increased her appetite and broadened her culinary scope; while she was taking it, she'd eat anything, even fish. Taking her off it reduced her appetite to its usual disappointingly low level and weakened her desire for culinary exploration; she went back to her old "white diet" of pasta, rice, milk and bread. Her headaches, which came primarily from the insult to her brain and skull, could be controlled with Tylenol and eventually disappeared completely. Her balance took a while to re-establish itself but later became excellent. She had few, if any limitations, and best of all, the prognosis was good because this type of tumor is usually slow growing. Anna would get frequent MRIs. If the remaining part of the tumor didn't grow, the interval between MRIs would increase from 3 months to 6 months and then to a year. If growth were noted, the time interval would decrease, and if the tumor grew large enough to cause trouble, another resection would be considered. As the neurosurgeon said, "By the time you've done a few resections, they'll either have new surgical techniques or they'll have found a cure."

The night we got home, Anna lay in bed talking for four hours, too keyed up and relieved to sleep despite her exhaustion. She spent the next day in bed, whining about her pain. This was hard for me, but Alan knew how to handle it. For every pain, he invented a nonsense word: "bing bong" was for her cranial incision, "mumphia" was for a headache, and "beep beep beep" was for her abdominal incision. That took the sting out. Anna's balance improved enough so that she could use the toilet without help. Then, as she got better, we noticed a number of cognitive changes that made us realize how much the tumor and the resulting hydrocephalus had been affecting her skills.

Eighteen days after the tumor resection, she designed a necklace. This was the first time she had actually planned and executed a pattern. Previous necklaces had been random affairs. Twenty days after the surgery, I read her some fairy tales. This was the first time that she appreciated the death of the evil queen and rejoiced in the happy endings. Before that, the tales were too complex and the presence of evil too frightening. On the twenty-sixth day, she began to get organized, putting her tapes and books in order and her get-well cards in her scrapbook. Her handwriting and other fine motor skills improved and, for the first time, she was able to color within the lines of a picture. A month later she made a bracelet for a friend, in three separate sessions. Not only was this her first spontaneous act of generosity, but she was more focused than we had ever seen her.

She also got better at telling stories and was more willing to accept a logical justification when something didn't go as planned. One day we arrived at the neurosurgeon's for an appointment, which had been canceled due to a surgical emergency. Instead of screaming and yelling, as she would have done previously, she listened to me closely as I said "Imagine that the doctor was doing your surgery and he had an appointment with someone else. Do you think he would stop what he was doing and run over to his appointment leaving you lying on the operating table?" "No," she giggled, and that was the end of the story. And her peers became more important. She started bringing home stories about what they did at school: mostly about the children who were sent out for disruptive behavior. Stories about what she had done with other kids and even playing with other kids would have to wait. She began to participate more in conversations with our friends, and they remarked that she seemed more integrated. One even thought that she had been on the verge of making some developmental leaps before the surgery and that the increased brain activity may have helped precipitate the crisis. Dr. W.'s take was slightly different. Although she did see some improvement in fine motor skills and in other areas, she thought it unlikely that Anna's deficits stemmed from the brain tumor and its associated hydrocephalus. Since the brain adapts over time to subtle increases in intracranial pressure and the tumor had been slow growing, Dr. W. theorized that an early operating-table incident or a period of hypo-oxygenation was responsible. Now that we have more information, we think that unlikely.

Third Grade

Anna went back to third grade in September with the other kids. We began to monitor the tumor. The first post-baseline MRI was scheduled for November. Alan's email describes what happened.

> The one-liner:
>
> Good news overall, with a tinge of doubt.
>
> In slightly more detail:
>
> Anna had a clinic visit a couple of weeks ago, which went very well. Last Thursday she had an MRI. The good news is that the MRI shows no irritation at the surgery site, and fine intracranial pressure. That means that the operations did what they were supposed to, without consequences (the tissue wasn't "angry," as the neurosurgeon put it). The doubt is that the radiologist thought there might be some slight change in the part of the tumor that remains. The neurosurgeon isn't sure; he doesn't think it's clear one way or the other. If there is a change, it's slight, so the neurosurgeon says that no treatment other than "wait and watch" is called for. But, because of the doubt, the next MRI will be scheduled for 3 months from now – if the case were crystal clear, the gap between MRIs would've been longer.

All we could do was watch, wait, hope and try to live as normal lives as possible. Anna continued to enjoy school, and her teachers noted many changes.

Everyone said that she was much more focused and calm and that her language skills had improved. She took the school bus home with no problems but hated to take it in the morning because she was so afraid of being late. Her social skills also seemed to have improved, and the other kids began to help her with her assignments. Then she started to tell tall tales. In one, she was driving Alan's car in the rain when a dog fell through the moon roof into her lap. Most important of all, she began to develop a stronger sense of self. She had always been stubborn (you have to be to survive what she'd been through), but now the stubbornness had a different quality. One day, she and I were walking the dog and discussing two of Alan's upcoming trips: the first one, which was one night in DC, and the second, which was to be two nights in DC and two in New York. Anna was convinced that they were reversed, and the argument that ensued sounded exactly like similar arguments I've had with Alan. She was now aware enough of herself to have an investment in being right. Her growing self-awareness took on another dimension as she learned to express her likes and dislikes more effectively. When invited to her friends' houses, she made it clear that she needed to be the only one: "I don't like to come over when there's another kid," she'd say. While listening to me read aloud, she noted, "I like it when I'm the only person being read to, but I don't like it when someone is reading to the whole class."

Although she appeared to be physically unchanged, she grew more cautious. Perhaps she'd had her fill of fear during the surgeries; perhaps she felt somewhat less coordinated; or perhaps she was merely older and more sensible. In any case, she seemed to have lost her daredevil spirit, and her reckless gymnastics became a thing of the past. She explored play structures slowly. She inched her way up the slide, holding tightly onto its edge, and slowly made her way down the staircase. When she went up the slide the right way, which was rare, she would spread her legs wide like a snowplowing skier and bump slowly down.

SHUNT FAILURE (WINTER BREAK 1996)

That winter we went to New York for our annual family visit. It was a pleasant visit, complicated, as usual, by our attempts to spend as much time as possible with each side of the family and by whirlwind visits to Manhattan. On December 30, we were at Alan's mother's house when Anna threw up. Since we were ready to leave for my parents' house in Queens, we took a paper bag in the car and drove over. Once we got there, Anna's temperature was 101.5 and she lay still, with none of her usual bounce. Although everyone insisted it was just a virus and although fevers aren't usually associated with shunt failure, I wasn't convinced. I called our neurosurgeon in California and he suggested a trip to the emergency room. Alan scooped her up and put her in the car. She was too tired to walk. He carried her into the emergency room, which was luckily not too busy, and she just lay there sprawled across my lap. We had never seen her so lackadaisical outside of the hospital. Alan's email continues from there.

> When [her temperature] was taken at the emergency room it was 102.9; an hour later in the pediatric emergency ward it spiked at 103.9. (Tylenol and antibiotics soon brought it down.) A neurosurgical resident tried to get a sample of cerebrospinal fluid from the shunt without success (a bad sign, meaning that the pathway to it was blocked) and arrangements were made, in consultation with Anna's California team and a New York pediatric neurosurgeon, for the shunt revision the next day.

I was numb, and my mouth was so dry I could barely speak, but I felt somehow prepared, as if I had known this was coming. Alan was blindsided; he turned deathly pale and, before I knew it, was lying prone on a gurney. A couple of nurses had grabbed him before he hit the floor. His email continues.

> The hospital is very good, and we lucked into a hotshot surgeon – this guy is a star (a force behind the creation of new board certification for pediatric neurosurgery), and our kind of straight-talking fast-talking New Yorker to boot. He explained the problem with down-home metaphors and straight technical language, and then went in and fixed it. . . . What had happened was that the catheter into the brain had gotten clogged (which happens, alas, 10-20% of the time during the 1st 6 months after a shunt is installed). When the shunt clogs, pressure builds up. That's what caused the symptoms Anna had, and it requires almost immediate remediation. Anna's pre-op CAT scan the next morning confirmed that the ventricle was enlarged. The remedy is to redo the shunt. In this case, since the proximal end was the problem, it meant opening up the valve and replacing the catheter. . . . (Luckily, this means the distal tube – the one that's threaded subcutaneously from her skull down to her stomach – remained untouched.) "Piece of cake" said the neurosurgeon; "I do this procedure all the time."
>
> So he did, about noon on December 31. The operation took an hour and a quarter, after which Anna spent some time in the recovery room and went up to Intensive Care. The surgeon came by early afternoon on New Year's Day, looked at the CAT scan that had just been taken, and said she could leave the hospital – that she'd be weak and

have headaches for a while, but that she could fly back over the weekend. He said she could go to school Monday – six days after the surgery! – though how much of the day she'll make it through we can't guess. In the meantime, Anna is somewhat weak and pale. Her headaches continue to respond to Tylenol and they are becoming less frequent. In her amazing fashion, she's bouncing back from the surgery. When we got home, she wanted to show Jim (who was house and dog sitting) how she can ride the unicycle! Needless to say she, and we, are very glad to be back home.

Alan's next email showed that our return wasn't quite as easy as predicted.

Yesterday I took Anna to school for the beginning of this term. About an hour later I got a call saying that she wanted to be picked up – she had a headache and tummy ache. I went to school to get her, and she threw up right after she got out of the car. Oh, joy...

Jane came home panicked from work. I called the neurosurgeon, who said that since she didn't have a fever and seemed alert there was probably no problem, but since he hadn't seen her, he might as well... So late afternoon, after Anna had recovered from her barfing and was exuberant as she could be, we headed to the surgeon. He declared that the valve is working, she's in fine shape (an eye exam reveals whether there's extra pressure), and the throwing up must've been "a coincidence." It may have been Anna moving too hard, too fast: when she gets overly excited she can throw up (she's done this on airplanes), and she was, after all, suffering from jet lag and post-surgical tiredness. Anyway, she's certified healthy; we're certifiable.

Anna's tenth birthday was on January 10th. To celebrate, we went to the neurosurgeon and got her stitches removed. It was then that we were forced to contemplate the bigger picture. The surgeon explained that the brain tumor was not just an isolated problem; it was part of a condition called tuberous sclerosis complex (TSC). He had implied as much early on when he justified refraining from chemotherapy. As part of this justification, he had given us several studies, which showed that the growth of subependymal giant cell astrocytomas (Anna's type of tumor) could be stopped by tumor resections in patients with tuberous sclerosis. The neurosurgeon we'd met in New York had confirmed the diagnosis in response to a question from me: "Of course, she has tuberous sclerosis," he'd said. "The calcifications in her CAT scans are clear signs."

TSC is a genetic disorder characterized by tumor growth. It can be very severe, causing multiple tumors in the brain, heart, kidneys, and lungs, retinal lesions, seizures, learning differences, autism, mental retardation, and small acne-like bumps or large rough patches of skin on the face, but patient manifestations vary. TSC occurs in one out of every six thousand live births and has been diagnosed in 50,000 Americans. A patient whose condition is carefully monitored can have a normal life span.[7] Anna's manifestations include the type of brain tumor characteristic of TSC, areas of calcification in the brain, a few ash-leaf shaped areas of hypocoloration on her limbs, retinal lesions (which should not affect her vision), renal angiomyolipomas (which are too small to be measured but which will have to be carefully monitored for they may start to bleed), learning differences and some autistic-like behaviors. But she does not have seizures or mental retardation. Her heart defect is completely separate from the TSC, and her heart appears to have no tumors. We wondered what the odds were of having two such different genetic mutations.

BACK TO THIRD GRADE

To celebrate Anna's tenth birthday for real, we held a party at the YMCA's swimming pool. The kids all had a good time swimming and the food and presents were expeditiously, and noisily, consumed. But Anna was somehow out of place: one girl tried to get her to join a water train without success and she did not participate in the banter around the table. It was sad to see that, at her own party with people that she had chosen to invite, she couldn't participate. I wondered whether she would ever truly fit in.

Anna had her next brain MRI in February 1997. The news was good. The residual tumor had not grown since the last MRI in November, and the surgeon felt we could wait a full year for the next MRI. So we could try to live normally. But it wasn't easy. Giggles and bead wrappers could not long hold the line against disease. I took her to the cardiologist on August 5, and the doctor reported that her ventricular pressures were up slightly; the heart was working harder than it should. He scheduled a visit in six months, rather than in a year, and suggested that a catheterization might be advisable. The conduit substituting for her pulmonary artery had already lasted nine years, a year longer than expected. In October, he called to say he had thought that a balloon angioplasty might open up the conduit, thus precluding more open-heart surgery. But he had now changed his mind; because of the extreme left pulmonary stenosis, which made her left lung essentially useless, he realized that it wouldn't. Instead he suggested a transeptal catheterization, which would enable the doctors to get a good look at the left pulmonary artery and to then discuss options for fixing both the conduit and the left pulmonary artery. He asked us to meet with him. During the meeting, he made it clear that there was no hurry: that we could do the catheterization during spring break and then, depending on the results, schedule surgery for the summer. So that's what we decided to do.

We could, once again, try to have a normal year. But it was not normal. Alan and I were tired, terribly tired: tired of hospital waits, tired of fearing diagnoses, tired of the same routines, and tired of, once again, seeing our little girl helplessly lying on a hospital bed and trying to talk the tears from her voice. That's what hospitals did to us – we felt weariness, rather than fear, and numbness. But Anna, refusing to admit her fear, claimed she loved hospitals; she talked about them constantly, looked for them on trips, demanded to visit them, and knew that, when she grew up, she was going to be a nurse.

No, life was not normal. I worried constantly. Every time Anna got sick, every time she got tired, I worried. I scrutinized her lips and nail beds for any signs of blueness. I looked into her eyes when they seemed momentarily unfocused. Anna worried too. She did her best to hide any physical discomfort and wouldn't, or couldn't, accurately report on how she was feeling. If she threw up, she would try to hide the vomit in her trashcan and do her (ineffectual) best to clean up what she'd missed. She didn't want us to know. She didn't want us to take her to the hospital. One day in her speech class, she cut her lower labial frenum, the piece of skin that holds the lower lip close to the gum, with a small pencil sharpener, and it bled profusely. Although she understood the risk of heart-wall infection and the need for prompt administration of antibiotics, she didn't tell me what she'd done when I picked her up. The speech therapist did, and I ran for the phone.

Colds were anathema. All hell would break loose if we even suggested she might have one. "I don't," she'd scream. "It's just allergies." One day, she sprained her ankle badly ice skating; she refused to talk about it, explain what happened, or tell anyone how much it hurt. We spent four long hours in the emergency room, and she was scared, terribly scared that she would end up in the hospital again. She always had, after all. No matter what all the doctors and nurses said, she knew better. She cried almost more from fear than from pain.

Anna worried about other things too. My mother was in a wheelchair when my parents came to visit. Anna was anxious about the visit and about the extent of Grandma's disability. She handled this anxiety by asking question after question about their arrival. I finally suggested she email her questions to her Grandpa, since only he could provide definitive answers. Here's the list of questions, which he meticulously answered. Typos and misspellings have not been corrected.

If your the last off the plane will you be first on?

Is it a big plane or a small one?

How many bags on the carousel?

Woutch corousel number?

what seet on the airplane?

Do you have your ticket?

What size weal chair large medium or small?

Please write back and answer all my questions in this order

111

Third grade continued. Anna was growing up. Despite the persistence of FDQ's (Fairly Dumb Questions), dialogs with her became more like conversations than stereotyped repetitions. If adequately prepared, she was able to play quietly by herself during the two-hour conference calls I led from home each month. Alan could still make her laugh, and she even enjoyed the local street fair, which had previously been too frenetic for her. She also began to enjoy Western Day, a school-year-end tradition. She had only tolerated the previous three, but by the fourth, she knew what to expect; she was finally comfortable enough to learn from the experience. The books we were reading aloud at night were more complex too. She began to enjoy the *Lyle Crocodile* books by Bernard Waber and seemed more willing to listen to stories that she hadn't heard before. The highlight of the year came in April with our Passover seder. I'd been taking her to a Sunday school whose purpose was to gently introduce the children to Jewish culture. The teachers explained the holidays and traditions, sang songs, and taught a bit of Hebrew. But these teachers weren't terribly good at relating to the children, so, using a tape I found, I took it upon myself to teach her to sing the Four Questions, which are traditionally asked by the youngest child at a seder. Anna has an excellent ear and a pleasant singing voice. Although she was ten years old that April, she also entirely lacked self-consciousness. When it came time to sing the questions, her performance – clear, strong and melodious as it was – brought tears to everyone's eyes. I had also prepared her to perform some short scenes relevant to the Passover story. The tears turned to laughter as she pretended to be King Pharaoh, singing out in a voice as deep as she could make it, "NO, NO, NO. I will not let them go!"

Fourth Grade

When fourth grade started in September, Anna was glad to be back in school. But the work was getting harder, and this teacher had trouble understanding why Anna, the comfortably middle class child of two Ph.D.'s, was not performing as she expected. In October 1997, the teacher told us that Anna's reading was only at second-grade level. Even though we had been reading to Anna since she was a baby, she could not read chapter books and had no interest in having complex books read to her. She did fairly well reading picture books with large print, but as the print got smaller and the lines closer together, she would miss letters, reverse them (making "bop" out of "pop," for example) and overlook important words like "not." Despite these perceptual difficulties, sounding out words was comparatively easy; the big hurdle was comprehension. When her reading skills were tested in fourth grade, she read the fourth grade passage with 92% fluency and 33% comprehension.

Reading comprehension was difficult because of the way she saw the world. Just as she saw only the details of the drawings she made, rather than the whole picture, her reading comprehension was limited to plot details. That made it difficult for her to see overarching themes and to understand how these themes contributed to the plot. Since she didn't see the big picture in her reading, she didn't see it in her writing either. Her stories were generally linear; they consisted of events connected only by their place in the story and did not seem to have an overall plot structure. They also lacked meaningful detail and emotional content. Here's an example from December 1997. All punctuation and spelling are hers.

The Plane Trip

One day a boy and a girl were going to New York. There names Nathen and Anna They were twins. They saw a dog named Mirld Snitzer crying loud. Whats wrong they asked there is something in my paw she said Colose your eyes we said and we pulled it out it was long. It was a thorn. She thanked them and liked her leg. That night she ate chocolate. She loved it. then she flew on a plane to Washington and saw a duck and the duck yawned and fell asleep and never woke up again for 15 years and he lay so still he died. They berryed him in the washer he became fresh water to drink from the well. he walked on the piano and played au clair de la lune we loved it. We fell asleep and died they berred us in the washer we became fresh water to drink we played au clair de la lune on the piano and the duck loved it.

The End

We wondered whether, in her effort to be creative and funny, she had merely glued bits of random stories together. She was somewhat more coherent in this plan for a trip we were going to take.

A Trip

On February 13 I will go on a plane to my aunt Laurie's house to visit Laurie, Tony, Joseph and Tova. I have to bring my gigapet because Joseph and Tova want a virtual pet but there mom and dad don't like em so they can play with mine. His name is spot. They will love him. I will also meet Scratches the cat. she is Tova's cat. Her name is Scratches because she Scratches everything up. For there birthday I got

Tova Beanie Babys named Patti and Sly. Patti is a platipus and Sly is a fox. Tova has a few beanie babys I don't know how many because I didn't ask Laura and Tova want to pick us up at the airport so my mom said they can for Joseph I got him a balloon animal kit. on the plane they will serve drinks. We get to choose our seets I will have 7 up the plane. there will be no food for a short ride. I will take Casey and browney. They're both bears and maby other animals like cats or dogs. They can sleep with them if they want. In their basement they have a trapise, a bar, and a rope I think that is all but I don't know And they have toys in their yard too. We will go some places but I don't know whare but I'll find out. I might play with there presents if they let me we will take Spunky to the kennel. After 3 nights we will go home and get Spunky when Laurie and Tova pick us up Joseph will be at school and Tony at work. We will arrive at the airport at 1130 AM And there house at 230 PM have to get 3 bags off the carrisell. then we will go their

The End

When it came to more complex concepts, Anna was lost. She couldn't use language effectively to discuss emotions or even verbally identify the emotions she was feeling. She could say that she was happy, that she was sad and that she didn't want to get angry again, but she couldn't go any deeper than that. And she certainly couldn't get into another person's skin. One day, her class was supposed to write a story from a point of view other than their own. She wrote a cute story, which was almost entirely coherent, but she did not understand the goal of the exercise. She didn't know what point of view was.

Even if she had, she couldn't imagine what it would be like to be someone else. The teacher had to drag her through the assignment. The final product met the goal of the assignment but was superficial with no reference to thoughts or feelings.

Anna often missed the point of an assignment, but she always wanted to try. When the school was holding elections for student-council representatives, the students who were running for office had to give a speech. Other kids promised to work on improving the cafeteria food or organizing school dances, but Anna had different ideas. Here's the speech she gave smiling naively throughout.

> Hi! I'm Anna Louise Schoenfeld. I would like to have fun field trips. I would like to go to a science museum and do science projects. I also would like to go on a plane to anywhere. I want to go to Fairyland and Water World such as Raging Waters. But it might not be open. I would also like to go to Ripley's Believe-It-or-Not Museum, the LA museum and the Lindsey Museum and museums in another state like Natural History, Modern Art and other museums. I love this class and Mrs. R. I would like to be your student-council representative. Vote for Anna.

She really didn't understand political speech-making conventions or what it meant to be student council representative.

Her teacher was also concerned because Anna was not really relating to the other kids and didn't seem to know how to fit in. She saw some of Anna's long-standing friendships merely as examples of the other children's amiability. Anna did have trouble relating. She avoided close physical contact and had difficulty perceiving social cues. If she wanted to talk to someone, she would barge right in, not realizing that that person might be otherwise occupied. She didn't understand the concept of personal space, and would often get so close that people would back off. These differences made many children shy away. But Anna was not deterred. She followed the other children around and, when they were not there, talked about them incessantly.

The teacher was even more concerned about Anna's increasingly disruptive behavior; Anna was calling out in class, screaming "NO!" when she didn't want to do something, cursing students who got in her way, and refusing to do her work when she didn't understand exactly how. The work was getting harder, and Anna, who wanted so desperately to do well, erupted when she didn't understand an assignment. Reading was hard, writing was slow and laborious, and verbal instructions went by too fast.

But Anna was learning from her assignments, despite her teacher's concerns. That year, she had to write a biography of a well-known African American. She chose Louis Armstrong only because we found a simple book about him, and she listened to some of his music as part of the assignment. That was enough to get her started; jazz was her thing. Aided and abetted by her dad, she began to collect jazz CDs and could often identify a piece just a few notes after it started playing.

At home, she was growing and changing. She was finally learning to ride a two-wheel bike. I was self-conscious as she tootled shakily around the playground, afraid that other kids would laugh at such a big kid who was just learning to ride. But she felt no stigma and cycled proudly round and round. She was also putting more effort into her schoolwork, with appropriate scaffolding from me. She was becoming easier to talk to and more cooperative: she was happily doing chores like setting the table, and she always accompanied us on dog walks and errands. Day trips were more fun because she was having fewer tantrums. We'd take BART to San Francisco, go out for lunch, and walk around a museum as Alan and Anna discussed their favorite art works. She was soon able to identify many of the artists we saw. Sometimes, we'd just spend a few hours walking around the city. Anna was game for anything as long as the routine had been previously established and the plans thoroughly described beforehand.

Then routines began to lose their power. Anna's anxiety was very strong even when she wasn't in school. Her tantrums became more frequent. She was asked to leave a social-skills group because she was loud and disruptive. In doctors' offices she would yell "no talk" and refuse to let us ask any questions. One day, after a particularly loud doctor's visit, she concluded she'd hurt the doctor's feelings, screamed all the way home, and immediately called him to apologize; she was afraid she had angered the man who could put her in the hospital at a moment's notice. Her anxiety was becoming more complex because it was fueled by an increasing sensitivity and a better, although still limited, understanding of the world. One day, after an enjoyable visit to San Francisco, as we rode down the BART escalator, Anna saw a train. It wasn't our train; it was, in fact, going in the opposite direction. But she wasn't up to such fine distinctions. All she knew was that it was a train and it was leaving. She ran down the escalator, heading for the train. Alan took off behind her, grabbing her just before she got on, while I stood there frozen with fear. But increased sensitivity and understanding of the world were not the only things fueling Anna's anxiety.

THE BRAIN TUMOR REVISITED (1998)

Anna had her next MRI on March 9, 1998. It had been about 11 months since the one that had showed no change. This time the news wasn't good. The tumor was growing; it had encysted and was leaking a protein-like substance, which had created a dense pocket in the brain. The pocket was also growing, impeding the flow of cerebrospinal fluid. Anna's neurosurgeon wanted to remove as much of the remaining tumor as possible, clean up the pocket of encysted proteins that had developed, and open the drainage system once again. He would also have to consider implanting a second shunt if drainage did not improve. And since the tumor had grown, post-operative radiation might be called for. We asked if the surgery could wait until the summer, so that Anna could finish up the school year. But it couldn't.

We couldn't believe it was happening again, and just to make sure the surgery was necessary, we decided to get another opinion. Even though Anna's neurosurgeon always reviewed complex cases with a surgery board consisting of other neurosurgeons, we had to see for ourselves. On April 8, Alan and I took Anna's scans to a pediatric neurosurgeon who was using a new radiation technique for dealing with small brain tumors. The technique, called gamma knife radiosurgery, uses highly focused beams of radiation to cut out the tumor and leaves other parts of the brain untouched. If this doctor endorsed Anna's doctor's recommendations, then the path would be clear. If not, then of course, we'd get another opinion.

This doctor confirmed the diagnosis and supported the recommendations we had received. Given the encysting, he said, the surgery was essential. Moreover, it had to be done soon, before the circulatory system was completely blocked and Anna succumbed to headaches, vomiting, and more. He did not define "more." He said that our doctor should be aggressive: he should remove as much of the tumor and the encysted materials as possible and, to insure effective drainage through the existing shunt, open a new pathway between the fluid chambers in the brain. He also said that he vehemently opposed general radiation treatment because of its potential damage to healthy brain tissue and that the kind of tumor Anna had did not respond well to chemotherapy. He suggested that any portion of the tumor remaining after the surgery be frequently monitored by MRI. There was a chance it wouldn't grow further. If it did, he would urge quick use of the gamma knife.

We got a call from our own doctor the very next day. He had consulted with the cardiologist to make sure that Anna's heart was strong enough for brain surgery. Although the cardiologist had wanted to do a catheterization during spring break so that he could decide when to replace Anna's conduit, he thought there was no hurry; the heart surgery could wait as long as a year. So the brain surgery was scheduled for April 21.

In the meantime, we tried, once again, to live a normal life. We didn't tell Anna about the impending surgery because the anxiety would have been too much for her. Alan left for a previously planned business trip and Anna went off to school. But normal wasn't to be; she threw up just before leaving and didn't tell me because she was still trying to hide any signs of illness that might send her to the hospital. I began to suspect something, though, when she dragged her way through her after-school gymnastics class. That night it got worse: she threw up and her temperature rose to 102°. I called the neurosurgeon to make sure it wasn't shunt failure, and with his concurrence, decided to wait it out. Kids with chronic conditions are just as susceptible to viruses as are healthy kids. Tylenol brought the fever down, but she threw up again at midnight. I thought of going to the emergency room, but since a fever is not usually characteristic of shunt failure and since sitting in the emergency room is a trial, we struggled through the night. The next day, her stomach was better but the fever was not, so we hightailed it over to the pediatrician. A blood test was ordered. When Anna heard the plan, she screamed her legendary scream. But then came a miracle: she took herself in hand and decided to handle this one like a grown-up. Plastering a smile across her face, she sat down in the chair, put her arm on the armrest and watched the phlebotomist's every move. She even decided she wanted tape rather than a band-aid because that's what the grown-ups get. The test showed that it was only a virus. When it disappeared the next day, Anna was exuberant and I was ready to die. So it goes with normal childhood illnesses.

We told Anna about the surgery a few days beforehand. She faced it bravely, knowing there was no choice. At the hospital for pre-op testing, she whirled around the waiting room announcing "I'm having surgery tomorrow." She sailed through the tests, not protesting even when blood was drawn and lying patient and still (except for her mouth) for the echocardiogram. Alan's first post-op report came the day after surgery.

Dear Family and Friends:

To sum things up in brief, things are looking good.

As before, Anna was as much of a trooper as anyone could be. When the anesthesiologist walked up and introduced himself early Tuesday morning, Anna grabbed his hand, said "OK, let's go," and marched off into the surgical suite. She remains strong and positive.

It was a long day Tuesday, with the pre-op visit starting at 6 AM, anesthesia starting at 7:30, the neurosurgeon making his way to the parents' waiting room to tell us how pleased he was with the results at about 4:30, and Anna making her way to the recovery room at 5:30. Everything went very well. The surgeon repositioned the shunt so that it will drain both ventricles. As he predicted from the pre-op MRI, he was able to remove much more of the tumor this time – he got about 90% of it. He also cleaned up the messy encysted materials that had formed in a pocket around the tumor, and made new passageways between the two ventricles so that there is very good drainage. This is all excellent news. It was confirmed today by an MRI.

Waiting through this surgery was easier on us for, unlike last time, we knew what to expect. We knew not to speculate or to visualize disaster as the hours passed. We also understood that it took so long because the surgeon was working slowly and carefully, and we were prepared to give him all the time he wanted. Plus I had my knitting. So we sat there – stolid, stoic, but not silent. Alan's note continues.

> There are always ups and downs in recovery, and I won't take you through a guided tour. Overall there were many more ups than downs and Anna has made excellent progress. A number of her IV lines have been removed, and more importantly, an external drain (which drained blood from the site of the

surgery) has been removed – indicating that the surgical site is healing well. We expect that tomorrow she will sit up on her bed with her legs dangling over the side, and when her balance is solid, she will progress later in the day to walking (with assistance of course). She should be able to move tomorrow from the Intensive Care Unit to the Monitored Care Unit, and after a couple of days to the regular care floor. After another day or two, we hope, she'll be out the door. Convalescence will be another 3 weeks at home.

It's time for me to hit the sack – I've gotten about 2 hours of sleep during the past 43 or so. This is in part because Anna has pretty much reversed day and night. After all, she'd spent much of Tuesday in (pharmaceutically induced) sleep! When she woke up late Tuesday evening, she was ready to roll... and so she did, through the night. Now I'm at home for my turn at walking the dog and for a regular night's sleep. I did want to get this note off before I crashed, though. I head back to the hospital tomorrow AM and I will be there through Friday night. So, you can expect another report – which I hope is as positive as this one – either Friday night or Saturday morning.

The surgery had gone well, and the doctors saw no need for radiation or chemotherapy, but, as Alan's note said, there are always ups and downs. The day after the surgery I walked into the ICU after spending the night at home with the dog. Alan had stayed at the hospital. About five minutes after I arrived, Anna's sats plummeted, her lips turned a deadly blue, and she began to flail uncontrollably. She was having a full-blown seizure. Words died in my throat, I too began to shake, and Alan almost hit the floor. But the medical staff took it in stride. They administered oxygen, saying that post-surgical seizures were typical and that they saw no need to postpone the baseline MRI scheduled for that afternoon.

After that, Anna's progress was astounding. She was quickly booted out of Intensive Care and sent to the Monitored Care Unit (MCU). Since the MCU was quieter, she was able to sleep a bit and even reverted to a more normal schedule. All her lines were pulled and she was free to walk only a few hours later. She walked so much, in fact, that the doctors moved her to a regular room. And she walked there too. A mere 72 hours after the surgery, she made it all the way around the entire fourth floor on her own steam. And thanks, once again, to steroids, she was eating up a storm.

But then came another downer. Balancing post-op medicines is a delicate art. Patients are typically given steroids such as Decadron (which controls swelling of the brain tissue and helps avoid murderous headaches), anti-seizure drugs, and more. The idea is to get therapeutic/prophylactic doses of various drugs into patients' systems in order to prevent problems, but then to wean the patients off the drugs as soon as possible. As it happens, an attempt to lower Anna's Decadron dose one day led to very bad headaches that night and the next day. When the headaches proved resistant to Tylenol, the staff tried codeine, only to discover that Anna has a strong aversive reaction to it – it stayed in her stomach less than a minute and left it in turmoil. She had a rough twenty-four hours. But reverting to the earlier Decadron dose eliminated the headache and raised her spirits, and the next day, she was well enough to beat Alan at Connect-Four, to walk and to socialize with every single patient and staff member. Soon she knew the complete family history of every nurse on the fourth floor. She went home to sleep in her own "friendly bed" on April 27th, only six days after major brain surgery.

We kept pretty busy for the month she stayed home. A teacher came to the house to provide some home schooling and Anna willingly did his assignments. We did some cooking, listened to music, and read books together. When we didn't have time to play, Anna amused herself partly by drawing up patient lists. She had always been fascinated by the lists of patients posted at nurses' stations. These lists generally contained information about current patients including their name, nurse, disease, health status and gender, as well as their location. At home, Anna would often draw tables with the appropriate column headings and make long lists of patients with silly names and sillier diseases. She would sit side by side with her friends as they'd draw up parallel lists, and the names grew more creative. Diseases like "mojo" and "fleka" gave way to diseases like "Can't stop talkingitis." She often returned to writing up patient lists when hospitalization loomed or her anxiety became too great. She also invented a dance she called the tootsie roll, which involved rotating her hands in front of her chest while knocking her knees together and had a successful run teaching it to various high-level medical professionals.

Anna visited her school about a week before she went back. Her class was performing some songs, and although she felt self-conscious about her shaved head and her scars, she insisted on joining them. She was back in school full time on May 29th. When summer started, she hurled herself into her usual day camp routines, and we even tried to take a brief vacation in Lake Tahoe. But the vacation gods were against us. As soon as we reached our cabin, Anna started complaining of a headache, and her dinner came up as soon as it went down. We knew it couldn't be shunt failure because she'd just had a good MRI, but we were all worried. Anna fell asleep babbling on about nurses she'd had, while I made several calls to the doctor and then decided we had to leave. The headache vanished at 3,000 feet. Distinguishing shunt failure from altitude sickness was as difficult as distinguishing it from gastroenteritis had been.

FIFTH GRADE

Fifth grade started with a bang. I got home from doing errands one day to find Alan gone and six messages on the answering machine. Anna had had a seizure and been taken to the hospital by ambulance; Alan had gone to her school. He was told to follow the ambulance in his car and will always remember the ambulance driver's words as he ran to get in the driver's seat: "Take it slow, man. We're in no hurry. You shouldn't be either." No one had been able to reach me. Anna had been sitting on a bench in the cafeteria when she let out a yell, her hand flew up, and she fell backwards banging her head on the cement floor. Teachers surrounded her, doing everything necessary to keep her from hurting herself; her fifth-grade teacher held her head so she wouldn't keep banging it. He also timed the seizure because he knew its duration was important. It lasted only 60 seconds. Her fourth-grade teacher cradled her in her arms until Anna's "other mother" Sally could leave her class. When I arrived at the hospital Anna was lying on a gurney in the emergency room and Alan was standing at her head. She was crying because the gurney was so hard, and she was exhausted from the stress of the seizure, but she was determined to go right home. After six hours of monitoring and a CT scan, which found no damage, that's just what we did. We took along some anti-seizure medication and instructions to make an appointment with a neurologist.

We saw the neurologist a few days later. Since the only other seizure Anna had had been provoked by brain surgery, the neurologist speculated that the seizure was a glitch caused by some unusual electrical activity. She thought that Anna was probably not prone to seizures, unlike many children with TSC, and she suggested that we wait to see whether Anna had another before turning to medication.

Even though she had no more seizures, that sudden convulsion, those six hours in the emergency room took their toll. Anna began crying more in school. Once again, she was afraid to take the school bus. All this came to a head one day when the bus driver told her that her stop would be the last one. She couldn't stand to be last, especially when she was in such a hurry to get home. The very next time I tried to put her on the bus, she began screaming, crying and choking so hard I thought she'd have another seizure. After all, how could she live her life as before when she couldn't understand what had happened to her body? How could she (and we) have any sense of control, any level of comfort, if she could lose it any time – on the climbing structure, swings, or balance beam – riding her bicycle or just walking down the street? It was hard not to be anxious.

Meanwhile we continued to monitor the tumor and the shunt. The July MRI had been good, showing that the post-operative swelling had gone down and that the shunt was draining properly. The doctor was so pleased that he scheduled the next MRI for October, instead of September. We hoped that, once again, the interval between MRIs would gradually increase. But the news in October wasn't good. The radiologist thought he'd seen some change in the tumor, although the neurosurgeon disagreed. He scheduled the next MRI for December, saying that more change might indicate the need for another resection and that the tumor might now be accessible enough to get the whole thing. I started having flashes: flashes of the surgery waiting room, the doctor reporting to us, the ICU, that bag – the dreaded drain which told us the first time that she needed a shunt – the ambulance ride with the drain for the post-op MRI, and now a new fear, a fear I didn't know enough to feel the other two times – the fear that this tumor was not going to stop growing. And flashes of the sleeper chairs, the long sleepless nights, the tension filled dog walks, the hospital food, the lack of appetite, the sick feeling in the pit of my stomach and the thought of going through it all again. How would Anna take it if she had to have yet another surgery? She felt healthy. Any new surgery was bound to be a surprise, an apparently random hit. It would be even more difficult for her to contain her anxiety if surgeries came out of nowhere when she wasn't even feeling sick. The MRI she had in December was better; the surgeon didn't see enough change in the tumor mass to "warrant surgery at this time." The gamma-knife specialist agreed. We moved to a four-month interval and scheduled the next MRI for March. Meanwhile, the cardiologist reassured us that the heart was stable enough to cope with anything that needed to be done. We were relieved, but we decided to take advantage of the extra time to get a third opinion.

We took several of the MRI films, left Anna at school, and went to see the chief of neurosurgery at UCSF. The traffic was horrendous because San Francisco was in the midst of a huge power failure and the traffic lights weren't working; a one-hour trip took more than two hours. The clinic was dark when we finally arrived. Our spirits were darker when we left. The doctor agreed that surgery was not necessary at this time, but he disagreed with our doctor about the surgical outcome: he felt that the entire tumor was too deeply embedded in the brain to be removed. He also disagreed with the gamma-knife specialist citing the danger of the intense radiation required and saying, "there's no point in just attacking the easy part and leaving the roots." He proposed a third alternative. If the tumor grew, he would apply focused radiation in fractionated doses over a six-week period. What were we to do? Right now, nothing because the tumor might not be growing. But what would we do if it did? We had three entirely different opinions from three top surgeons. How were we supposed to decide, when even the neurosurgeons couldn't agree? Luckily, we didn't have to. Anna had the next MRI on March 22, and the films looked so good that the surgeon moved us to a six-month interval.

Meanwhile, Anna was trying to make more friends – giving her lunch to anyone who asked for it, but not knowing what to do next. She didn't know how to participate in conversations: she didn't understand give and take, wouldn't listen well enough to respond in kind, and would constantly interrupt with irrelevancies. Her peers knew she was different, but she didn't, and that absence of self-consciousness enabled her to keep trying. It gave her strength and persistence.

On the medical front, she was taking her MRIs more in stride. We had always tried to schedule them first thing in the morning, so she wouldn't have to be hungry and anxious for long. Once, however, our appointment was later. Instead of spending the whole morning wandering aimlessly around the house, she spent it reading picture books and writing poems. She knew that she wasn't allowed to eat until afterwards and accepted the prohibition without complaint. In the waiting room, she played with a three-year-old girl and obsessed about the time only a bit. And she didn't cry when the IV was inserted for the anesthesia. She revealed her anxiety only later, crying inconsolably while waiting to see her neuropsychologist, Dr. W. who was a bit behind schedule.

At home, Anna was helping out more around the house, willingly doing many of the chores I asked her to do. She would vacuum, do the laundry (but only if I didn't touch it after sorting), fold the clothes and put them away. She would set the table and take out the trash. She was getting more self-contained and not talking to every stranger she saw on the street. She was playing somewhat more interactively with her friends and began to have long telephone conversations consisting primarily of silly noises and giggles.

She was also becoming more intense about her homework and more focused. Her reading was improving, though it wasn't at fifth grade level, and she was learning how to skim for key words. She could work at home for longer periods than she could at school, especially since I was providing enormous amounts of structure and scaffolding. I never left her alone to work. I sat with her, explained what was required, and, if necessary, guided her through it. General concepts were hard for her, and her thinking was very concrete. We made progress in small increments. She worked diligently and could, with my help, write clear essays. Here's an excerpt from the autobiography she wrote for school. Her spelling and punctuation were much improved, partly because she knew when to check with me. The focus on detail and the lack of emotion are typical. Interestingly enough, she didn't mention the brain tumor or two of her four heart surgeries.

> I was born at 7:00 p.m. at Alta Bates Hospital on January 10, 1987. My parents, a nurse and Dr. Risa Kagen were at my birth. The birth took 48 hours.

I had a serious heart defect. I was turning blue because I didn't have enough oxygen in my blood. They took me to Childrens Hospital in an ambulance. My dad and my mom drove. They put me in the ICU.

When I was 2 days old they put in a Blalock-Taussig shunt on the left side. When I was 1 month old my parents went to the fourth floor and couldn't find me. I was about to go home when I turned totally white. The doctor was playing with me. A nurse named Gwen said "she is back in the ICU." They put in another Blalock-Taussig shunt on the right side. When I was 2 months old, I went home.

Now I am fine and everything is okay.

Then, her anxiety started to increase once again. Although we didn't tell her about our doctors' visits, she undoubtedly sensed our concern. Besides, schoolwork was hard, she was starting to realize how important it was, and a big change loomed on the horizon: the move from an elementary school with about two hundred fifty students to a middle school with almost a thousand. Small schedule changes became difficult. She would refuse to comply and then, after accepting the inevitable, would call me multiple times to make sure I knew. She couldn't handle many of her assignments. She would scream when she didn't understand what to do, refuse to make an effort, and disrupt class by writing "I want my mama" or "I have to go to the bathroom" on the board. The teacher tried negative reinforcement: he gave "0's" for refusing to do assignments and sent her out of the classroom when her behavior became too disruptive. She only screamed louder, and the work remained undone. He worried about what would happen in middle school.

She brought her anxiety home with her. When the morning school bus was late, she'd become progressively more anxious, even though we'd agreed to drive her in if the bus hadn't come by 8:05. She insisted on doing her homework as soon as she got home, and on doing it quickly. Homework sessions were often punctuated with loud cries of "Noooo!" Going over to her friends' houses became more difficult as her friends' circles expanded and we never knew exactly who was going to be there when we arrived. One extra person, even someone she liked, would send her screaming back to the car. We couldn't talk on the phone. Every time it rang, she screamed and ran to answer. She usually gave us the handset willingly when the call was for us but would then stand by trying to hear every detail and loudly telling us to get off the phone. We could talk in peace only if the call was business-related, and when it wasn't, out of desperation, we sometimes said it was. If the call was from one of her doctors or teachers, she would bark "what do you want?" before reluctantly relinquishing the handset. We couldn't make calls without saying whom we were calling and why, and when the call was over, she always wanted to know how long it had lasted. Leaving the house was difficult too. She would start pushing us to go at least half an hour before we had to. When Alan went on business trips, she worried that his plane would crash (just like his father's had) and worried to the point of screaming when he was late calling home. "I know he's dead," she'd say. His trips wore us all out.

Anna did try to control her anxiety and sometimes did very well – up to a point. Her last elementary-school Halloween parade went much better than the first, although she didn't seem to enjoy it much. She put on her costume and marched stalwartly, dutifully in the parade.

This was a task she had set herself. She was determined to participate but could not enjoy it. Halloween had always been more frightening for her than exciting. Disguises were scary – perhaps because she didn't know they weren't real – and she was still afraid of masks and face paint. The piles of candy she always collected couldn't balance out the fear. When her class put on a shortened version of "As You Like It," she steeled herself and did what she had to. She stood up there in her Elizabethan cap and fairytale gown looking like a princess. Her lines were wooden, but she said them clearly. She also had some narrator lines, at which she excelled, and even had the courage to step up at the last minute and replace a missing student narrator. But then she was done. When one of the parents led the students in an unrehearsed rendition of "Give My Regards to Broadway" and presented the teacher with a gift of appreciation, Anna broke down. She had done her best. Singing the song, even listening to it, was more than she could handle.

The summer before middle school, Anna started getting headaches. She'd never had them before, except with increased intracranial pressure, so we didn't know if we could safely attribute them to anxiety. Since she was now beginning to understand the implications of her headaches and knew that they often portended surgery, she became even more anxious. The headaches intensified. But she couldn't talk about them; she couldn't say how scared she was. Instead, she denied having them and filled the house with tantrums, baby talk and silly noises. We did our best to convince her that everything was all right, that she was probably not having shunt failure, and that reporting her physical symptoms was essential.

In June 1999, we decided that something had to be done about Anna's anxiety level. We tried a non-medical approach at first, taking her to a psychologist specializing in cognitive therapy. After spending an hour with him describing Anna's background, we took her in for a session. Neither one them could handle it; he brought her out after ten minutes, implying that she did not have the self-awareness necessary for cognitive therapy, and then he opted out. Next, we took her to a psychiatrist specializing in psychotropic medications. The psychiatrist noted her anxiety as she flitted all over his office picking up whatever struck her fancy and endlessly repeating his first name. He prescribed Buspar, the most innocuous of the anxiety drugs, because he wanted to avoid medications with possible cardiac effects. Then, he sent us on our way.

SIXTH GRADE

About halfway through Anna's last year at Jefferson, I began to look at middle schools. The few private middle schools I saw either were fast tracked or filled a specialized niche that was not appropriate for Anna. The teachers, unlike elementary-school teachers, were inclined to focus more on academics than on the whole child, and the homogeneity of the school population, even in schools that were reasonably ethnically diverse, would have made Anna stand out. We feared that this would mean that the teachers would be less understanding of Anna's differences and that they would focus on her deficits rather than on her strengths. Once again, we turned to the public schools with their ethnically, socially, socio-economically and intellectually diverse student body.

We chose the public school whose teachers seemed most structured and in control of the classroom. Our job didn't end once we'd made our choice though. We couldn't choose the teachers, but we could do our best to allay Anna's anxiety by introducing her to the school before classes began. We also wanted to make sure that her teachers knew what they were getting into. Anna's IEP, the Individualized Education Plan that describes the special services to be provided, specified that she would be a full inclusion student: that is, a special-education student whose program consists entirely of general education, rather than special education, classes. She would receive whatever support she needed to keep up with the work. We met with the vice principals before school started and they urged us to authorize the provision of a one-on-one instructional assistant (IA) to sit in class with Anna and provide academic and behavioral support. Anna had never had an IA, but the school was large and she'd be changing classes for the first time, so we agreed. A few days later, I took her to meet her two main teachers and the full inclusion specialist – the woman who supervised the IAs, informed the general-education teachers about her students' special needs, oversaw specialized services like speech and occupational therapy, and coordinated the IEPs. To ensure that all her teachers understood both her strengths and weaknesses, I hand delivered a letter describing her special needs and health status to each one.[8]

The weekend before the first day of school was very difficult. Anna's anxiety was sky high, despite the pleasant weekend we'd planned. As we were standing in front of the house talking to a neighbor, another neighbor, Jerry, came strolling by. Anna disliked Jerry because he talked incessantly, rarely listened to what Anna said, and always seemed to come over just as we were about to leave. Naturally, he began to talk, and naturally, she started to scream, "Not Jerry! I hate Jerry!" The dog's tail went down. He shook and she wailed. Then the next day, after a delicious lunch and show at a local jazz club, the clouds reappeared. The club stamps the hands of its customers so they can leave and return if necessary. Anna was very uncomfortable about her ink-stained hand but was willing, after some persuasion, to leave the stamp on until the end of the concert. Then she ran to the restroom. She scrubbed and scrubbed, getting more and more agitated as it became apparent that the stamp would not come off. Some fast talking convinced her to wait for the special soap we had at home. Then Alan refused to buy the performer's CD. He'd bought CDs at previous performances, but this time, he wasn't interested. That was too much. We had altered the pattern, changed the rules, and Anna wasn't having any of it. The storm hit as we entered the parking garage – she screamed, she yelled, and she hit us both with flailing fists. We had to call Dr. W. right away; she was the only one who could help Anna get this anxiety under control.

The first week of school went reasonably well. On the first day, I met her outside her classroom and she introduced me to the pleasant, motherly woman, Heather, who was to be her IA. She came home every day bubbling about the candy Heather had brought her and sat down immediately to work. The next school day followed a three-day weekend. On Tuesday, she forgot we had another appointment with Dr. W. and came home determined to do her homework immediately. She rushed through one of her three assignments. When I told her it was time to go, she dug in her heels screaming. She wanted to do her homework, so I should cancel the appointment. She was NOT going. And then she started pushing me. I had to think fast. If she didn't go, I told her, she'd have to spend the rest of the day in her room. That convinced her. I was very glad we had made the appointment. When we got there, Dr. W. made sure Anna understood there were things for which you have a fixed appointment and things for which you don't. She said you have to plan around appointments and figure out when to get the other things done. She also made her apologize to me. In the car on the way home, I tried to prepare Anna for the upcoming homework session. I outlined a structure that would, I hoped, slow her down. When we got home, I said, she was to:

> Figure out what assignments had to be done and when they were due,
>
> Make sure she understood the directions on the assignment she had chosen to do,

Work slowly and carefully.

I was exhausted and so was she.

The next day, I picked her up with some trepidation. She had clearly been crying. Heather hastened to assure me that she'd been doing just fine and that she'd simply "had too much energy." It turned out that she had responded to the teacher's homework assignment with her usual cry of "I don't want any homework," and had been sent out of the room. Her increased anxiety was making her loudly oppositional. At school though, she only yelled. At home, where she felt free to let loose, she would scream, call me names, shout, "You can't have your way," and even hit me. I was at my wit's end. Time-outs were impossible because she wouldn't go into her room, and shoving matches were out of the question. When her behavior began to get aggressive, I could only lock myself away and try to deal with the source of her anxiety before it became overwhelming.

The worst time was when I picked her up from school. First of all, I still had to be precisely on time – she would scream if I was even one minute late. Secondly, she insisted on going home immediately with no stops en route; this meant I couldn't talk to her teachers or do errands unless I was prepared for a tantrum. She had worked hard all day and done as well as she could to control herself. When at last she saw me, it was time to go home and "take the girdle off." Warnings, threats and punishments did nothing to silence the screams; only home would do.

Anna's anxiety decreased during the first part of the school year. We had increased her dose of Buspar and, with help from the community that had surrounded her at

Jefferson and that remained solid at King, she was settling in. One day, Anna's P.E. uniform disappeared. A classmate who'd been part of the Jefferson community saw another girl wearing it and reported what she'd seen to the vice principal. The uniform was immediately returned.

Anna was doing well academically. Although her reading comprehension was poor, her writing was improving to the point where she could write clear, though superficial, essays. At the beginning of sixth grade, her teacher asked the students to write a letter of introduction. She helped structure it by asking a series of questions. Here is Anna's letter. As always, the punctuation and spelling are hers.

> I am smart and beautiful. I am a very great reader and I can relax while reading a good book. I like to write stories. I don't like to run because it makes me tired. Since I was born I've had 4 heart surgerys.
>
> I learned that King [her new school] is different from Jefferson [her old school] because it is a lot bigger. King also has a good snack bar, hard work, and many different teachers.
>
> I am surprised we will be able to swim at King swimming pool. I don't know how to swim so I will learn a lot.
>
> So far or right now I am not afraid of anything. I am afraid the work might get too hard.
>
> One of my goals this year is to spend the night at point reyes [the standard sixth grade field trip]. Another is to be a great swimmer. I will also learn to be more patient.

She seemed less compulsive about starting her homework the minute we walked in the door and more willing to do it carefully. She was even beginning to enjoy doing some of the assignments. One day, the teacher asked each student to design a game. This was an assignment Anna could really get into; her game was called "Hospital." Similar to Monopoly, it requires players to throw a die and move their markers around the board. The spaces on the board refer to hospital locations and events, and each one has a positive or negative score attached. Players who land in the ICU, for example, lose twenty points, while those who land in the playroom gain twenty. The winner is the one who reaches a hundred first. The players begin by drawing Disease Cards, which indicate a medical condition and a place on the board: those with brain tumors start out in the ICU and immediately lose twenty points, while those with less serious conditions go to the floor and gain ten. There are also Direction cards, which send the players to particular spaces, and a space labeled "You're Dying." Players who land on that space must take a "you're dying" card and if they get three of these cards, they die – that is, they lose the game. This game made such a hit that we briefly considered trying to get it published or at least giving copies to hospitals.

And there were good times too. One day, we joined a group doing charity work at a nursing home. Anna was uncomfortable at first, but the minute she saw food, she knew what to do. She would serve, and off she went moving purposefully and solicitously around the room. She threw me a surprise birthday party in December. She had attended two surprise parties and wanted to do one of her own, so she conceived, planned, and executed it all by herself. She called all our adult friends, took Alan to order (and pay for) the cake, suggested that our friend Sally baby-sit while Alan and I had our birthday dinner, helped Sally decorate the house, put together loot bags, and kept the secret for two whole weeks. Alan and I returned home from our birthday dinner to shouts of "surprise!" This was also the year we discovered *Harry Potter*. Whenever we had time, all four of us, including the dog, would snuggle up as Alan read aloud. Despite the violence that pervades the series, these books meant so much to Anna that she saved her money and bought each new volume as soon as it came out.

Anna was doing well neurologically. Her September MRI looked good and the interval between MRIs remained at six months. Then we met with the cardiologist. To avoid giving Anna another source of anxiety, we didn't include her in the meeting. The cardiologist had previously talked about doing two surgical procedures: inserting a shunt to encourage growth of the left pulmonary artery and then later hooking up the newly enlarged (he hoped) pulmonary artery to restore blood flow to the left lung. He now told us, that before considering these two procedures, the surgeon would require a transeptal catheterization, which involved poking a hole through the septum or the wall between the heart chambers. This was more than we'd anticipated. The cardiologist felt that three surgical procedures would be too much, especially since there was no guarantee they would work. We breathed a sigh of relief: guilty relief because we knew doing nothing meant Anna would have only one functional lung, but not so guilty because the quality of her life would not be affected. What was necessary, the cardiologist went on, was to replace the conduit that was serving as the central portion of her pulmonary artery. We had known that was coming. Not only was Anna outgrowing the conduit, but the conduit was calcifying and, therefore, decreasing in diameter. Since, in addition, the conduit's valve was no longer working, the blood flowing through the right side of her heart was splashing back. This made the heart work harder than it should, and overworked hearts become enlarged. Anna's heart was now one and a half times its normal size. But the cardiologist was in no hurry. Anna had had her last brain surgery only six months ago, and he felt that heart surgery could wait until the summer. So as long as we didn't let Anna know and as long as our frequent doctor visits did not include discussions of future cardiac procedures, we could go back to trying to live a normal life.

During the second quarter of the school year, Anna's anxiety increased partly because her beloved Nana, who called every week and gloried in her granddaughter, was very ill. One day when she'd lost some work she'd done, she cried so hard that she got a headache and began to throw up. When she felt better, she explained that she'd been crying, not from pain, but from sadness. This was the first time she was able to put her emotions into words, the first time she distinguished physical pain from emotional pain, and the first time she saw that talking about feelings could be more helpful than denying them.

Her headaches became more frequent. At first, we thought shunt failure, but then it became clear that she had them only on Mondays. That suggested stress. It became clearer still that there were two very specific causes of her stress at school: band and her IA. Band was scheduled first thing in the morning before school actually began. That was hard enough. There were 90 kids in the class, one lackadaisical teacher, and occasionally a volunteer. The teacher made no effort to teach. He would just assign pieces whose difficulty far surpassed Anna's clarinet playing skills and the musical skills of many of the other students and stand there conducting cacophony, while the less talented kids ran wild. The class was too much for Anna, and we resolved to drop it for the second semester.

The IA was a motherly woman who had never been an IA before and had received no training. Although she was thrilled at the possibility of helping this "poor little girl" who had so many health problems, she had no idea how to do it. She would constantly call Anna at home and buy her treats. She would brag about Anna's achievements when I picked her up not realizing that Anna wanted to be the one to brag. She would do Anna's work for her when she could, and, when Anna didn't understand an assignment, merely tell her to reread the instructions. Anna likes to please. She wanted to do assignments right, and she wanted to finish them quickly. Simply telling her to reread an assignment didn't help her understand it. Assignments had to be explained and structured in a way that would enable her to complete them to her satisfaction. She found Heather's approach terribly frustrating, and she responded by crying, screaming and refusing to do the work. Not knowing what else to do, Heather would take her out of the room and mete out one detention after another. The detentions upset Anna even more: she was missing class; she would, therefore, not be able to keep up with the other students; and by not keeping up, she felt she was making her teachers angry.

We had a reasonably good winter break visiting our parents in New York, although Nana's condition was worrisome. Then it was time for school and Anna jumped bravely back in. But her stress level was just too high. One day, at the end of the first week, as she was struggling with a particularly difficult assignment,

Heather bent over her a little too closely. The difficulty of the work combined with Heather's suffocating presence brought on the screams, and the teacher responded by sending Anna to detention. That was too much. Anna couldn't take it. She punched Heather as hard as she could and school-district policy came down on her head; she was suspended for three days. Something had to be done to reduce the stress.

Our strategy was multiple. First, we devised a checklist for Anna to follow while working. We hoped that it would give her a structure, make it easier for her to ask for help and simultaneously help her become more independent. We promised Anna we'd get Heather to back off if she used it. Here's the checklist we devised.

<u>Anna's checklist for doing her work to be done with every helper</u> (Mom, Dad, at school…)

1. Do I understand what I'm supposed to do? Yes _____ No _____

If yes, proceed to step 2.

If no, then read it again and see if I understand it.

If still no, ask for help.

2. Do I know how to do it? Yes _____ No _____

If yes, proceed to step 3.

If no, think about it some more.

If still no, ask for help.

3. Do the work. Did I do it slowly and carefully? Yes _____ No _____

If yes, proceed to step 4.

If no, do it over, slowly and carefully. Then proceed to step 4.

4. Check the work. Did I check it slowly and carefully? Yes _____ No _____

If yes, proceed to step 5.

If no, check it over, slowly and carefully. Then proceed to step 5.

5. Am I sure I understand the work? Yes _____ No _____

If yes, hand the work in.

If no, ask for help.

The checklist was never used. Heather was not sensitive enough to use it properly and Anna resisted since it made everything take longer. But Anna and Heather both learned from the incident; Anna tried harder to rein in her impulses, and Heather learned to keep off Anna's back.

Anna's full inclusion specialist was also working to improve the situation. She devised a behavioral plan with the help of the school psychologist. She planned to use a series of positive and negative re-enforcers to help Anna replace inappropriate behaviors with more appropriate alternatives. She hoped that she could teach Anna to chew gum and work quietly instead of picking her nose, jumping out of her seat, and shouting. More important, she replaced Heather with an IA who had more experience dealing with behavioral issues. The behavioral plan was ineffective because Anna's anxiety, the source of the disruptive behaviors, was too strong.

The replacement IA was only somewhat helpful. Ms. R. did not smother Anna with love, as had Heather. She kept her distance in a professional manner and was consistent in punishing disruptive behaviors. But after a while, the number of detentions increased, and Anna, who wanted desperately to please her teachers, grew even more anxious. Now the main problem was that Ms. R. did not know how to teach; she did not know how to structure assignments so that Anna felt she knew what she was doing. One day, the class was given an assignment involving the Pangaea Hypothesis, according to which South America and Africa were once part of one large continent. The students had to cut out maps of South America and Africa and try to fit them together. Since Anna's spatial perception is poor, this assignment was very difficult for her. She grew more and more frustrated, refused to focus, and was sentenced to detention for the following day. When we got home, her refusal to do any homework and her tear-stained face told the story. Later that day, when she was more relaxed, Alan decided to help her with the assignment. Afterwards, he wrote the following letter to the IA. Its purpose was to clearly outline some teaching strategies in hopes that Ms. R. would be able to implement them.

Dear Ms. R:

Anna and I worked on the plate tectonics exercise. When we started, she did not understand the concept, so she was very frustrated. When I explained it to her, it began to make sense, and then she was able to do it.

This is very typical of Anna. She needs to know what she is doing and why, and she often finds it difficult to understand things. When this happens, she gets frustrated. Sometimes, if you are dealing with a complicated concept, such as plate tectonics, it is necessary to repeat the explanation of the background until she gets the concept. Then she may be able to do the work.

Even when she gets the background ideas, it may be necessary for her to work through the task one step at a time. Often what we have to do is break the task into smaller pieces, until she does understand. Sometimes a paragraph is too much for her to "swallow" at once. She should use the checklist we wrote to help her structure the way she works on things. If she does not understand a paragraph, then she should work on the paragraph a sentence at a time. She should try to make sense of things by herself, and check with you. But if she really doesn't get it, you should explain it to her.

By the way, Anna came home very worried about being sent to detention tomorrow. I assured her that since she did the work this afternoon, she will not be sent to detention.

Thank you very much for your help.

Anna was not sent to detention the next day. And she was doing well academically despite her anxiety.

Afternoons were difficult. Each day, I picked her up from school, stomach knotted, wondering how long her screaming would last. If she'd had a good day, I could prolong it by taking her directly home. If the day had been bad, even going directly home couldn't stem the tide. She had worked so hard to hold herself together at school that she had to let it all out as soon as she saw me.

Once we got home, there was always homework. Anna plugged away at it patiently because she wanted to finish all her assignments and she wanted good grades. She'd work for hours with me at her side. She and I read all her English and history assignments out loud, discussing them as we went. I then helped her write up her ideas. Math was easier. Once she understood a concept and its associated algorithms, she could work through the assignment by herself. But I still had to sit there; I had to reassure her that she was doing just fine.

The telephone was still a major source of anxiety. After all, it brought bad news. It told us when Nana was sick; it told us when Anna had a doctor's appointment; and it told us when medical tests or surgical procedures were scheduled. It also took us away from her while we were talking. Incoming calls were the worst; our friends called us only if absolutely necessary, and they never called after 9:00 PM. One night, when our good friend Sally called shortly before 9:00, Anna couldn't contain herself. She pulled her arm back and hit me as hard as she could. She was more cautious about hitting Alan, possibly because of his six-foot frame and deep voice. But a phone call timed a bit too close to her bedtime once made her spiral out and let loose on him. On the advice of her psychiatrist, we increased her Buspar.

The increased dose seemed to help. By dampening Anna's anxiety, it allowed her to become more reflective and to make the most of our familial routines. She could finally relax. She became more responsive and our conversations grew more natural. We took the dog for long walks together, chatting comfortably. Dinners were a pleasure, and weekends a breeze, once we got the homework out of the way. When Mother's Day found me in New York, Alan and Anna celebrated by themselves. He began by asking her what her perfect day would be, and she didn't hesitate: lunch at a very good local restaurant, a visit to the Exploratorium, and a walk over the Golden Gate Bridge. She was ready for almost anything.

Nana died that year. When we went to her funeral, we wondered whether we should take Anna. We didn't know how she would handle it, and she was afraid to go. My parents even offered to baby-sit. But Dr. W. said she had to go, so we took her. Anna regressed enormously on the plane; she whined for the entire six-hour trip. It was scary – she'd never been to a funeral – and it made her way too sad. But when she got there, she knew she had to say good-bye and she was terrific. She talked seriously and appropriately with the officiating rabbi and connected with him during the service. At the cemetery, she joined us all in putting her shovelful of dirt on the grave. She was "helping to bury Nana."

She was doing better in school too. By the end of sixth grade, her teachers felt she was fitting in nicely. They were more than complimentary on her final grade report, and three of her teachers made especially nice comments.

> "Anna comes to class prepared, completes her daily work, is punctual and has a good classroom attitude and behavior."

> "Anna has grown tremendously this year. She is much more mature and more in control of her impulses. She comes to class prepared, completes daily work, turns in homework, is punctual and has a good classroom attitude."

> "Anna has stopped fighting with me and is trying to the best of her ability [in P.E.] to do the class work and is a pleasure to have in class."

We breathed a sigh of relief.

THE LAST (WE HOPE) HEART SURGERY (2000)

With the tumor temporarily out of the picture, we could take another look at the heart. The surgeon had done the full repair when Anna was fifteen months old. He had replaced the missing section of the pulmonary artery with the largest conduit he could fit into her infant chest, but we knew that she would outgrow it. The cardiologist had said that the conduit would probably last no more than eight years. It had lasted twelve. Now, the conduit was too small, its valve no longer functioned, and Anna's heart, which was enlarged, was working too hard. In May, she had a catheterization, and the cardiologist saw what he expected to see. It was time for cardiac surgery #5.

Anna's face crumpled when we told her she would be having more surgery that summer. Then she took a deep breath, pulled herself together, and announced: "I love the hospital. I want to have surgery." The surgeon, impressed with her attitude and her strength, predicted she'd be out of the hospital in no time. During her pre-op visit, Anna interviewed all the parents and kids who had come for surgery that day, announcing that this was her ninth surgery and that she loved it. One of her subjects was a large, imposing 15-year-old boy, whose mother we later met in the parents' waiting room. Her son, she told us, had known that he needed surgery but had resisted it. That morning, he'd said that he would come to the hospital but that the cops would have to drag him into the operating room. Then he saw Anna. "If she can do it," he said pointing her out, "so can I," and he marched right in.

Here's Alan's description of the surgery.

> Surgery began about 8 AM Tuesday. There's anesthesia and extensive prepping before the patient

gets hooked up to the heart/lung machine; these took nearly 2 hours. The heart/lung machine is an issue. In the past, Anna's been on the machine 3+ hours, and that can be problematic. This time, when the surgeon looked at her plumbing, he decided that there was no sense trying to open the LPA [left pulmonary artery] – it wasn't really visible, and trying to thread a pathway to the left lung would be like trying to find the proverbial needle in a haystack. That meant he wouldn't meddle with the left-hand side of her heart – and that meant he could use a new technique on the right hand side. In the old days (5 years ago), the heart/lung machine would literally replace the heart and lungs, doing the oxygenation and pumping for those organs. The patient's blood was chilled, and the heart was stopped during surgery. This time they did a "warm" conduit replacement. The heart/lung machine was used for oxygenation, but the heart itself was kept in action. The net result: Anna was on the heart/lung machine for only 40 minutes, and she was out of the operating room by noon. FYI, the conduit that was installed – the main branch of the pulmonary artery – is 27 mm wide. The surgeon said that mine [Alan's] is probably 25 mm wide – which means that Anna's is more than big enough, and should last for a very long time.

Anna went up to the ICU about lunchtime. By 2 PM she was waking and dozing frequently, and making it very clear when she was up that she wanted to be taken off the respirator. That couldn't happen until she was "over-breathing" – breathing more frequently, both asleep and awake, than the number of times per minute that the respirator was set for, and staying well oxygenated. She got stronger through the day, and the respirator was removed at about 10 last night. She slept well, and this morning the nurses removed a number of her IV lines. She continued to do well. At 4:30 this afternoon she got out of bed and sat in a chair for about an hour. Then a bed opened up in "monitored care," and Anna and her possessions were moved to that unit. The MCU has a two- or three-to-one nurse-to-patient ratio, it's much more serene than the ICU, and being moved there is a sign that you no longer need constant observation. We'd hoped she could make it there in 2 days. Getting there in one day is amazing.

Anna continued to improve as Alan describes.

When I returned to the hospital yesterday morning, her surgical drain tube had been removed, and she was able to walk around the MCU. However, as she was weaned from her powerful pain medicines, she became more aware of her pain and tired somewhat easily. Last night she had a decent night's sleep. She was more rested this AM. As a result she had more stamina and, while still complaining of pain at the site of her incision, was visiting other patients. She's always loved babies, and she was happily tracking the medical courses of the two infants who'd fallen out of a window and off a balcony respectively (!), and of an 8 month-old who'd swallowed a penny that got stuck in her throat. (You should've seen the baby's X-ray!)

Anna's X-ray and echocardiogram showed that her new, improved conduit is functioning well, and that the conduit's valve is also working well. In consequence, the pressure in her right ventricle, which does the heavy pumping, is much reduced. That's what counts for the long run.

Anna was home in her own bed just 72 hours after the surgery ended. She was determined to get out of the hospital, but things slowed down to a more normal pace after she got home. Alan wrote this note two weeks after the surgery.

The one-liner: everything's proceeding more or less according to schedule. Given that the recuperation process typically takes about 6 weeks, Anna is about where one would expect.

As you know from previous reports, Anna's recovery got off to a very quick start. Like a sprinter out of the starting block, she raced out of the ICU in one day and home from the hospital after two more. But, recuperation is more like a long-distance race than a sprint, and (given the law of averages) the quick start was bound to be followed, at some point, by a leveling-off.

Needless to say, Anna's levelings-off have to have unique Anna-like twists; our kid couldn't possibly do things in ordinary fashion. At various times during the week and a half since her return from the hospital, Anna has had headaches, nausea, and decreased appetite; she's been extremely tired, and on the irritable side. For those of you who know the symptoms, these are signs of ... yes, indeedy: shunt failure. Perhaps her brain craved some of the attention her heart was getting?

Of course, each of the aforementioned symptoms has a logical explanation. Who wouldn't be tired after surgery? Anna's hemoglobin count was low, and that contributes to tiredness. She'd returned home on "hospital schedule," waking up promptly at 3 AM most nights and staying up for a few hours. All that could explain extreme tiredness easily enough. Headaches are not uncommon after anesthesia, and they can, of course, be stress-induced. Anna's never been a big eater. The iron pills Anna was prescribed for the low hemoglobin count were the most likely cause of nausea, and when we discontinued them, the nausea stopped. Nonetheless, the neurosurgeon suggested a CT scan to check, just in case....

So, at 1:00 this afternoon we had a cardiology clinic visit. The cardiologist said that Anna's conduit is working well, there's no fluid around the heart, and that he can hear very little heart murmur (pre-surgery, there was a huge murmur). The regions around Anna's incisions are all healing nicely, so Anna can bathe once again. All told, a very positive report. At 2:45 Anna had a CT scan. It showed that Anna's ventricles (the liquid chambers of the brain, which hold and transport cerebrospinal fluid) were small, so her shunt is draining properly. Her various neurological symptoms, then, are "simply" the concomitants of recovery from major and stressful surgery.

In short, Anna and her parents are all tired, headachy, and cranky (though Anna's father almost never loses his appetite), and that's to be expected. The recovery is on course. We have to keep reminding ourselves that the full course is 6 weeks, and it's only been 2 weeks since the surgery. All told, it's pretty amazing.

Anna's recovery proceeded more smoothly after that, and life began to feel more normal. We immersed ourselves in *Harry Potter*. We'd already read the first three books and were well into the fourth when a friend lent us the tapes made by a Broadway actor named Jim Dale. Anna listened to all three sets several times. Then, one day, a package arrived. Jim Dale had sent Anna the audio version of the fourth book along with a card praising her courage. Our friend had forwarded Alan's email notes to him and he wanted to join the ever expanding community that surrounded and supported her.

She was doing very well four weeks after the surgery when Alan wrote the following email note.

> Anna has been sleeping through the night most nights, and her energy level is returning to normal. She hasn't needed a nap during the day for the past few days, and on a calm day she makes it straight through to her normal bedtime. Her headaches have pretty much disappeared, and she's gotten her appetite back. (Anna was hardly Rubenesque pre-op, standing 5 feet tall and weighing 73 pounds. After surgery she was down to 66 pounds, meaning she'd lost a full 10% of her body weight – she looked somewhat like the pictures of refugees in the newspapers. But now she's eating as much as Jane, if not more, and she's gaining some of her weight back). The cardiologist was very happy with what he saw. An echocardiogram showed there's no fluid around the heart, her incision scars are healing well, and her color is good. (This means her hemoglobin count must be improving – both the cardiologist and pediatrician, whom we visited Friday, said she looked so good that a blood test for her hemoglobin

level wasn't necessary). In short, we couldn't ask for better.

Two weeks later, Anna had completely recovered and was going to day camp full time. But she was anxious, and her anxiety was making her insufferable. Alan took her to the camp bus every day, and every day it was the same thing. She didn't trust him to get ready on time.

"Did you have your shower yet?"

"It's almost time to go."

"No pee."

"Put on your shoes."

Then when he pulled up behind the bus, she just knew it would leave without her and ran to get on. A short time after she started camp, I got the worst head cold I'd ever had; my head was so stuffed up that I couldn't sleep or think, let alone go to work. I had made it through the surgery and Anna's recovery, and now it was my turn to collapse. That made Anna more anxious; she had trouble sleeping and tantrums shook the house. She started to relax when I got better, camp ended, and summer vacation continued, but she relaxed too much and wandered around the house all day doing absolutely nothing. That drove us crazy so Dr. W. suggested a schedule and I created one; Anna was to spend an hour reading, an hour doing an art project, an hour watching a video, and it worked. Structure was what she needed: she was productive and cheerful, and her anxiety at last started to abate.

SEVENTH GRADE

We had learned a lot in sixth grade. We had learned how to communicate with the teachers and with the school district. We had learned that the IAs, although generally very nice people, were not adequately trained and had little understanding of how to help Anna learn. We wrote long letters describing Anna's need for an IA capable of structuring and providing support for Anna's academic work and social-skill development. Dr. W. backed us up with a letter describing Anna's strengths and weaknesses, explaining the kind of support required, and noting that untrained IAs did more harm than good. We then decided to find our own IA. After contacting the School of Education at UC Berkeley (where Alan worked) and posting notices without success, I called everyone I knew and finally struck gold at Dandelion, Anna's preschool. The teachers recommended a caring and sensitive woman who knew how to work with children and who, coincidently, was just then applying for IA positions. We met with her, went to the school district, and did what we could to facilitate her appointment. The letters that we had written ensured that Anna's needs would be met by a qualified IA. This woman, who was more than qualified, was hired less than a week before school started. She made all the difference.

The first week of school was torture. Anna screamed in the morning, screamed when I picked her up, and screamed because she wanted to do her homework as soon as she got home. She was actually controlling herself quite well in school however. The tantrums were held in check until she felt safe enough to relax – that is, when she got home. In the morning, they helped her get ready for school; Alan got the brunt of those tantrums. I got hit in the afternoon. The minute she saw me waiting, her tightly wound spring would uncoil and she would noisily collapse. Nevertheless, as the introductory letter she wrote to her English teacher indicates, she really did like school.

"Dear Ms G.," she wrote.

I love to read and what I love to read is chapter books. The one I am reading now is "The Westing Game." It is very funny. I read it out loud at nighttime to practice reading. My parents are reading me "Charlie and the Great Glass Elevator." They are both good books. I also love to swim, eat and sleep because they are very peaceful. I like to talk. I also like talking on the phone. I also love jazz musicians like Louis Armstrong and Ella Fitzgerald.

The kinds of writing I like to do are I like to write stories and essays because they are fun to write. I also like making silly lists. I also like making cards and gifts for people that I know or know of in the hospital. I made a card for a friend's minister's daughter who had heart surgery.

This summer I had open-heart surgery, as you already know. The reason I had it is the conduit that replaces the pulmonary artery was too small. Do you love that? I do. So they put in a bigger conduit. Do you love that? I do. I have had 9 surgeries: 5 heart surgeries and 4 brain surgeries.

What I am looking forward to this year is cooking meals in the kitchen because when I was at King last year, I cooked meals in the kitchen from different countries and I want to do it again this year. I also want to learn how to translate in French this year.

With the help of the new IA, Anna began to calm down. Alan and I met with her teachers in November to keep in touch and to make sure there were no problems. They said she was doing very well in school. They liked her, appreciated her, understood the sources of her difficulties, and were doing a good job of accommodating them. They all praised the new IA's understanding of Anna's needs and her ability to help Anna calm down, to stand back when help wasn't necessary and to help other students.

The teachers also appreciated Anna's unusual perspective. When asked to write a short essay about collections, for example, Anna wrote the following.

> Hello. I am going to collect hospital equipment because I love the hospital. I love it because I go there a lot. They fixed my heart defect and my brain tumor. They remember me and my parents and they are nice to us.
>
> I am going to call a company called Slatabee's and order the equipment. Then I will go to the hospital and give the equipment to people like Smadifia who has a disease called Bell's Palsy. That is when half of your face is paralyzed (it can not move). Giving the equipment to these people will help them get better. They need to use it at home.
>
> What I want to collect is IVs, respirators, pulse-oximeters, etc. IVs give you food through your veins. The respirator helps you breathe. The pulse-oximeter is used for measuring the oxygen in your blood. When I am in the hospital, I use them to help me get better so that I can go home.
>
> I am going to learn how to use these machines because I want to be a nurse some day. The reason I

> do is because I love hospitals. If I am a nurse I get to help patients get better. Do you love that? I do.

Anna was obsessed with the hospital and referred to it whenever she could, even if the assignment had to be twisted to make it fit. She loved to make her writing funny and invented funny names, even if the topic was serious, and she had certain stock phrases like "do you love that?" which she always tried to include. She still focused on details and had difficulty perceiving the whole picture. This is clear in all her seventh grade writing. Here is another example.

> This is a comparison of Japan and Europe during the feudal times. In Europe, feudalism started when Rome fell in 814 AD because the people needed protection. It started in Japan in the 1100s also because people needed protection from the invaders. Even though they were two totally different cultures, they had a lot of things in common.
>
> Part of feudalism was a class of warriors trained to protect others. The warriors were called knights in Europe and samurai in Japan. The knight began his training to fight as a page and then a squire. In Japan, the samurai practiced with a sword and studied martial arts. The European knights had horses, armor and chain mail. The samurai wore armor made of lacquered steel plates with leather strips. The knight was a Christian and the samurai practiced Buddhism and Shintoism. The European knights had a code called chivalry and the samurai had a code called bushido. They were both codes of honor. The samurai and the knights had to be loyal to their lords because they swore an oath of loyalty. They had to

serve as examples of virtue for people of the lower classes.

In 1454 feudalism ended in Europe. People could live in growing towns instead of the castle. The knights wanted to oversee their land so kings started to pay their soldiers. In 1854 feudalism ended in Japan because the people did not need as much protection.

The people of Japan and Europe had feudalism in common and some of them were warriors who fought and protected others.

Anna was still having language-processing and expressive-language difficulties. She didn't always understand what she was supposed to be doing and had difficulty phrasing her answers to questions. She was no longer receiving speech therapy in school though because she had tested out of it in 1996. But, now in 2000, the full inclusion specialist pointed out that those tests had been administered shortly after the first brain surgery and that even under those circumstances, the dramatic improvement documented at that time was not entirely credible. She and the current speech therapist had observed Anna's social-skill deficits. They noted her failure to make eye contact, her inability to maintain a conversation by responding appropriately to what was being said, and her tendency to repeat the same questions over and over without listening to the answers. They worked together to ensure that speech therapy was reinstated and that it focused on pragmatics, the social aspects of speech. Anna began to receive therapy in a group with a few other fully included special-education students. Although the therapy's effectiveness varied, we were glad that the need had been acknowledged and that some remediating measures were being taken.

At home, when we weren't helping Anna with her homework, doing errands or taking short family trips, we were still reading aloud. One of the many gifts Anna had received after that summer's surgery was a book called *The Bad Beginning* by Lemony Snickett. The cartoonish dilemmas of the Baudelaire children and the comically predictable narrative voice appealed to her sense of humor. And, except for the occasional big word for which the definition was immediately provided by the narrator, it was an easy read. Anna wanted to read these books herself, and so she read every single one in the series. But she did not read them silently because, for her, reading was a social activity; one or both of us would always sit with her while she read them aloud.

We were still cooking together too, and Anna began to take on a more significant role in our weekend breakfast tradition. She was no longer merely playing sous-chef and following Alan's instructions. Instead, she learned to use the food processor and the stove and became an expert crepe maker. Weekend mornings would find her whirling a flour mixture in the food processor and flipping crepes for Alan to fill.

Other aspects of our life were getting easier. We could now talk to Anna, even if she didn't always respond as expected. We could reason with her; we could justify our actions and convince her of their necessity. She was helping out around the house more consistently too. Now, when Alan was out of town, I no longer felt solely responsible for all the housework. She was even beginning to let us talk on the phone. At that time, my mother was terminally ill in New York, and I spent hours on the phone while Anna played quietly by herself. She was willing to call her paternal aunt regularly, even though it meant that Alan would be on the phone for an hour after she got off. And when a friend's call interrupted a read-aloud session, she waited anxiously, but she waited. Of course, we still had to report every phone call we made, and she refused to do anything at all when a call was expected because she feared she wouldn't hear the phone ring.

She was also feeling her oats a bit. Although she was still afraid to try new things, when she did do them it was on her own. One day, she was invited to a birthday party on a chartered fishing boat. The group was to sail around San Francisco Bay and under the Bay Bridge. She refused to go until I had described the event several times in great detail. Then she accepted the challenge. The boat was beautiful with gleaming wood paneling on the inside and an adorable, self-contained kitchen. The sky was California blue, and the salt-sprayed air exhilarating. I really wanted to go along, but she wasn't having any of it.

As always, she handled the big problems like a champion. When Alan went in for shoulder surgery, she was very worried. We explained it all in detail, but she knew only her own surgical experiences and couldn't imagine this one would be any different. On the day of the surgery, she did amazingly well. She was calm until it came time to leave for the hospital. Then she started the usual routine of pushing us to make sure we would leave on time. She didn't break down until I dropped him off. Then, she began to cry. But she was crying sadly, not screaming anxiously, and had recovered by the time we got to school; she clearly understood at some level that her dad was going to be all right.

Anna was becoming more "normal." But as she became more "normal," our expectations increased, and we became less tolerant. Some days stood out. Once, while I was driving her to a birthday party, she thought we were late. She kept screaming, pounding me on the shoulder, and pulling my hair. On the way home, she refused to do any of the errands I had planned because she needed to get home. When we got home, I got stuck on the phone with AT&T for half an hour. She didn't scream but she did curse me, call me names, and tell me to get off the phone. On another, particularly difficult day, she had four major tantrums: one because she didn't want to go to the post office for her passport, the second because she'd mislaid the essay she'd just written, the third over dinner, and the fourth because an untrained friend made the mistake of calling at 10:15 PM and woke her up. We could avoid such behavior by preparing her carefully for everything and reporting afterwards. But such preparation, such reporting, was exhausting and made us feel like prisoners.

As Anna became more "normal," her social-skill deficits stood out. She still didn't really know how to interact with her peers. She had only one good friend, Erika. Erika didn't have any other good friends either, but she knew it and was very dependent on their relationship. Anna was more distanced. She didn't seem to realize the difference between this friendship and the many acquaintanceships she cultivated at school. She was very aware of Erika's disabilities, especially since Erika would often initiate discussions about disability and special education with me. She would make fun of the way Erika spoke and tease her relentlessly. When they sat in the car together, she would poke at Erika, refusing to stop until I reprimanded her. One day, Erika's mother called to say that Anna had been cutting off pieces of Erika's hair and hiding them around the house. Anna was lucky that Erika was so forgiving.

Scoliosis (2001)

Then came another showstopper. Anna had developed a teenage slouch. Although not uncommon, this one looked serious. The cardiologist noticed it during a follow-up visit and referred us to the scoliosis clinic at Children's Hospital. Since children who have had many cardiac surgical procedures are more susceptible to scoliosis and since I have scoliosis, there was a good chance that she did too. X-rays showed that she had a forty-degree curve, and the doctor was concerned because her scoliosis appeared to be progressive. If left unchecked, the curvature could become so severe that it would compress and damage her internal organs. To slow down the progression, he suggested she wear a Boston Brace twenty-two hours a day until two years past her first period, but he also noted that the brace doesn't always work. Then, he ordered an MRI of the spine to make sure the scoliosis wasn't caused by a tumor. Although spinal tumors aren't generally associated with tuberous sclerosis, he wanted to make sure. That was just what we needed: something else to worry about. But this time, there was no tumor.

Meanwhile, Anna's heart was doing well. Before the surgery, the right ventricle had enlarged to about one and a half times normal size. Four months after the surgery, it had already decreased by forty percent of the overage. The small piece of the brain tumor that remained wasn't changing. So I made an appointment with the brace maker. Since these braces are designed to prevent any increase in curvature, they are custom made and must be carefully fitted. Anna was at her most cooperative. First, giggling all the while, she put on a tiny open-ended body stocking, which expanded to cover almost her entire torso.

Then the brace maker covered the stocking with a viscous paste. When the paste had hardened into a mold, he sliced it down the back and removed it. The brace was finished a week later. Anna tried it on, so the brace maker could mark its length. He cut and sanded it while we waited.

The doctor had said that his patients had little difficulty wearing the brace and that their main concern was that it made them look lumpy. But Anna was more sensitive than most. As a toddler, she would take off her clothes at every opportunity and, when she was older, getting her to wear a watch was a struggle. The brace was made of hard, thick plastic. It covered the torso from armpit to waist, and it had three Velcro straps in front. Anna was supposed to put it on like a jacket and pull the straps tightly closed. We wondered how she would do. But Anna is compliant, strong and courageous, and she always follows the rules. We tried to work up to twenty-two hours gradually. One day, she wore the brace for an hour; the next day, she wore it for two. When we got to twelve hours and her bedtime approached, she really did try to wear it to bed. But she couldn't sleep with it. Whenever she managed to fall asleep, she would wake up in the middle of the night feeling very uncomfortable and take it off. We went back to the doctor in March. Seeing little change, he decided to see what would happen without the brace. But he was not hopeful; he expected the curve to increase rapidly, and he urged us to plan for a summer surgery.

For the first time, we felt we were confronting elective surgery. It wasn't really elective, but the consequences of doing nothing were long term, rather than immediate. The gradual compression of internal organs did not impress us quite as much as oxygen deprivation or increased intracranial pressure; Anna was not turning blue or throwing up. And there were three months before the summer: time for alternative approaches and a second opinion. My trusted massage practitioner suggested we try cranialsacral therapy. According to the website of the Upledger Institute, cranialsacral therapy

> is a gentle, hands-on method of evaluating and enhancing the functioning of a physiological body system called the craniosacral system - comprised of the membranes and cerebrospinal fluid that surround and protect the brain and spinal cord.
>
> Using a soft touch generally no greater than 5 grams, or about the weight of a nickel, practitioners release restrictions in the craniosacral system to improve the functioning of the central nervous system.[9]

Practitioners claim that the therapy can help manage scoliosis, but Alan and I were both skeptical; Alan's a mathematician, and neither one of us is into New Age therapies. Nevertheless, I felt I had to try something. During Anna's first appointment, the therapist had Anna and me rolling around on Styrofoam noodles and brushing each other. The work was so subtle that it looked like nothing was being done, but Anna became very jumpy after a half hour. Although physical contact with us was becoming easier for her, it was still very difficult if it involved strangers. When the session was over, the therapist asked if she could bring in another therapist who specialized in children to work with us the next time. I agreed and Anna had her second appointment the following week. The therapists rolled her on noodles, brushed her up and down, and massaged her lightly. I left wondering whether the session had been worth the money I had paid, but I was still hopeful. That night, my hopes were shattered. Alan was out of town. At 11 PM, Anna woke up screaming. She had the worst headache she'd had since her 1998 brain surgery. I gave her a Tylenol, she started to throw up, and she couldn't stop retching, even when nothing was left. Was it shunt failure? I called the advice nurse, although Anna was dead set against it, and the nurse sent us directly to the emergency room. Then I had another job ahead of me. If Alan had been here, he could have picked her up and put her into the car, but I had to rely on my persuasive powers and Anna listened. She understood that she could die if she didn't go. So she went.

In the emergency room we got in line to wait for the triage nurse with Anna yelling "skip them" at everyone ahead of us, and we quickly got a room. Hospital staff do not fool around with possible shunt failure. Anna lay down on the gurney; she was exhausted, but not lackadaisical as she had been during her first shunt failure. "The bed's too hard," she cried. "I wanna go home." We waited. After some time, a doctor arrived, did a neurological examination, and agreed with my assessment: the neurological signs were good. But she also thought the shunt was filling a bit slowly and ordered a CT scan. Then we waited some more. When the tech arrived, he wanted to use sedation because it didn't look like Anna would lie still, but I assured him she would. She didn't. Once again, the tech suggested sedation, and once again, I insisted it wasn't necessary. So I went in with her. The tech encased me in a lead apron that brushed the floor and handed me a huge glove. Anna lay still as I held her head with my gloved hand. Then we waited some more. The CT scan was normal. I wondered if the cranialsacral session was to blame: whether Anna's neurological system was so sensitive that the session, innocuous as it seemed, had caused the headache and vomiting.

The next day, I called the cranialsacral therapists, who claimed that they'd never heard of such a reaction, but that healing can be traumatic when the body is working through traumatic memories. I didn't know whether Anna's body was working through its traumatic memories, but I did know that she was done with cranialsacral therapy.

Every cloud has a silver lining though, and that night had two. The first was that Anna showed that she was mature enough to accept responsibility for her own health. She didn't want to go to the emergency room, but she knew she had to. She was getting ready for the day when she'd have to make these types of decisions on her own. The second was the long talk I had with the emergency room's attending physician. The doctor assured me that I had done the right thing by bringing Anna to the emergency room. She speculated that the symptoms could have been caused by a virus or that the cranialsacral therapy had produced a headache severe enough to induce vomiting. Then we had a long discussion about the scoliosis. She felt that the surgery was not elective. She spoke to me not only as a doctor, but as a mother with two children and as a human being. She understood what we were going through, but she stressed that you just have to make the best of what you have. She said that, as parents, we all have to make hard decisions. Since her kids have asthma, she had to decide whether to give them steroids, which are bad for the heart but which usually alleviate the symptoms; she had to balance the benefits of the drugs with their dangers. She said that Anna would hate me for making her have the surgery, but that she'd hate me even more at the age of thirty-five if I didn't. And she catalogued the effects of scoliosis: inability to carry a baby to term, heart and lung involvement, and a greatly shortened life. Then she said, "Get that kid dressed and take her home." When we left the hospital, I knew we had to do the surgery.

Scoliosis surgery consists of a spinal fusion and the insertion of one or two titanium rods to straighten the spine and prevent further curvature. Timing is critical. Waiting too long before doing the surgery can reduce the extent to which the curve can be corrected, but performing the surgery before a major growth spurt would dangerously increase pressure on the spine. By the spring of 2001, Anna had reached puberty, which is a crucial milestone for this particular surgical procedure, and had essentially finished growing. Any extra growth would probably be confined to her limbs. We discussed the surgical options with the doctor. The usual technique, the posterior surgical approach, involves making a long incision on the back of the spine, but many surgeons also recommend an anterior release of the disc space or removal of the disc from the front. The combination of these two approaches allows for greater curvature reduction and produces a stronger fusion. At first, the surgeon was leaning in that direction, since the anterior release could be performed arthroscopically and would leave only a small scar. But he soon realized that Anna probably had too many adhesions from previous surgeries for an arthroscopic procedure. More important, though, was the fact that this procedure required deflation of one lung, which is not a good idea when the other one isn't working. We would have to be satisfied with the posterior surgical approach and accept the fact that the correction would not be as good.

But we didn't have to make a decision right then. For once, we had some time; no one was rushing us to the hospital. What Anna had wasn't going to kill her – yet. We took that time to get a second opinion at Stanford's Lucille Packard Children's Hospital. After looking at Anna's X-rays and listening to her history, the other surgeon completely agreed with ours. In fact, he felt the procedure should be performed sooner rather than later. It would hinder spinal growth only a bit, and, if the spine did continue to grow, the worst effect would be some crankshafting, spinal twisting, with some loss of correction. He confirmed that kids who've had multiple cardiac surgeries have a much higher incidence of scoliosis, and reassured us about the sturdiness of the hardware used. He also felt very strongly that the anterior approach would entail too many risks because of Anna's other complicating conditions. This was a very different experience from the one we had had with the neurosurgeons, when each doctor advised something completely different. This doctor was confident and straightforward. He made it clear that a posterior spinal fusion was the way to go, and we believed him. So we scheduled the surgery for the first available date, July 31. We would have preferred to do it earlier to give Anna more time to recover before school started, but surgical procedures are difficult to schedule. Besides, we didn't want to miss a long-planned family trip to France.

Anna was really excited about the trip. When a good friend gave her a French tape, she rushed out of the room to listen to it. Anna's not a "material girl" – far from it. Very few toys interested her; she never went through the "mine" stage and would barely look at newly received presents. Even now, she'd rather spend her money on junk food. But she loved this tape. We were excited about the trip too. We were going to spend some time with good friends in the south of France and then a week in Paris. After that, Anna and I would head home, while Alan went on yet another business trip. Anna had become a great traveler and had gotten used to Alan's absences, so we had a hiatus from worry for about two and a half months. It worked partly because we had broken out of our routine, in which a countdown would have been implicit, and partly because Anna didn't know about the impending surgery. Her anxiety made it imperative to avoid telling her too far in advance. For all she knew, she'd be going to her usual day camp when we got home from France. (She did, for a few weeks.) But on May 23, the answering machine broke the spell. Anna's obsession with the telephone didn't stop at the receiver; she would check the answering machine for messages first thing whenever she walked into the house. That day, she heard the message from the orthopedic surgery scheduler confirming the surgery date. Of course, she screamed. But once she calmed down she accepted the inevitable, saying "I have surgery every summer, don't I?" She was able to compartmentalize well enough to thoroughly enjoy our vacation and her three weeks of camp. That doesn't mean she didn't obsess about it; we heard about it every day. But she did manage to keep it under control. She even went on a two-night camping trip with her camp a week and a half before the surgery date. Anna had learned, in a huge psychological growth spurt, that the surgery wouldn't be bad until it actually happened.

July arrived, and we began the intense series of medical visits and tests that, for Anna, must precede any surgery. We saw the cardiologist, who said her heart was stable. Anna had a brain MRI and managed it very well: even though our favorite nurse wasn't there to help sedate her, she went through her paces like the professional patient that she is. The films showed that the tumor had not changed and that the shunt was functioning well. All systems were go. Then we were thrown into a tizzy. The orthopedic nurse called on the day of the MRI saying she'd just had a cancellation and asking whether we'd like to reschedule for two days hence. I was tempted because that would give Anna an extra week and a half for recovery before school started. But then I began to realize how many plans we had both for doctors visits and just plain fun. I realized how our work schedules would suffer, leaving too many tasks unfinished, and how it would rob us of our few remaining days of pre-surgery time. We just couldn't do it.

July 31st finally came and, as always, Anna marched right in. She was ready. It helped that we knew all the medical professionals. We were in a line of three waiting for surgery in the early morning. One anesthesiologist came out of the surgical suite, gave us a big greeting, and then went on to his patient. A second anesthesiologist came out and did the same. The third anesthesiologist came for Anna. He knew us too. After the surgery, we were greeted by a recovery-room nurse who had been Anna's nurse in the ICU after her first surgery in 1987.

But let's not get ahead of ourselves. Anna marched into the surgical suite and we repaired, as always, to the parents' waiting room. The operation consisted of two parts. First, the surgeons placed two titanium rods against the spinal column and anchored them with plates screwed into the vertebrae. You can actually see all this hardware in Anna's X-rays. The rods kept the spine from moving and corrected the curvature as much as possible. Then, to prevent curvature increase, the surgeons performed a spinal fusion, which, in overly simple terms, involves roughing up the spinal tissue so badly that it will scar over and rigidify. This scarring process, which takes about a year, completes the spinal fusion.

The surgery was not straightforward. As Alan reported in the email note he sent to friends that night,

> During surgery, the medical team monitors electrical impulses transmitted along the spinal cord. About half-way through the surgery, when various screws had been put in place for the titanium rods and they were putting some clips in for the top of the rods, the monitors showed a significant drop in the "evoked potentials" – that is, electrical activity in the spinal column. That's bad news; if the drop continued there could be spinal cord damage, muscle weakness or even paralysis. Indeed, it was possible that the surgeons might have had to remove all the hardware they'd installed to that point, and just hope for the best. They woke Anna up and asked her to wiggle her toes. Since she could and since, after a forty-five minute wait, the evoked potentials returned to their normal level, the surgeons decided to proceed. But a larger spinal correction was out of the question; the electrical problem indicated that the risk of fiddling with the spinal column was too high. So instead, they bent the rods to (more or less) the shape of Anna's spine, and continued putting them in place and doing the spinal fusion. As a result, things won't get worse – but they won't be much better than they were before either. That's not what we might've hoped for, but it did achieve what was essential....

If the evoked potentials had not returned to normal, the surgeons would have had to remove all the hardware and stop the surgery; the curve and the risk of increase would have remained as they were, and the entire endeavor would have been for naught.

Anna's in-hospital recovery went well. Alan described it via email.

> Anna's recovery has proceeded in pretty straightforward fashion. This kind of surgery is, alas, very painful. Fortunately, enlightened hospital policies give kids their own PCAs (patient-controlled analgesia), which administer baseline doses of pain reliever and in addition small doses when the patient hits a button that's at her side. So, Anna is a main player in her own pain management. Of course, she's a stoic, and we have to keep reminding her that the PCA is there to be used. But it's a nice touch. Since she came out of surgery the baseline dosage has been steadily reduced, as has Anna's use of it, one sign that she's recovering.
>
> A second good sign is that it looks like Anna will make it through the night without an oxygen cannula – another step toward independence. (Patients are always monitored for oxygen saturation levels (O_2 sats) post-op. 100 is a perfect score, and we like to see figures in the high 90s if possible. If they drop below some threshold when the patient is left on her own – say 93, though the number is variable, depending on context, etc. – then the patient is given a continuous boost of oxygen via a cannula. Typically patients start with a reasonably heavy rate of oxygen flow, and then they're weaned – the flow rate is lowered when the O_2 sats stay above the threshold level, then lowered again, and then stopped when the patient can maintain sats at or above the

threshold level without assistance. It looked like Anna was just about there when I left the hospital this evening. That's one less thing around her neck....

And a third is that she is starting to eat, albeit slowly. The first 24+ hours, nutrition comes via IV, because post-anesthesia one's stomach is likely to respond violently to any input. After that come ice chips or little sips of water. If that stays down, clear liquids are next, then more substantial stuff. Anna had some yogurt this afternoon, so she's on the way.

(We've eaten much better than she, thanks to the kind solicitude of friends who've made sure that we don't have to go near the hospital's cafeteria except for water or breakfast (and bagels are safe). We have a steady input of good things, for which we are most appreciative. I have always been shocked at the quality of the hospital food – it's generally unhealthy (a lot of fried things, for example) as well as unappetizing. I intend to contact Alice Waters after this is all done and see if she'd be interested in helping the hospital serve the kind of food that will make families get better....)

Needless to say, it hasn't all been great. Anna's in pain a fair percentage of the time (perhaps an unfair percentage of the time is a better way to put it). She's hyper-vigilant, finding it hard to fall asleep and startling awake at the slightest sound. (No surprises for this kid, she's on guard.) So, it's not surprising that she's kind of gaunt and more than a bit on the tired side. But, it's only 2 days after surgery, and she's making good progress. She sat up in bed a bit today, will sit up in a chair tomorrow. She'll also be fitted for her brace tomorrow. And once she gets the pain under more control and has the brace on, she may be able to start her sociable tours around the MCU.

The hospital stay went quickly, but it was, as usual, full of ups and downs. On the evening of the fourth day, Alan wrote the following email.

Through this morning, her progress was slow and steady. After the initial scare during surgery, everything went according to plan: each day Anna's color was a bit better and she had a bit more energy. There was measurable progress along all the lines I mentioned in the previous report: Anna's O_2 sats stayed high enough to keep the cannula off, and her persistence at breathing exercises brought the sat levels up yesterday and today. The amount of painkiller she self-administered diminished over each 8-hour period, another good sign. In some ways, this was better than many recoveries – we're used to "two steps forward, one step back," and there were no steps backward. On the other hand, progress was slow. Anna spent a lot of time napping and/or in pain, and her literal steps forward (we walked a few steps together) exhausted her.

This morning, in fact, she was tired and grumpy, and ate and drank so little that we were afraid that we might have to take a big step backward and increase the amount of nutrients coming through her IV. Then, a nurse came by and gave Anna the best motivational speech I've ever heard. She asked if Anna wanted to stay in the hospital forever. "Can someone really?" asked Anna. "Yes," said the nurse, and she told Anna the story of a patient who'd decided she didn't want to drink. The patient, a girl about Anna's age, was in the hospital for an extra four days, with sustenance through the IV instead of her mouth, until she realized it was true that you can stay forever. Once she figured that out she started drinking as fast as she could, and was out of the hospital the next day. Having told this story, the nurse then said that she would be delighted to adopt Anna and keep her at the hospital if Anna wanted to live there – she'd see her there 8 hours a day, and take care of her two boys the rest of the time. Anna's response was essentially "thanks but no thanks," and she got serious about her liquid intake. In a couple of hours she was re-hydrated, more energetic, and eating better.

By mid-day Anna sat up, walked, and showed real signs of life – perhaps the most important of which is that she regained her sense of humor, returning to her wacky old self. We were able to trade her pain pump for pills, and then remove her IVs. She got fitted for her brace and has started wearing it, so there's progress there too. Assuming that she stays energetic and eats reasonably well, she can come home tomorrow.

As you might imagine, Jane and I are very relieved. Exhaustion is par for the course – on average our hyper-vigilant little one is up about once an hour during the night, which means that the accompanying parent is too. (I read this week's New Yorker last night between midnight and 6 AM.) But exhaustion just comes with the territory, and it'll stop once Anna's secure at home. Tonight, having seen her terrific progress, we can be much more hopeful of a speedy recovery and begin to relax ourselves. (Well, I'll sleep well tonight. It's Jane's turn at the hospital, so I don't know how well she'll do. But starting tomorrow....)

Anna was naturally hyper-vigilant. She was even more so because of an encounter we had with another scoliosis patient. This patient had had her surgery on May 9 and was, on May 30th, still quite uncomfortable. We ran into her again, on July 31, right after Anna's surgery; she was back in the ICU. The doctors had used the minimally invasive procedure – deflating one lung and making two small arthroscopic holes. She had been doing well, despite her discomfort, when a routine X-ray showed that some of the screws holding her titanium rod had worked loose. Although Anna's doctors had not used the minimally invasive procedure and had used different hardware, Anna feared the same thing would happen to her. It took a discussion with the doctor, a detailed analysis and explanation of the X-rays and everyone's emphatic reassurance to put Anna's fears to rest.

Anna came home five days after the surgery. Her shoulder blade still stuck out because the drop in evoked potentials had allowed only a partial correction. But she'd gained an inch and was now all of 5' 2" tall. Her back was also noticeably straighter than it had been. Alan's August 5th email tells the story.

> Anna is now in bed. Here's what the future portends, if things go according to plan. Anna has a brace, which she'll have to wear for about four months. This is, to put things in perspective, a pleasant alternative to a body cast: the idea is to keep the spine from bending or twisting while it heals. (And it's better than her previous brace, because it's protective rather than coercive – it's designed to

keep her from doing something traumatic to her spine rather than to coerce her body into shape.) Once Anna's back heals, she can stop wearing the brace and ultimately, go about her business as normal. In the meantime, there's no lifting – I get to serve as porter and carry her books to school, for example – and no horseback riding, gymnastics, or skydiving. More down to earth and the one silver lining related to this event, Anna is delighted that she can't take Phys Ed for a year....

At this point Anna's shot, physically and emotionally. But she's as tough and resilient a kid as I've ever met; I assume she'll be up and at 'em in short order. Her parents are doing fine, thanks to all the support we've had. Our gratitude to all of you for in some cases physical and in all cases emotional sustenance.

At home, life was not easy. Anna's recovery from heart surgery and brain surgery had gone far more smoothly. She'd be walking around the house less than a week after coming home, getting restless within two weeks, and doing errands with us in three. By the fourth week, she could usually do just about anything, except for strenuous physical activity, and by the end of the sixth, she'd be back to normal. When the surgeons predicted a six-week recovery, we thought we knew what that meant. But we didn't. Two, three, and even four weeks after surgery, Anna complained of serious pain, which wasn't completely alleviated by Tylenol. She didn't want to get out of bed, even for meals. This reaction seemed so extreme that I called the hospital, asking whether her pain and tiredness were cause for concern. "Oh, no," the nurse said: "Children prefer to recline for some weeks after the surgery, and there is some discomfort." Recline? Ha – Anna couldn't get out of bed. Discomfort? Anna wouldn't even mention what most of us would consider discomfort. What she felt was pain, real pain. But she kept her sense of humor and would, in her few comfortable moments, recite a particularly appropriate poem by Shel Silverstein, "Standing is Stupid."

Standing is stupid

Crawling's a curse,

Skipping is silly,

Walking is worse.

Hopping is hopeless,

Jumping's a chore,

Sitting is senseless,

Leaning's a bore.

Running's ridiculous,

Jogging's insane –

Guess I'll go upstairs and

Lie down again.

That seemed to sum things up.

Sleep was impossible. Anna would go to sleep, wake up after a very short time and then stay up for hours crying and screaming that she couldn't fall asleep. I slept in her room because my room, which was right next-door, was too far away. I had never done that before. We knew she was terrified; she was afraid she'd have to repeat the surgery as the other girl had done. We knew that her nervous system, which was very sensitive, had been upset by the surgery because of the spinal-cord manipulation involved and that waking her up during the procedure had upset it even more.

There was also something else. The girl with cystic fibrosis – the one who'd gone through elementary school with her and whom she'd visited in the hospital – had died that summer while we were in France. She was thirteen years old. We had decided to tell Anna after the surgery so as to avoid increasing her anxiety. But she found out beforehand from a fellow camper, and she never told us. Her fear that she would need a second operation was heightened by a new fear, one that had not previously occurred to her despite her array of life-threatening illnesses: the fear that she herself would die. Her dreams became nightmares. She had the same dream over and over, and it frequently woke her up: a balloon was losing air and was going to pop at any second. As she waited, she became tense, hyper-vigilant and ready to pop herself. We wondered whether she was dreaming of the surgery and whether the balloon referred to a piece of surgical equipment. We wondered whether she herself was the balloon and whether popping was a metaphor for death.

Anna adores older women, and they adore her. So while she lay in bed whining and moaning, all our women friends came to visit. Some of them came every day, taking turns sitting by her bedside so we could pay bills or maybe even get a little sleep. And they brought sweets, which was all Anna would eat for some time. Life began to settle down when the doctor prescribed a sleeping pill. But we didn't settle down quite so quickly because, just like parents of a new baby, we had forgotten how to sleep through the night.

EIGHTH GRADE

School began on August 29. Anna wasn't ready, but she was determined to start with everyone else. Since she'd spent most of the previous four weeks in bed, we knew she couldn't make it through an entire day. We thought she could spend a few minutes in each class and then go lie down in the inclusion teacher's office. Alan would be near the phone and ready to pick her up at a moment's notice.

She woke up that morning scared and sad, thinking about the girl who had died, but ready to go. So she and Alan went. But getting there wasn't easy. The construction project that had begun during the summer was not quite finished, and construction equipment seemed to be everywhere. When Alan and Anna got to the entrance they'd planned to use, they found it locked. Since they couldn't get to the other entrance by car and Anna couldn't manage the long walk, Alan set out in search of the full inclusion specialist. Anna sat calmly in the car until he found her and unlocked the gate. This was a great leap forward: he could never have left her alone like that the year before without precipitating a meltdown. But the effort Anna made took its toll. The phone rang at 10:15. She had to come home. She was so exhausted that she could barely get up the four steps to our front door, but she settled in calmly and lay down for a nap. All told, she coped remarkably well with a very stressful day. After that, progress was slow but steady. Anna made it through two class periods and then reached a plateau; a few days later, she lasted three periods. We tried to make sure that she sampled all her classes, taking her there some days in the morning and some days in the afternoon.

At home, life was difficult. Anna was putting all her energy into coping with school and would collapse the minute she got home. We were all having trouble sleeping. One weekend morning about a month after the surgery, she refused to get out of bed. When she finally did, she had to support herself for some time by holding onto the kitchen counter; her foot was numb. The day before, there had been brief periods when her foot "felt funny," and it seemed to be getting worse. We were afraid that this was the muscle weakness that the surgeon had said could occur as a result of the drop in evoked potentials. Anna wouldn't give us any details; she wouldn't tell us how often it happened or how long it lasted. Even the surgeon was somewhat concerned because it had been so long since the surgery. But upon seeing her, he decided that the numbness was a "transitory positional phenomenon," which was caused by the body's efforts to readjust its alignment. The episodes seemed to diminish once Anna was convinced that they were nothing to worry about. Then her neck and head started to hurt. Those pains also subsided, but her anxiety remained high. She wasn't sleeping well, and she didn't want to go to school, even though she always insisted on going. Dr. W. noted that Anna was having difficulty disentangling her own condition from the recent death of her classmate; Anna was afraid that she, too, would die.

Homework was hell. She was terrified of each assignment and would scream until she realized it wasn't as hard as she had thought. But she didn't limit herself to screaming. She pinched, punched, and kicked when her anxiety or fatigue grew too great. Alan and I fought like we never had before; we, too, started screaming, but at least we didn't punch each other.

Finally, things began to improve. Alan wrote the following email on September 14, six and a half weeks after the surgery.

I'm writing with good news twice over.

Anna seems to have turned a corner. She made it through the full school day on both Thursday and Friday, and even had some energy when she got home. Thursday is especially tough in terms of schedule: Anna made it through double periods of math, science, and "core" (English/History)! She did spend some % of the time lying down in class – her teachers are wonderfully accommodating – but making it through the day is a major accomplishment. It's a strong contrast with only a week ago, when one double period (an hour and a half) was as long as she could handle before I had to pick her up and take her home. She's also sleeping better. She's made it through the night twice this week, the first time since the surgery six weeks ago. (It might've been 3 times, had it not been for a wrong number last night at 2 AM.)

We saw Anna's back surgeon this afternoon. He's very happy with her progress. A side-by side comparison of before-and-after X-rays shows that a lot of the spinal curvature has been corrected. The surgeon tested her leg strength, flexibility and mobility, and said she's doing just fine....

More generally, Anna seems to have more spark and is more of her old self. Good news all around.

This was the hardest recovery of all. It took three full months for Anna to recover her ebullience and her stamina.

On the bright side, Anna enjoyed the restrictions placed on her for the year following the surgery. Since she couldn't lift or carry anything weighing more than a few pounds, she didn't have to carry her schoolbooks; that was the job of her dad in the morning, her mom in the afternoon, and her IA or the random classmates she enlisted during the school day. Since she couldn't take P.E. she gained a tutorial period, which she held onto throughout high school because it gave her more time to do her work.

Eighth grade was challenging. Apart from P.E., Anna was carrying a full load with Core (a combined English and history class), beginning French, algebra 1 and general science. The workload was tremendous. What made it even more overwhelming was that, in order to maximize her reading comprehension, Anna needed input in as many different modalities as possible: she had to see, hear and speak the text she was reading. We read everything out loud. She wrote slowly, and her organizational and time-management skills were poor. Even her French assignments, which were so easy for her, took more time than they would have if her handwriting had been better. The tutorial period enabled her to do some of the work at school, but there was always more, and she felt impelled to start working the minute she got home. She wouldn't pause for relaxation, and she wouldn't slow down either because minimizing time spent meant more to her than quality. So much for the daily assignments. She tried to forget about the longer-term projects because they were harder, they required fairly high-level organizational and conceptual skills, and they took too long. She would ignore them until I reminded her and then she would angrily assert that they were not required. Trying to help her set up a reasonable work plan for these projects would precipitate major explosions.

I wondered what high school would be like and whether a special school would be more appropriate. There was a school for children with autistic spectrum disorders a short drive away. Although Anna did not have an autistic spectrum disorder, she often behaved as if she did, so I went for a visit. I didn't like what I saw. The school had only twenty-four students, an awfully small peer group within which to find friends, especially for a big-school kind of girl. I was also concerned about the role models available and wondered what kind of behaviors Anna would learn from her peers. And there were only three girls at the school. This worried me, so I asked how they handled gender issues. "The girls love it," the director said giggling, "because they've never been so popular!" So much for female empowerment and the development of strong female leaders. Finally, although there were many special-service providers, there were only four teachers. I was concerned about the limited perspective that would be provided by such a small academic staff and I wondered what students did in cases of personality conflicts. Perhaps a special school was not the answer.

Then I looked at several non-selective private schools. The staffs were stultifyingly small and the peer groups too homogeneous to tolerate difference. The teachers I observed weren't very good, partly because private schools don't have as many hiring constraints as the public schools. I saw kids fresh out of college without any teacher training struggling to control classes of fifteen, while the public-school teachers seemed to be more experienced, more organized, and, even though their enrollments were larger, better at managing their classrooms. I saw a French teacher who had clearly been hired because she was a native speaker spend an entire class period gossiping in English with her three students. "They look at me blankly when I try to speak French," she complained. The boy/girl ratio was also of concern; the schools all seemed to have many more boys. Finally, these small private schools didn't have the financial resources to provide as many services as Anna needed, and we weren't eager to pay untold extra amounts for special services in addition to the high fees. Alan and I agreed that the public school with its diverse student body, its multiple course and teacher options, and its range of special services would serve Anna's needs more effectively.

Despite the homework problems, Anna was doing well in school. At the parent/teacher conferences in November, we heard nothing but praise and empathy. Her French teacher praised her pronunciation, her command of the language, and her enthusiasm. Her math teacher understood her facility with number facts and her difficulty grasping concepts. Her science teacher could only express admiration for her attitude and unusual perspective. "What happens," he had asked, "when you turn over the test tube with the solution in it?" "I get it all over my hands," she'd replied. He told this story laughing with sincere appreciation. Then he told us how, when the students had designed egg containers and were dropping them from the top of a ladder to see if the eggs inside would break, Anna – even though she was still recovering from scoliosis surgery – had zipped up the ladder before anyone could stop her. That was typical of Anna, he said; she was enthusiastic in everything she did and determined to do it well. "So," he added, "I wish I could clone her." More objectively speaking, she was doing very well in

French. She needed help in algebra but, with Alan's expert support and my help, she developed a good conceptual understanding. She also seemed to understand her science class work. It was Core (English and history) that concerned me. I often wondered how much of the literature and history she really understood. I knew how difficult it was for her to understand the movies I watched with her and the conversations we had with other people. I knew how little knowledge she had of the world, knowledge that was the basis for the literature and history she was studying and that could serve as the frame on which new concepts would be built.

One area in which Anna's knowledge base was secure was the hospital. She obsessed about the hospital and based some of her best work on it. When she had to write a mystery poem, for example, she chose the hospital as her subject.

Mystery Poem

Buzzing machines

helping people feel better

people dressed in white all over

people caring for people

babies being born

night and day

people are frightened to go there

and happy to go home

Her writing was getting more organized, but she had little concept of motivation. Her stories tended to be linear recitations of tangentially related events. The following story was intended to be a myth describing how the Grand Canyon was formed.

"Oh shoot, life is getting boring on this beach," said Jack. It was the year 700 and there were no stars in the sky. There was no sun. It was dark. Jack was tired because the beach was boring. There was nothing to do and Jack slept all day. He had one friend named Spunky. Spunky was a very mean dog and growled at the other animals. Jack was also very mean. He wanted a hole in the beach, because he was tired of the beach. He thought it would be great to explore.

So one day, he called all the animals to help. He yelled at them. He yelled, "Get over here you rats, come right now or Spunky will eat you in one gulp." Spunky barked, growled, bared his teeth, and bit the animals. Animals came from everywhere! Coyotes, deer, lizards, snakes, roadrunners, fish, donkeys, jack rabbits, foxes, and tortoises. They were very scared and their tails were down. They started crying. Jack yelled, "Get to work and start digging." They all began to dig as Jack had ordered until the hole got big. The hole was as deep as an abyss.

As they dug a family appeared. They were midgets like munchkins. In the hole there were also factories and stores with chocolate inventions. Everything and every invention you could think of were in the hole. It was brilliant! The animals', Jack's and Spunky's mouths opened wide because it was a beautiful sight. They started doing all sorts of things in the hole, such as eating, camping, hiking, swimming, etc. They even went to the factories and the stores with chocolate inventions. Jack, Spunky and the animals loved it. They all became friends. That is how the Grand Canyon was formed.

Literary analysis was also difficult. Her thinking was still very concrete and she was not ready for abstraction. Nor did she understand degrees of emotion. To her, everything was either very good or very bad. This made it hard to analyze a character's motivation with any subtlety. The following essay describes Steinbeck's attitude toward euthanasia as indicated by his novella, *Of Mice and Men*. The teacher had told them the title had to be catchy, and so it was.

Euthanasia Ain't Easy

The vet killed my auntie's dog because the dog was in bad shape. This is called euthanasia. In Of Mice And Men by John Steinbeck, George killed Lennie because he'd rather do it instead of the men who were trying to catch Lennie. Carlson killed Candy's dog because the dog was too old and sick. Steinbeck showed sometimes it's necessary to kill, but it is always difficult.

It is not good to kill. Carlson killed Candy's dog; it wasn't nice because the dog didn't cause any trouble. Candy said " I don't mind takin' care of him." (P. 45) It wasn't good to kill Lennie because he was retarded and he didn't mean to kill Curley's wife or the pup. George said " 'Course he ain't mean. But he gets in trouble alla time because he's so God damn dumb." (P. 41)

Another reason euthanasia is always difficult is that people kill because they are angry and they don't stop to think about whether it is right. Curley was very angry at Lennie for killing his wife and wanted to kill him. " Curley's face reddened. 'I'm goin',' he said. 'I'm gonna shoot the guts out of that big bastard myself, even if I only got one hand. I'm gonna get 'im.' " (P.98) Curley didn't realize that Lennie was retarded and didn't mean to kill his wife. Carlson wanted to kill the dog because it smelled bad. Carlson said " God aumighty, that dog stinks. Get him outa here, Candy! I don't know nothing that stinks as bad as an old dog. You gotta get him out." (P. 44) He also said, "Well, I can't stand him in here." (P.44) Carlson wanted to kill the dog because the dog was bothering him.

Another reason euthanasia is always difficult is that people are sad when their friends or relatives die. After Carlson shot the dog, Candy went on his bunk and looked at the ceiling. George was sad when he had to kill Lennie, but he had no choice. " And George raised the gun and steadied it, and he brought the muzzle of it close to the back of Lennie's head. The hand shook violently, but his face set and his hand steadied. He pulled the trigger." (P. 106) You can see that having to kill Lennie upset George because his hand shook violently.

Steinbeck thought that euthanasia is always hard, but sometimes it's not a choice. It's difficult because it is hard to take lives, people kill out of anger and retaliation, and people are sad when friends and relatives die.

Once Anna had fully recovered from the scoliosis surgery, she began to do better at home. We could now both make and receive telephone calls without triggering major tantrums as long as we announced whom we were talking to and, afterwards, how long the call had been.

But a ringing phone was still a source of major anxiety. Each time the phone rang, Anna would jump up cursing and run to answer it. It didn't matter where she was or what she was doing. She would even jump out of the shower. She had to be the first one to get the bad news, whatever it was. I decided it was time to take the behavior in hand and told her she could answer the phone only if she did so calmly. Anna loves structure because it makes her feel safe, and she usually follows rules strictly. It was apparently the right time for this rule because it made a real difference. For a while at least, we no longer had to rush out of her way when the phone rang. She would always answer it, but no one would be hurt in the process.

We began to look for other annoying or inappropriate behaviors that could be eliminated by making a new rule. The opportunity arose shortly thereafter. Anna had just turned fifteen. We went into San Francisco with a woman friend to see "A Christmas Carol" and then out to dinner. As we were coming out of the restaurant, a homeless man approached asking for spare change. Alan muttered "sorry" and we shook our heads. Anna, however, was not used to street people, and the man made her nervous so she stared at him and giggled. This made him angry. He followed us for three blocks yelling, "it's not fucking funny," calling Anna a bitch and bellowing, "That's no way to raise a child." Anna was scared, and Alan was concerned enough to walk behind us in case physical intervention was needed. But the man finally gave up, and when we discussed the incident, Anna learned another rule: don't stare or giggle at strangers.

SHUNT FAILURE AGAIN (WINTER BREAK 2002)

Our holiday break started a few days early with the flu. Alan's email told the story.

> The first recipient was Anna, who lost the last two days of school to a stomach flu. Anna did give us a scare. Headaches and throwing up are two major symptoms of shunt failure, the others being lethargy, flakiness, irritability, and lack of appetite. Anna hadn't been especially lethargic, but flakiness and irritability ... well, she's a teenager, right? And then one morning she refused not only breakfast but lunch, saying she wasn't hungry. Up, up, up went the parental anxiety meters, until Anna mentioned to Jane mid-afternoon that she'd knocked off a whole bag of M&Ms that morning...
>
> Anna got better, and we were able to join friends for their traditional Xmas eve dinner. (I went in blue and white, with a 6-pointed silver star doing double duty – it not only completed my Alan-as-Chanukah-bush costume, it covered part of my bald spot as well.) The friends were rightly concerned that the bush looked wilted and wasn't as talkative as usual. I spent that night throwing up, and the next two days barely able to get out of bed. I won't trouble you with descriptions of my multiple symptoms, though I will say that they were tailor-made for a Stephen King-like exposition... Anyway, with a call to the doctor and a Jane-and-Anna pilgrimage to the one pharmacist in Northern California who was open on Xmas day, I was placed on the pathway to recovery. Not only that, since the drug of choice for what ailed me was Cipro, I'll be ready for anthrax when it comes my way. Or at least I will when my body

recovers. My fingers are fine, but the rest of me moves and feels like Dorothy's metallic Oz companion. Would that oil or WD-40 would work!

Anna and I had recovered enough for all of us to have a lovely Saturday in SF. We saw an appropriately creaky performance of "A Christmas Carol," walked around the city, had a superb dinner. Then at 3 AM Anna complained of a vicious headache and stared throwing up. It didn't stop. At 8 AM we called the advice nurse (it being Sunday, a visit to her regular doctor wasn't in the offing), who said we should trundle along to Children's Hospital. We had a nice relaxed corner of the emergency room. For the first 8 hours, Anna would seem to be recovering. She'd rest calmly, we'd get our hopes up, she'd have a little liquid, and then she'd barf... In the interim, the staff did major tests to check out the possibilities of serious stuff. Shunt failure? Do a CT. Ventricles look fine. Stomach adhesions? Do an X-ray. Stomach and intestines look fine. The silver lining: Anna gets a clean bill of health on the critical issues. The bottom line: probably a very bad case of gastroenteritis, there's been a lot of it. To avoid an overnight stay, which was looking increasingly likely, the doctor gave Anna a large dose of liquid through an IV. We got the rehydrated Anna home and into bed, where she slept through the night. She's spending the day in bed. And we once are again thankful for the wonderful medical care (skilled and sympathetic doctor and nurses) we have available.

Today's December 31. So, what is Jane, who thus far has played only a supportive role in our drama, doing to celebrate the end of the year? Not to be outdone by Anna and me, she got the bug. An impressive performance, rivaling the rest of us for best in show (though I think when the curtain comes down on the year, Anna will get the honors for this performance, not to mention her lifetime award). It's kind of scary to think that although I have functional fingers only, I'm the healthiest in the family. Well enough to go get a 2-day supply of penicillin soup, at least – and to hope 2002 starts off a hell of a lot better. Best for a great start to everyone.

There was no school that week since it was winter break. So for the next few days, we all tried to take it easy. But that didn't seem to work. Anna was a mess. She wouldn't get out of bed. Her neuropsychologist, Dr. W., saw her several times and observed that she was starting to ask "Why me? Why can't I be healthy like other people?" She was finally realizing that most people did not take regular trips to the emergency room and that most people were not continually watching out for shunt failure. We all thought she was depressed because we'd just spent ten hours at the hospital. School was going to start on Monday, and, on Friday, I did everything I could to lift her spirits. I read her children's books since she was also regressing and we baked cookies. The next day, she refused to get up, and Sunday threw us into a panic. We had to get her ready for school. She was scared, she was refusing to go back, and she was almost as depressed as she had been after the scoliosis surgery. So we worked her hard. She and Alan made crepes – or rather she did, with Alan playing sous-chef. She and Alan made ginger cake, and she and I made a lamb stew. She was on her feet cooking all day. But she still wasn't ready for school.

She began to cry when we put her to bed, and she didn't stop until she'd worn herself out.

Monday was another day though. She got up, gathered her forces and, trouper she is, went off to school. The day passed normally. That afternoon she reported only one thing out of the ordinary: "two Richards" had been sitting in one Richard's seat. What was going on? Why the double vision? We hoped it would go away, but it didn't. It just got worse. The next day was Tuesday. Anna spent about half the day rubbing her head and covering one eye to make the double vision go away – you can't have double vision if you don't use two eyes. On Wednesday, the full inclusion specialist called me about three quarters of the way through the day. Anna needed to come home, so I left a message with the neurosurgeon and went to pick her up. Alan took the return call while I was gone, was told to bring her right in, and packed his clothes. He had decided that it was his turn to spend the first night with her in the hospital. When Anna and I got home, we led her back to the car, but she was adamant. "NO," she screamed. "I'm not going." There was no question of picking her up and putting her in. She had just spent ten hours in the emergency room. Now she was angry – and she was strong. But anger soon gave way to reason, and she realized she had to go.

Everything moved quickly at the hospital, except the neurosurgeon. We were admitted, and got a room, a CT scan and the admitting physician in what was, for the hospital, quick succession. The admitting physician didn't see much difference between this CT scan and the one that had been done only days before. She wasn't sure whether Anna's shunt was failing or whether there was some other, as yet unidentified, reason for the double vision. We waited some more. Where was Anna's neurosurgeon? We had never met the one who finally showed up, but we were impressed. His bedside manner was perfect: he knew just how to talk to a fourteen-year-old girl, and he was very direct. After greeting us with a handshake, he sat down next to her and looked her right in the eye. She asked what he was going to do. "I'd recommend a shunt revision," he said. He explained that the double vision was caused by pressure on the optic nerve, which was, in turn, caused by increased pressure in the cerebrospinal circulatory system, and that this increased pressure was due to shunt failure. We didn't know that double vision could be a symptom of shunt failure. "When do you want to do it?" Anna asked. His reply was quick: "How about now?" he said. Her reply was even quicker: "Let's do it," she said. It was 7:30 at night.

The neurosurgeon left and preparations for the surgery began. We had only a few minutes, but as we waited Anna's eyes began to wander in separate directions. We wondered whether she'd kept them under control until then by the sheer force of her will and whether the relief of knowing the problem would now be fixed allowed her to relax her hold on them. When we got to the surgical suite, we recognized the anesthesiologist as yet another old hospital friend. But he was more than that; he was the hospital's famous anesthesiologist-musician and he wheeled Anna out of the anteroom singing a quite respectable version of "Double Vision." This time, because it was so late in the day, the parents' waiting room was unavailable, and we were ushered into the quiet luxury of the MCU waiting room. We breathed a sigh of relief as a nurse unlocked the room, knowing we could wait in peace, insulated from the continual blare of the television sets. Since we hadn't had dinner, we ate vending-machine sandwiches, and we just sat there, too tired to do anything else. The procedure went quickly. It was a proximal revision, which is the easiest kind and which involves replacing only the clogged tube in the skull. The doctor assured us that the failure had been purely mechanical and that it did not imply any changes in the tumor. He didn't think the shunt failure had anything to do with the scoliosis surgery either, but we remembered the drop in evoked potentials, thought of the debris which must have been generated by the scoliosis surgery, and wondered.

Less than two hours after she was rolled into the surgical suite, Anna was back in the ICU. She was fully conscious and chatting away, just like she always did, with the night nurse, and once again, it was old-home week. She was in the same bed and had the same nurse and the same attending physician she'd had after her first brain surgery in 1996. The nurse and the doctor were both surprised by how much she'd grown up, but not by the strength and the courage she had shown.

Alan spent a calm night in the ICU, while Anna was recovering. The next day was her birthday. "If you have a good breakfast and sit up," the doctors promised, "you can celebrate your birthday at home." Not only did she eat and sit up, but she walked all around the third floor, and at 1:00 PM we were on our way home. But there was to be no birthday celebration that day. As I was unpacking the clothes I'd brought to the hospital in case we had to spend another night, I heard a scream from her room and ran in. Anna lay on her bed shaking uncontrollably. She didn't respond to my cries, didn't seem to even know I was there. And it got worse: her face contorted in a rictus;

her fists balled up; her arms twisted; and she began to turn blue. I didn't know what was happening. I thought she was dying. I tried to give her CPR, but her teeth were clenched and nothing was getting through. "Call 911," I screamed and Alan did. Then I realized what was happening: she was having a full-blown tonic-clonic seizure. "It's a seizure," I yelled. "Call the neurosurgeon." Alan did. When he told the assistant that the paramedics were on their way, she said they should bring Anna in to the emergency room.

Then the paramedics arrived. They assessed the situation and called for an ambulance. They tried to give her oxygen, but she pushed it aside. Then, they picked her up using the bed sheet as a sling, carried her to the ambulance, and helped me into its cab; they wouldn't let me ride in the back with Anna. Alan followed behind in the car, stopping long enough, in his usual thoughtful way, to pick up what I needed for a night at the hospital. I never thought an ambulance could move so slowly – no sirens, no flashing lights, just big, solid transportation. That ride was the slowest part of our adventure. Even the shunt revision had seemed to go more quickly, but then, we had known what to expect. When we arrived in the emergency room, we urged the staff to send us directly back to the ICU, where Anna, at least, would be more comfortable, but they didn't feel it necessary. It was, after all, only a seizure. As Anna lay on the gurney, tired but alert, waiting to go for yet another CT scan, it happened again – the shaking, the clenching. I ran for medical help and the team moved quickly around her. Alan stayed at her head, but I couldn't bear to see another one. The team watched as the seizure ended and then pumped her full of Dilantin to prevent any more. The nurse arrived soon after to escort her to the CT-scan room. She carried a syringe full of Ativan in case there was another seizure, but there wasn't. The scan looked just fine. The neurosurgeon said that the seizures had most likely been provoked by the irritation of the surgery and the withdrawal of the anesthesia and that no major intervention was required. The staff then monitored her for two hours, gave us a prescription for Dilantin with instructions to see a neurologist, and sent us home again. Anna went home twice for her birthday! She improved rapidly once we got home, eating up a storm because of the Dilantin and spending less time in bed than she had the week after her second episode of gastroenteritis.

Anna would have been ready for school on Monday, five days after the surgery, if it hadn't been for the seizures. They'd worn her out. So we waited until Wednesday, but the timing was terrible. The sister of Anna's wonderful IA had died unexpectedly over winter break, and the IA was taking a three-day bereavement leave starting that very day. Since Anna really had to go back to school, the full inclusion specialist got the best substitute she knew and gave him explicit instructions for handling a seizure. I felt safe for he was huge and soft and I could picture her in his cushiony embrace. He went to advisory with Anna and then he took her to French. But he didn't know French. So what did he do? He left! Anna looked around and he was gone. Naturally, she had a panic attack – headache, nausea, the works – and the French teacher had to ask a student to take her to the full inclusion specialist's office. And naturally, Anna came right home after that. There was no substitute IA for Thursday, so we kept her home then as well. For Friday, the full inclusion specialist herself promised to serve as IA. And she did. By January 19, only ten days after the surgery, Anna had recovered enough to invite her best friend for a long-delayed birthday sleepover.

We went to see the neurologist shortly thereafter. She agreed that the seizures were probably provoked by the surgery and the anesthesia, and she was, therefore, willing to bet that anti-seizure medication would not be necessary. But she ordered an EEG just to make sure. An EEG or electroencephalogram is a test that detects abnormalities in the brain's electrical activity. Finding no abnormalities would confirm the neurologist's opinion. Since the test requires the patient to sleep for part of the time, the neurologist recommended that we keep Anna awake till midnight the night before and then wake her up at 5:00 AM. When we protested that our hyper-vigilant daughter would never fall asleep on a table with twenty-four electrodes stuck to her head, the neurologist suggested we keep her up all night. That would have been too much for all of us, so we opted for only partial sleep deprivation and crossed our fingers. We had a party that night. We watched "Dr. Doolittle" and "Little Rascals," we ate popcorn, we read aloud from *The Hobbit*, and, throughout it all we had to keep poking Anna so that she wouldn't fall asleep.

At 5:00 AM I stumbled out of bed. Anna was more awake than we were; she had an unerringly accurate internal clock and would always wake up exactly on time. At the hospital we were escorted into a small room that held only a table, three chairs and a computer strung with a large number of electrodes. The technician carefully attached each one of the electrodes to Anna's head while she sat quietly. The rebellious patient of her youth was long gone; Anna couldn't have been more cooperative. The technician went through the first part of the study, flashing strobe lights and asking Anna to move around and cough. Then came the big moment. He dimmed the lights. When we wondered aloud whether she'd fall asleep, he responded quietly saying, "everybody falls asleep." Then he asked her to turn on her side and close her eyes. She fell asleep, just as he had said she would. This technician had a hospital-wide reputation: he'd been putting children to sleep without fail for forty-two years. So we watched the squiggles on the screen wondering what they all meant. Happily, they meant she was fine. The EEG confirmed the neurologist's opinion that Anna was not prone to seizures, so no anti-seizure medication was prescribed.

BACK TO EIGHTH GRADE

Nine days after the surgery, Anna was back at school full time. She wanted to do well and she didn't want to miss anything. But she was embarrassed about her partly shaved head. The school strictly prohibited hats: teachers wanted to see their students' faces; they didn't want to encourage team or gang-related rivalry; and other kids' hats were irresistible lures. So she was in a quandary. We assured her that this was an exception and that she could certainly wear any one of her multicolored scarves or the glittery hats she had acquired after previous brain surgeries. She covered her head for a few days. Then – whether because of the rule, because of her extreme sensitivity to bodily encumbrances, or because of her usual lack of self-consciousness – she quickly discarded all head covering, declaring, "bald is beautiful."

Anna recovered quickly, but then, in mid-February, she got a bad headache. This time, it was only stress, or was it? We tried not to scrutinize her, not to ask too many questions, but we didn't recover as quickly as she did. There was fear with every symptom – stomach-clenching, dry-mouthed fear. What is it this time? Shunt failure or stress headache? Shunt failure or virus? We couldn't be sure, and I was always one step away from calling the neurosurgeon. But, this time, I didn't have to.

She was doing so well that we spent spring break in Spokane with my sister's family. Anna and her ten-year-old cousin, Tova, had a blast. They went for walks, tried on clothes, ate junk food, played games, and ran all over the place making silly noises and inventing silly words. They even disappeared together long enough to require a parental search party. Although five years younger than Anna, Tova was a perfect match for her. The only thing they didn't share was athletic ability. But that didn't detract from the adventure, as Tova gently pushed Anna up steep paths and waited patiently when she couldn't keep up.

Anna was doing better in school. She loved French and, with Alan's help, was doing well in algebra. Her reading was improving. Although we had always read her assignments aloud, that March she was able to read some short sections of her history text silently and report on the important points. But that didn't mean she would move to silent reading. Reading assignments were getting harder, and the social component of reading was very important to Anna. She didn't want to read silently. She wanted to read with me or with anyone else willing to join her. For her, reading (like almost everything else!) was an intrinsically social activity.

Her writing was also improving. In order be eligible for an "A" in Core, the students had to do two independent reading projects and write two short stories. Anna wanted to do these assignments. She wanted that "A." But her first efforts were usually skeletal. To help her flesh them out, I asked for details and descriptions; I told her the descriptions had to appeal to all five senses; and I asked her what came next and what came after that. The second story she wrote was based on an incident that had really happened while we were visiting some British friends in the south of France.

A Bashed Car in Avignon

Avignon is a beautiful city with a lot of food shops. There are bakeries making croissants, cakes, pizza, and bread. You can smell the delicious aromas. There are restaurants serving French food, Chinese food, and Spanish food. There are clothing shops with elegant dresses and sophisticated pants. There are florists with irises, daisies, poppies, and roses. There are also flowers growing in the gardens and by the river. The river flowing under the famous bridge through Avignon is long and pretty.

Jerry and Rosa were looking at the scenery in Avignon. Jerry was a very short, fat British man with purple eyes, blue hair, a red nose, and a purple mouth. He liked to read books about science, and had lots of animal friends. He had a dog named Patchi and a turtle named Zatchi. Jerry understood everything the animals said. Rosa, his wife, was beautiful. She wore sparkling dresses and had purple hair, which she wore in a spiral on top of her head. She could shrink until she was so small that no one could see her. Then she could grow to be tall again. Jerry and Rosa had a small yellow car that would start whenever you said "stadle." The steering wheel was on the right, like on all British cars. They were in the car looking for a café and finally, they found one.

"Let's have some coffee here," said Rosa.

"Good idea," said Jerry. They parked the car, went into the café, sat down at a table and ordered coffee. They were relaxing. There were a lot of people in the café, so it took them a long time to get their coffee. But they didn't mind because they were reading. They smelled the coffee from miles away and wanted to taste it. The waiter brought it after 19 minutes and they lapped it up with their tongues. Then they paid and went out.

They walked to their car and discovered something shocking. Their car had gotten bashed. Someone had hit the front, back and sides of the car with a hammer and broken all of the windows. There was broken glass all over the ground. They stared at the car and began to cry.

"I wish I knew who did this," said Jerry.

"So do I," said Rosa. "We need to call the police." Jerry took his cell phone out of his pocket and dialed 911.

"911 at your service. This is Rasty."

"Someone has just damaged our car," said Jerry.

"Do you know who did it?" asked Rasty.

"No," said Jerry.

"You need to find out who did it," said Rasty.

"We'll find that out now," said Jerry. He hung up the phone and he and Rosa walked to the river. There were fish swimming the river, dogs running along side, and cats cleaning off their fur. Jerry ran to a tabby cat and asked him if he knew who damaged their car.

"I don't, but my friend Chenchka is a psychic and knows everything. He is a blue and white polka dotted fish." Jerry walked to the river and peered into it. There he spied Chenchka.

"Good morning Mr. Chenchka, we were in a café in Avignon and somebody bashed our car. The cat that lives over there says that you know everything. Do you know who did it?"

"Yes, I do," said Chenchka. "His name is Chatana Chonkers. He has red eyes, blue hair, a green nose, and a purple mouth. His hair stands up. He's in his house now at 669 Chunky Street. Go find him." Jerry and Rosa walked to Chunky Street and found 669. Rosa said, "chocka chok chok," and shrank to the size of a pinhead. Then she crawled in through the crack under the door and saw the villain. She knew it was him because he looked exactly the way Chenchka had described. He was talking to a girl with rainbow colored hair.

"I'm so proud that I wrecked their car." I don't want any British people in my country," he said. "I went up to it, hit it with a hammer and threw a bunch of big rocks at it. It was so much fun." Rosa was terrified and ran out of the house. She ran to Jerry and said "jocki" and grew to her normal size.

"I saw the villain," said Rosa. "I saw him talking to a kid. He looked like what Chenchka said and he was saying how much he loved wrecking our car. I know he's the one who did it." Rosa picked up the cell phone and dialed 911.

"I found the villain who bashed our car."

"Oh that's terrific! I'm coming to see!" said the policewoman. A few minutes later, there she was.

"How do you know who did it?" she asked.

"Chenchka, the psychic fish, told us where he lived and what he looked like. Also I heard him talking about it. He said he did it because he didn't want any British people in his country."

"It's too bad he hates British people so much that he would do such a bad thing. I'll go arrest him," said the policewoman. She knocked hard on the door of his house. "Open up. Police," she said. The criminal didn't answer and hid behind his bed. The policewoman shoved the door open. The criminal ran out the back door and into the backyard. He was about to climb over the fence when the policewoman captured him. She put handcuffs on and took him to jail.

"I'm so glad that the criminal got arrested. It's just what he deserved," said Jerry.

"So am I," said Rosa. "Let's go get the car fixed."

Anna preferred describing something that had really happened because she still couldn't effectively separate fact from fiction and thought all stories had to be basically true. Her plots were linear; events piled up one on top of each other and had to be reined in to move the story forward. Her descriptions were concrete, usually consisting of lists of nouns, and when she wanted to be funny, which was most of the time, she gave her characters silly names and made them look as silly as possible. But silly names and lists were no longer enough for her. This incident had affected her deeply; she couldn't forget the sight of the badly dented car surrounded by broken glass, and she was outraged that the perpetrator couldn't be found. She wrote the story to make sure that justice was done.

Anna started worrying about high school in the middle of eighth grade. The middle school was big, but the high school was three times its size. Her IA tried to allay her anxiety by taking her to visit. But planned visits often fell through because of scheduling difficulties. Each time, Anna handled the uncertainty well. Since her IA was never sure when they were going, Anna told herself that they weren't. This consciously imposed strategy helped her avoid disappointment and reduced her anxiety. When Anna and her IA finally did make the visit, they met the full inclusion specialist who supervised the IAs, and they shadowed a freshman girl as she went from class to class. Anna came back excited and energized. She liked the teachers and enjoyed the classes. She didn't seem to mind the crowds either. They weren't any worse than the ones at the middle school and she had long ago developed her class-changing strategy. Charging full-speed ahead, she would elbow her way through the crowd pulling her rolling backpack behind her. She was always the first student to arrive in class.

But Anna's anxiety about high school, her upcoming routine MRI, and the standardized tests that she was taking with all the other eighth graders was getting worse. One day, I happened to see her taking a history test. She was shaking so much she could barely write; the matching questions seemed to run together and she couldn't think straight. Another day, when I picked her up from school, she announced, as she often did, that she had a chapter in her history book to read and outline, that she had to do it as soon as she got home, and that I had to help her. When I replied that I had to change my clothes and make a cup of tea and that our haircutter would be coming any minute, she had the tantrum to end all tantrums. She didn't care that our housecleaner was in the house. She didn't care that fifteen year olds aren't supposed to have tantrums. She cried, she screamed, she flailed. Since physical restraint is sometimes advised in situations like that, I put my arms around her and tried a hug. I should have known better. She didn't want to be touched, and she sank her teeth into my shoulder. When I managed to extricate myself, my shoulder was covered with red teeth marks and a two-inch wide bruise. I couldn't believe it. I shook with fury as we pushed her into her room. There, she spent over an hour yelling, cursing, and throwing anything she could, while Alan and I considered what to do. Anna had to learn that this kind of behavior was absolutely unacceptable. We came up with a three-part plan. Since all of us were scheduled for a haircut and she always went first as a concession to her anxiety, she would go last this time. This was a punishment she could really understand. To emphasize her position in the hierarchy and prevent her from hovering over us as we got our hair cut, we made her wash her hair. Finally, we made her write a two-page letter of apology. We hoped the point had been made.

Then, one week before the end of school, disaster struck. Anna's IA, who would, we'd hoped, move on with Anna to the high school, decided she was more comfortable at the middle-school level. She had fought with herself over this decision. She had cried at the thought of giving up her beloved student. But she and her older daughter had both gone to Berkeley High, and she realized how uncomfortable she'd be working there. Besides, she assured herself, Anna was more than just her student; she was a good friend that she could visit any time. So we had a problem. When Anna was in sixth grade, we'd learned the importance of having an IA who could support her academically. We'd had a jewel for two years, and now, we'd have to find another. That was my assignment for the summer.

But first came graduation from middle school. Anna had had a very good school year, despite a painful first quarter spent lying on the classroom floor and a January shunt failure. Her teachers loved and respected her. Everyone came to her graduation, including many of Anna's older female friends and even Dr. W., who usually tries to maintain professional distance. Once all the guests were seated, the band began to play a solemn march, and the graduates walked down the aisle. The boys, in T-shirts and baggy pants, weren't dressing up for anyone, except for one who rose to the occasion in a white tuxedo and top hat. The girls, some of them wearing heels for the first time, glided by in soft, filmy and occasionally too sexy dresses. Each graduate wore a carnation, turning this diverse collection of happy kids into a real procession. And Anna fit right in; no one could see how different she had once been from her fellow students. She strode down the aisle – no gliding for her – in her elegant, flowered dress and beamed with pride and dignity. She'd made the honor roll every year. She was one of the ten percent of the students who had received the Martin Luther King award for exemplary citizenship. And she was ready for high school.

A few minutes were set aside to honor the girl who had died of cystic fibrosis. Although they had never been friends, Anna had followed the course of her illness, keeping track of her hospital stays and worrying constantly about the state of her health. When she died, Anna contributed some of her own money to Children's Hospital in her memory and wrote the following poem.

<u>I Wish You Were Alive</u>

I wish you were alive

You were strong

And brave

Your beauty

I wish you were alive

Your smartness

Your sickness

Killed you

I WISH YOU WERE ALIVE

O how I wish it

I wish you were alive.

We all do

We wish you were alive.

When the time came to remember the girl, Anna spoke briefly from the stage, and her voice was strong and clear. But she was disappointed in this part of the ceremony. Although she had prepared a whole speech and was even then an excellent speaker, she was allowed to say only one line. Another girl had been chosen to speak for the students. Since this girl was not a special-education student, Anna's teachers felt that discrimination had been a factor in her selection. But Anna didn't suspect discrimination; she only knew that she had wanted to say more.

The summer was starting. Since Anna's last MRI had indicated that the remaining tumor was stable and cardiac ventricular pressures were good, it would be the first summer in three years without surgery. Anna would attend her usual day camp, and then we were going to visit Washington, DC. But in the meantime, I had work to do. The IA bidding process was held at the end of June. Each child's requirements had been established in his/her IEP and were outlined on a card posted at school-district headquarters. IAs who wanted to work with a particular student and who felt their qualifications met the student's needs could place a bid, and the child's IA would be selected from the bids that had been placed. Since Anna's IEP specified an IA who could provide support in college-preparatory academic courses, the coordinator thought that a qualified IA could probably not be found on the district payroll. If that was the case, we could initiate a search on our own and encourage the person we found to apply to the school district. That's exactly what happened. A week after the bidding process, during which no IA was selected, I began to contact everyone I knew. When I called a friend and neighbor who was studying to become an occupational therapist, she expressed strong interest. The program she was in had just been extended to five years, the fees had increased, and she was very interested in special education. She was smart, she was sensitive, and she already knew Anna reasonably well. Plus, she had taken college-level classes in math, biology and chemistry just recently. She invited Anna to her house to see what it would be like to work with her and then she applied for the job. The wait began.

Of course, Anna didn't know how uncertain the situation really was. She was back at her beloved day camp, and she was much more relaxed than she'd been during the school year. She took the camp bus every day from the North Berkeley Library to the camp location and back without complaint. There were no echoes of her elementary-school bus trauma. And I was almost always there to pick her up when the bus arrived. But one day, I wasn't, and she waited patiently, talking non-stop to the bus monitor who waited with her. That was a real breakthrough. Then another day, she went to the store to get some bread, reached home before me, and once again waited patiently – without the screaming we had come to expect.

This summer, too, Anna was doing other normal kid stuff. After years of checking in with the orthodontist and postponing orthodonture because of upcoming surgeries, Anna finally got her braces. She'd been wanting them for years since almost every kid in her school had them, and she was a model patient. But that night, reality hit: she woke up crying at 3 AM. Why did she ever want these stupid braces anyway? She began to regress. We remembered her slow recovery from the scoliosis surgery and we worried. But she was strong, the pain abated, and orthodontic ornamentation held sway. One day, her smile gleamed with pink and violet bands; on another, she chose blue and green; and, of course, she demanded red, white and blue for the fourth of July.

She was taking on more responsibility as a camper. When we decided that it would not be a good idea for her join her day-camp group camping in a remote Sierra Mountain location, she was allowed to be a "junior" junior counselor for the youngest group. She had a wonderful time helping the little ones with art projects, distributing snacks, and taking the kids to the bathroom. They even liked her enough to call her a "poophead." But her day camp didn't last all summer, and I still had to go to work. So Anna became a teen assistant at the local zoo camp. Of course, we were the first to arrive on the first day. The other teen assistants – two girls and a boy, all of whom had been coming to the camp for years – knew each other well. A difficult social situation. As usual, Anna wasn't quite sure how to proceed. But, also as usual, she plunged right in. She wasn't going to sit on the side as I would have. True, she asked some FDQ's, which earned her strange looks, but strange looks have never deterred her. When she made one of her standard comments saying a broken toy needed surgery, the other teen assistants took it as a joke and laughed in a friendly manner. When the teacher arrived, Anna asked her usual anxiety-driven questions about time and structure. But she also asked good questions about what they would be doing. She spent a week there working with kindergartners, making herself useful during both the morning and afternoon sessions and walking around the zoo with the other teen assistants during the lunch break. She managed just fine even though she wasn't part of this particular clique. And the little kids loved her. Months later, I met several zoo-camp moms who told me what a great counselor she had been. The girl was definitely growing up!

Meanwhile, we were still waiting for the school district to hire Anna's IA. Three weeks before school started, while we were vacationing in Washington, DC, we made daily phone calls to the potential IA (Eleanor) and to different district personnel. We called the Department of Special Education; we called the personnel office. Eleanor went to the district office and waited to speak with the personnel director because no one had called about the status of her application. Slowly, with our insistent help, the district's wheels began to turn. Eleanor was allowed to take the qualification test, which was easier than it should have been. Then, two days before school started, the district said she had to get fingerprinted. But the Berkeley police needed two weeks notice for fingerprinting. So the day before school started, Eleanor drove to a police station twenty miles away. She had to be there at 6:00 AM so that they would have time to process the paperwork, and she made it. Finally, Anna had an IA capable of giving her the academic support she needed in high school.

HIGH SCHOOL

Anna was healthy throughout high school. There were no surgical procedures, only the testing needed to monitor her heart and the conditions associated with tuberous sclerosis. She saw the cardiologist, the neurologist, and the ophthalmologist regularly. She had echocardiograms and brain MRIs. When she turned eighteen, kidney ultrasounds and CT scans of the chest were added to the mix to check for adult manifestations of tuberous sclerosis. But she was healthy. And because she was healthy, she could grow and develop as teenagers are meant to – with no major interruptions.[10]

Settling In

Anna was finally a high-school freshman. She handled the stresses of the first week just fine: the crowds, the noise, the confusion. Tough and determined, she knew just where she was going and she blasted her way through the crowd to get there. On the very first day the crowd was so tightly packed that Eleanor, the new IA, lost sight of her and had to make a detour to get the room number. When she finally arrived in class, Anna was there primed and ready to go. No breakdown, no problem.

But the math class was a disaster. Anna had done very well in the first year of algebra, but because of spatial perception issues, we felt she wasn't ready for geometry. To make sure she didn't forget the math she'd learned, we decided to have her repeat the second half of algebra. Bad idea! Because most students don't take the second semester of algebra in the fall, the class was filled with students who had failed math at some time. The students were difficult, and it seemed that the teacher had already given up. They were doing everything but math – listening to music, talking on their cell phones, playing games on their cell phones, drawing pornographic pictures, bouncing basketballs and, of course, talking. The teacher made no attempt to structure the class or teach, and the noise level was unbearable. When Anna's IA complained to the teacher, he told her not to worry. "Lots of the kids will stop coming to class," he said. "When that happens, the atmosphere will be better and we'll be able to get down to work." We were outraged and considered speaking to the principal on behalf of all the students in that class, but we had our hands full with Anna.

Anna's IA was getting headaches, and Anna was bringing home enormous amounts of math homework because she couldn't think clearly enough in that environment to do either class work or homework. By the end of the week, Anna's full inclusion specialist had pulled her out of the class and Anna had re-discovered the advantages of a tutorial period. She used that period to finish at least some of her homework, just as she had in middle school. Because the extra time soon became a necessity, we made it part of her schedule. But that addition created a problem. Taking only five classes a day would make it difficult for Anna to fulfill all the graduation requirements in four years. Adding an extra year would enable her to alternate the classes with the biggest daily homework load, science and math. Anna was willing, so we made the change. For the rest of her high-school career (except for her fifth or "super-senior" year) she took four academic classes, one performance or art oriented class, and tutorial.

We were all settling in. Much of the reason things were working so well was Anna. Despite her medical history, Anna was, and still is, a happy person. She sings, dances, jokes around, and can laugh non-stop. She found many things funny, although they may not have been as funny to other people. She thought it hilarious when, at her giggling request, her Spanish teacher read aloud from *Little Men* and when that same teacher helped her with a chemistry problem. She nearly fell out of her seat when, upon spilling coffee, another teacher used a forbidden expletive. She seemed to find comedy everywhere, and she reported it daily. And she has always been a survivor. Not only has she survived eleven major surgeries, but she has compensated for the resulting differences so successfully that Dr. W. called her the "best compensator I've met in my professional career." Anna works hard, talks hard, and is not afraid to ask for help. With only $1 in her backpack, one day, she asked a food-cart vendor if he had anything that cheap. "No," he replied "but you can have whatever you want." When she tried to buy a Coke and a bag of chips at the supermarket with only $2.00, the cashier made up the difference. (So much for teaching her money management!) One day she went off to school leaving her wallet at home, but she knew what to do: she solicited loans and collected enough money from her fellow bus riders to cover her bus fare and her lunch. They didn't want the money back either. When the Tuberous Sclerosis Alliance held a walkathon to raise money, she collected over $1,220. She asked people to donate wherever she was – at a school production or in the street – and she had no problem going door to door. She signed up thirty-seven people to walk with her, and she made $40 for the walkathon selling her old plastic toys at a garage sale. When she decided she wanted to read the high school bulletin over the P.A. system, she got the bureaucratic runaround and shuttled among three different administrators until she got the permission and guidelines she needed. When her best friend got sick during a large street fair, she took her to Safeway, found the nearest bathroom (by asking of course, since she doesn't usually see what she's looking for), led her friend to the front of the line explaining it was an emergency, and found an adult who could help. Anna always managed to get whatever she needed whenever she needed it.

Another reason high school was working so well was Anna's school placement. Berkeley High is a large urban school with approximately 3000 students. When Anna was a freshman, most of the students were placed in the comprehensive school, but there were also, within the school, a few semi-independent entities called "small schools," and Anna was in one of them. Small schools have several advantages. Everyone knows everyone else. The teachers know each other well and can, therefore, collaborate and share knowledge about their students. They also know each student well, and, having made the commitment to work together in this small-school community, may be more interested than other high-school teachers in the "whole child." Even the students know each other better than they would otherwise.

Anna loved her teachers, some to the point of infatuation. She talked incessantly about her ninth grade Identity and Ethnic Studies teacher. Although she was less infatuated with the others, they were all the center of her world. Most of them were sensitive to her problems and appreciated her strengths. Her freshman photography teacher enjoyed her unusual perspective; he selected an unsentimental portrait she'd taken of our dog for a local art show. And her French teacher appreciated her enthusiasm and her excellent oral skills.

By the time open house arrived, in February of her freshman year, she was feeling much more comfortable. The high school had become her domain, and she led me proudly all over the campus. Her favorite classroom was the photography lab. There, she eagerly showed me all the equipment, explaining the procedure for developing photographs in great detail and making sure I knew the exact number of seconds required to perform each task.

But her proudest moment came at the end of her freshman year, when, along with 149 other students, she received a mayoral award. Hers was for leadership in the classroom. She had been nominated for the award because she was always enthusiastic, always ready to volunteer, and always eager to jump in and forge ahead with the work.

She didn't understand that it wasn't "cool" to get excited about school. The ceremony was held in a tent, which overflowed with friends and family members. Since the crowd made it difficult for the award recipients to make their way to the front, they could only stand when their names were called. Anna waited patiently, on the edge of her seat, as the announcers waded through the names in alphabetical order. She took a deep breath when they reached the "S's," and, at the sound of her name, she popped up proud, tall, and beaming like the sun.

The Way It Went

<u>Medical Situation</u>

Anna was doing well medically. During her freshman year, the orthopedic surgeon lifted restrictions on all sports except gymnastics and football, neither of which Anna had any interest in, and her heart was strong. But we still worried. Whenever she had trouble reading, whenever her handwriting was particularly bad, whenever she seemed more distractible than usual, we worried that her shunt was failing or that the tumor was growing. In January, when her birthday grew near, she remembered the previous year's shunt failure and was afraid to celebrate. She kept it quiet at school, almost hoping no one would find out, although she couldn't resist telling her favorite teachers. She just didn't want her birthday to come. But that didn't stop the celebration. She invited Erika for the ritual sleepover, and both girls stayed up for the entire night.

At the end of her freshman year we went to see the cardiologist. Everything had been going well and Anna hadn't had a surgical procedure for a year and a half. The doctor said her ventricular pressures were good but expressed an interest in trying to get blood flow to the left lung. When we demurred, she admitted that the technology had not changed since the last attempt and that, as long as Anna continued to do well, there was no need for intervention. She then extended the time between visits from six to nine months, and we breathed a sigh of relief. But the conversation still weighed on us. We had thought that Anna was done with cardiac surgery, and it hurt to know that the cardiologist had been contemplating yet another intervention. The sword was still hanging over our heads.

Then, in December 2003, the sword began to fall. Anna had her periodic MRI scan. Although the tumor looked exactly the same as in the previous scan and the ventricle size showed the shunt was working and the cerebrospinal fluid draining as it should, the pituitary was slightly enlarged. The doctor made this observation casually, saying the enlargement was probably due to puberty, but he wanted to do another scan in six months just to be sure. This would be an entirely separate problem, since enlarged pituitaries are not associated with tuberous sclerosis. We didn't tell Anna, but we were worried. The next scan was performed shortly before her seventeenth birthday. This time, the doctor said that the pituitary looked fine, as did the remaining portion of the tumor and the ventricles. The shunt was functioning well. "But," he added, "something has lit up along the site of the tumor." During MRIs, a contrast medium is frequently injected to facilitate visualization of the brain's structures. The doctor meant that the contrast medium had indicated the presence of a nodule he hadn't seen before. "It shouldn't be another tumor," he reassured us "because it isn't in the right place and because kids usually start to stabilize at Anna's age." He thought it might be scar tissue and ordered the next scan for only three months hence. It was back to the waiting game.

We went to see the cardiologist a few months later. Anna's heart and conduit looked the same as they had the year before. That was good. The valve leak, which is expected in conduit replacements, remained small, the conduit itself was clear, the ventricular pressures were normal, and ventricular size was within bounds. Somehow, we didn't worry as much about her heart as about her brain. Perhaps it was because the first cardiologist had always had such a positive attitude;

perhaps it was because Anna seemed so energetic; perhaps it was because there was no alien presence in her heart like there was in her brain.

It was April 2004, time for the three-month MRI, the one which would provide more information about whatever it was that had "lit up" along the incision site. By this time, Anna was a pro. Of course she was worried, and even though we didn't tell her the doctor's concerns, she wondered why she was having another MRI so soon. But she handled the actual test with aplomb. Then the wait began. One day, I got home to find a message from the neurosurgical nurse on the answering machine. "The doctor said to call," she said, "and he said the MRI looks **great.** There are no changes." So I called her back to ask what the doctor had said about the new enhancing nodule and when he wanted the next MRI. She didn't know, and the doctor had just left for two weeks. The wait continued. The only answer we got when he returned was that he felt comfortable waiting nine months for the next MRI. That was good news.

Up to this point, I had been doing all the coordination for Anna's medical care. I had to schedule all her appointments and when surgery was planned, make sure that all her doctors were consulted. In mid-2004, Children's Hospital, Oakland opened the Jack and Julia Center for Tuberous Sclerosis Complex. That made a big difference. For the first time, the hospital's medical staff would oversee all aspects of Anna's care, and we could be sure that this care would be provided based on an understanding of Anna's unique medical needs.

Anna was scheduled for another MRI and a renal ultrasound in December 2004. The ultrasound was now becoming part of the routine because renal tumors are often associated with tuberous sclerosis. Her face crumpled when we first mentioned the upcoming tests, and she seemed more upset than usual. But then, for the first time, she was able to explain what was bothering her. Since kidney involvement typically begins in late adolescence, routine renal scans are not usually recommended until then, and Anna had previously had them only as part of pre-operative testing. She therefore thought that the upcoming ultrasound meant another surgery was in the works. She felt much better when we assured her that this was not the case and that the ultrasound was just routine. But she didn't ask why her routine had suddenly changed because she wasn't ready for the answer. She was, however, ready to talk. She was finally capable of articulating her concerns, told everybody who would listen, and was amply rewarded with hugs and sympathy.

The results of the MRI were good: nothing had changed. The small remaining tumor and the newly visible nodule both looked exactly the same as they had eight months before. Although the TSC clinic director, a neurologist, couldn't definitively identify the nodule, she thought it might be scar tissue and was not concerned. So she decided to lengthen the interval between MRIs to a full year. That was good news indeed. The findings of the renal ultrasound were not quite as good. For the first time, the ultrasound showed lesions characteristic of tuberous sclerosis. But these lesions were too small to be measured and probably wouldn't cause any trouble in the immediate future. If they did begin to bleed, the neurologist assured us, a minimally invasive clotting procedure would take care of the problem.

Anna was healthy throughout 2005. Our annual cardiology visit went well; her heart was strong and her ventricular pressure normal. The renal ultrasound and the MRI showed that her kidney lesions and her tumor had not changed. This was good news, but the neurologist had better news still. The brain tumors typical of tuberous sclerosis, she said, generally stabilize as the children get older. She thought that Anna's tumor had probably stopped growing and that we could probably discontinue monitoring it shortly. There would be no more regular MRIs.

When Anna turned eighteen, on January 10, 2005, several new sets of problems arose. The first was a possible additional manifestation of tuberous sclerosis. About 40% of women with tuberous sclerosis develop pulmonary disorders in the fourth decade of life, the most common of which is lymphangioleiomyomatosis (LAM). Doctors therefore suggest that girls with tuberous sclerosis have a baseline CT scan of the chest at the age of eighteen. Anna had the CT in 2006 and it showed a small number of cysts in the left lung, the lung that receives little or any blood flow. So now we had to see a pulmonologist. Although Anna had no shortness of breath, I was worried. It didn't help when I found out that LAM can lead to pulmonary failure and that the lesions associated with tuberous sclerosis can recur even after a lung transplant. But then, I thought, Anna does seem to have a milder form of tuberous sclerosis; she has no seizures, she has only one tumor and tiny renal lesions, and she is definitely not mentally retarded. Perhaps it wasn't LAM after all, but merely remnants of her heart surgeries. That was exactly what the pulmonologist concluded. Since the cysts appear to be limited to the periphery of the left lung, she theorized that there had been limited blood perfusion to the left lung, possibly through ancillary vessels, and that the cysts developed in the part of the lung that the blood could not reach. She promised to consult with the cardiologist and suggested scans only every few years. That was good news.

Anna was now legally an adult. That meant she could vote, but it also meant that we, her parents, were no longer allowed to make health care decisions for her. We consulted an attorney, who advised us to have her sign an Advance Health Care Directive so that we could continue to make these decisions until she was mature enough to take over. We quickly put the Directive in place.

Then the health insurance company began making unpleasant noises about moving to adult health care providers. We have good health insurance, and all of Anna's physical health care needs have been covered, but because the company is an HMO and because Children's Hospital is not officially part of its network, the company was hoping to move Anna to its own network doctors. We were willing to move for scoliosis follow-up since scoliosis is a common problem, and we waited patiently while the medical group worked to find a provider. But tetralogy of Fallot and pulmonary atresia are another matter because adult cardiologists generally do not have expertise in congenital heart defects. To address this problem, the cardiologists at Children's and Alta Bates Hospitals established an adult congenital heart disease clinic in which patients are monitored by both pediatric and adult cardiologists. Most patients move to this clinic at the age of twenty-two, and our insurance company agreed to let Anna follow suit. It also agreed to let her stay in Children's Tuberous Sclerosis Clinic for now. But there is no clear migration path for tuberous sclerosis patients who outgrow children's hospitals, and the Children's Hospital Jack and Julia Clinic was the only tuberous sclerosis clinic in Northern California. It consequently served adult patients, as well as children, and should continue to serve Anna.

Therapy and Other Interventions

Independent Therapists

When Anna was born, there was no blueprint for bringing her up. In 1977, ten years before she was born, "blue babies" like her required serious ongoing medical management if they survived, and they usually grew up somewhat physically impaired. Twenty years earlier, they died. Although brain tumor resections had been performed for many years, their accuracy improved with the invention of the MRI and its approval in 1984. So until recently, parents of children like Anna were grateful for mere physical survival; they did not look beyond to the psychological effects of surgeries or to the impact of these conditions on their children's development, and they did not understand the importance of early intervention.

To make matters even more complicated, Anna's neuropsychological profile was atypical. She didn't fit into any predefined categories, and she didn't have a neuropsychological diagnosis. This meant that we had no specific intervention plan. Anna had however been seeing a neuropsychologist, Dr. W., since she was five years old. Dr. W. provided individual play therapy that addressed a number of developmental issues, and she gave us the guidance we needed for responding to the problems as they developed. Since she also helped us through the public school's assessment process, making sure that we knew how to get the services Anna needed from the school district, Anna received occupational therapy, speech therapy, and academic support throughout her school career. But now Anna was ready for more.

Dr. W. recommended Dr. A., a communications specialist, to deal with presentation issues. Anna looked much younger than her chronological age not only because she was thin and physically immature, but also because of the way she carried herself and interacted with others. Dr. A. worked on voice usage – including inflection, tone, pitch and volume – facial expression, eye contact, courtesy, conversational and listening skills, appropriateness of behavior, and carriage. On our first visit, Anna showed how much this work was needed. She was anxious about the new doctor in her life and showed it in her behavior: she picked her nose, stuck her tongue out, made a variety of silly faces, slid around on the chair putting her feet up and down, and giggled at the sounds Dr. A. asked her to make. Dr. A. thought she could help. She was tough, she was consistent, and she gave homework, which addressed multiple objectives. The homework included reading aloud, repeating word lists, practicing phrases for a variety of situations, observing other people, greeting people, offering help, and walking with people (rather than ahead of them). She explicitly taught socially acceptable behaviors, and she made sure that Anna met her expectations. Anna "graduated" from her practice at Dr. A.'s suggestion after two years of hard work.

But the behaviors that Anna was learning with Dr. A. would not stick unless she used them. A structured group setting was essential, so I intensified my search for a social-skills group. Although most children learn social skills automatically while playing with their friends, children on the autistic spectrum and many of those with chronic health conditions do not. These children don't play or converse in a truly interactive manner. They don't see social cues and often fail to recognize the intentions of other people or the ways in which they themselves are perceived. I had been trying to find a social-skills group for quite some time.

Anna had been in a group for a few months during fourth grade, the period during which her brain tumor was growing. The group, which consisted of three intensely quiet girls and three rather loud ones, was unsuccessful because the psychologist was unable to resolve the differences in the group setting. She ended up summarily dropping the louder ones; she asked Anna, who was one of the louder ones, to leave and promised to set up a more appropriate group for her in the future, but she never got back to us. Since Anna really needed a group setting and since there were so few groups around, we went back to that psychologist when Anna was a freshman. I told her that Anna was a different person, and she was. But I should have known better. This psychologist did not understand or appreciate her. After only a few months, she told me that Anna needed a group in which social skills were explicitly taught and that she'd be setting one up shortly. She didn't. It was only when I ran into the mother of another one of the "loud girls" that I found out about a group led by another therapist. This therapist, Toby, met with us and we clicked. She appreciated Anna, loved her sense of humor, and was sensitive to her needs. We had finally found a social-skills group that would develop Anna's social awareness and enable her to apply what she was learning with Dr. A. Anna stayed with the group through most of high school.

Since Dr. A. was working on presentation, I asked if she could recommend someone to help improve Anna's gait. Anna had limited body awareness, and though her coordination and balance were good, she was somewhat asymmetric and lacked grace. Dr. A. recommended a Feldenkrais practitioner who had worked for some time in a brain injury clinic, and I quickly made an appointment. The practitioner remarked that Anna was fast and light, which was good, that she had excellent balance and that she was flexible in some ways and rigid in others. He told her that she was good at being fast and that he wanted her to "learn slow." He observed the way that one of her shoulders was tightly drawn up and noticed that she had limited understanding of degrees of motion and texture. He talked about the need to learn control of degrees, about understanding the differences between jagged and smooth movements, sudden and gradual movements, and about learning words to describe physical feelings. I suspected that addressing these deficits would help address similar deficits in the academic, social and linguistic realm. He did some gentle manipulation, which was reminiscent of the cranialsacral session but which did not cause traumatic retracing, and had her do gentle exercises. Anna worked with him throughout high school.

Then we had Anna evaluated at the U. C. Berkeley School of Optometry, which has a clinic specializing in learning problems. The doctors identified deficits in tracking and sustaining focus, so we made weekly visits where Anna learned exercises that she practiced faithfully at home. Her tracking and focusing improved substantially, but she still had reading problems and the doctors recommended a binocular vision and perceptual skills report. Some of the conclusions are quoted below.

> Anna has completed vision therapy. Her accommodative system (eye focusing) improved after vision training. Her eye movements and binocular vision system are adequate for her age.
>
> Anna demonstrates excellent auditory sequential memory skills. She has age appropriate phonemic awareness skills.

Anna demonstrates below average visual perceptual skills overall. She would benefit from a multi-sensory approach to learning: seeing, saying, hearing, writing and building words….

Visual sequential memory is important for remembering basic arithmetic facts and accurate spelling of sight words. [The body of the report indicates that these skills are poor.]

Visual closure is important for reading efficiency: quickly scanning a page, isolating each line, and completing each word in the mind's eye from just a few letters and the context. Visual closure is also important for note-taking: seeing in the mind's eye the picture that is being described in lecture in order to write down the important points. In addition, visual closure is necessary to visualize math, chemistry, and physics concepts as well as during essay composition. [The body of the report indicates that these skills are poor.]

Anna shows reduced spatial planning skills.

Anna has adequate fine motor skills for her age.

Anna reverses letters in forced choice situations.

Anna's memory sequencing skills are excellent as she can recall the maximum length of 7 digits in a sequence.

Anna has adequate decoding (sight word recognition) and encoding (spelling) skills for her age.

Anna's reading and listening comprehension for 7th grade level material are below average. Her reading rate is also 1.6X slower than the expected for her grade level.... [which was 10th grade][11]

This helped us to understand why Anna could copy a one-way arrow pointing in the wrong direction and why, when she was much younger, she frequently did not see the connection between a two dimensional picture of something in a book and the real object. The report recommended academic support strategies and games that could improve performance, but it did not recommend any specific therapies. It did increase our concerns about the geometry class scheduled for the following year, and confirm the need to continue the extensive reading support that we'd been providing. At Dr. W.'s suggestion, we had been reading all assignments out loud so that Anna could have auditory, as well as visual, input and so that she could feel her lips forming the words when it was her turn to read. We continued to do so. But it's tiring to read a whole book out loud, so to reduce fatigue and make sure she wasn't "spacing out," her tutor suggested we alternate paragraphs: Anna read one paragraph and I read the next. That worked, and it allowed reading to keep the social element that is so important to Anna. But then Anna's attention began to wander. She seemed to think that she didn't have to follow along while I was reading. So I devised a pop quiz. Every so often, I would stop and expect her to fill in the missing word. That kept her on track and made sure she was getting visual input even when I was the one doing the reading.

The summer before Anna's first senior year, I discovered a day camp with a special stream for kids with social skills deficits. Anna spent two weeks there and liked it so much that she went back for two sessions the following summer. The camp, which is affiliated with the University of California, has a large site in the Berkeley hills and focuses on sports. It has two social skills streams: one for younger kids and one for teenagers. Each stream is fully integrated with the rest of the camp and the teenagers, who are learning to be counselors, receive intensive support. Anna and the other Counselors in Leadership Training, as they are called, were closely supervised as they worked with campers. They learned social skills during lunch, and they met once a day to discuss their work and the qualities of a good leader. The staff, which seemed to consist mainly of graduate students in psychology, developed a clear set of goals for Anna. They worked on voice volume and what it conveys, pointing (which is an annoying habit that Anna has, I think, finally broken), using discretion in conversation, and anxiety. During the second summer, they also ran into some tricky emotional issues involving jealousy and inappropriate demands for attention, which were eventually resolved.

Throughout all this, Anna's anxiety remained high, so we decided to try cognitive behavioral therapy once again. We had tried it unsuccessfully when Anna was in fifth grade, but she was a different person now. Cognitive Behavioral Therapists teach their clients to identify the thoughts that are causing unwanted feelings or behaviors. Once these thoughts have been identified, clients learn to replace them with more productive thoughts or, as Anna's therapist put it, to "turn caterpillar thoughts into butterfly thoughts." With the therapist's help, Anna worked on identifying thoughts and feelings and developing strategies to replace the thoughts and feelings that stimulated inappropriate behavior. Instead of loudly informing restaurant hosts that she doesn't wait, she learned to internalize her reaction and will eventually develop other more effective coping mechanisms.

Teachers

Although Anna's reading had been improving steadily, she found high-school reading difficult, and I was exhausted. Working five hours a day, coming home to a cup of tea, then plunging into homework with Anna the minute she got home was just too much. So I turned to UC Berkeley's School of Education for a reading and writing tutor. Suzanne, a Ph.D. candidate specializing in reading and a former middle-school English teacher, was perfect. She helped Anna with her English and history homework several times a week, thereby taking some of the academic-support load off our backs. She was more patient than I because Anna was not her child. She made Anna more independent, insisting that she "use [her] brain" and periodically leaving the room while Anna worked. Anna loved Suzanne and she was much more willing to work with her – and much less likely to scream – than she was with me. Suzanne's help was invaluable.

Because Anna spent an extra year in high school and had met almost all requirements when her super-senior year started, she didn't have enough classes to fill up a five-period school day. P.E. was always good – and necessary – and Spanish was a winner, but those two classes, along with the required biology class and the ever-present tutorial only made four classes. So the full-inclusion specialist suggested Workability. Workability is a California state transition program, which provides vocational training to students with disabilities. Anna was given a job helping to clean the school cafeteria. Although she found it "BORING," she got some work experience, made money for the first time and did so well she got a promotion.

Parents

Anna was becoming more independent, so, during her sophomore year, I decided to build on that by weaning her from our car. I would teach her to ride the city bus. I began by taking the bus with her all the way to school for a week; I showed her how to flag it down, pointed out the stops, talked her through the route, got off with her, and made sure she crossed the busy street safely. Then for two weeks, I took the bus with her but didn't get off until after she did. Finally, the big day came. Alan accompanied her to the bus stop, waited with her, and watched her get on all by herself. She was doing it. But she was anxious, worried that the bus wouldn't come or that it wouldn't stop and that she'd be late. So Alan made a deal with her: he promised to drive her if the bus hadn't arrived by 8:05. That only happened once. After a while, Alan even managed to persuade her to go to the bus stop by herself.

But things were not going as smoothly as I thought. I happened to see her waving the bus down one day. She was so afraid that the driver wouldn't stop that a simple wave wouldn't suffice: instead, she was jumping up and down frantically waving both hands. She didn't care or didn't realize how unusual and inappropriate her behavior was. Drivers reassured her, they teased her. But only my insistence that this behavior was both unnecessary and unacceptable, several clear demonstrations, and a firm hand on her shoulder could stop her.

As she got to know the bus schedule, she realized that the northbound bus simply turned around at the BART station, and she figured out what time it would pass our house going north. A ritual began. Every morning, while sitting at the breakfast table, she would watch for the northbound bus. If it was on time, she knew that her bus would also be on time, and she could begin to relax.

We now had another hurdle to jump: taking the bus home. I broached the issue a few months later. "No," she cried, "I want you to pick me up." She was tired at the end of the day and didn't relish waiting for the bus with hordes of other kids. Nothing could persuade her; she didn't care how strapped I was for time or how much these car trips contributed to pollution. She didn't even care that taking the bus would give her more time to spend with friends. But I forged ahead.

We looked up the homeward bound bus schedule together. Unfortunately, she would miss the most direct bus, the one that stopped almost in front of our door, and would have to wait a full half hour. I went with her a few times just to make sure she could handle it. She'd pull up at the bus stop, park her pack in the middle of the sidewalk, and begin her litany pacing as she worried. "When's it coming?" she'd ask over and over again. Since I had no idea, she began to ask everyone else who passed. She couldn't enjoy the wait; she couldn't spend the time, like other kids, hanging out and chatting with her friends. I suggested she visit her favorite teacher for a few minutes before going out to the bus stop. That didn't work, especially since it occasionally made her miss the bus. Finally, after several painfully long waits, her friend Erika suggested she walk over to downtown Berkeley where she would have the choice of three different bus lines. We had hoped that wouldn't be necessary because of the crowds of students and the large numbers of homeless people, but the wait for the other bus was just too long. So Anna headed downtown on her own. There, she met such a large crowd of high-school students trying to board the bus that she decided, on her own, to wait at a different stop. She was independently handling a situation that made her uncomfortable. Another day she got on the bus only to discover she didn't have her bus pass. So she did what any normal 17 year old would do, but not what she would have done earlier in the year: she calmly paid for the trip with cash.

But the bus situation was not completely resolved. Anna came home several times announcing that the bus driver had yelled at her. We didn't understand what was going on until her IA's son explained. She had been waiting for the bus with a large crowd of high-school students in downtown Berkeley. When it came, she was so afraid it wouldn't stop, despite the crowd, that she jumped up and down waving her hands and would have jumped right in front of the bus if a woman hadn't grabbed her. The bus driver was, of course, furious. We warned her sternly, vividly describing the dangers and eliciting a promise not to repeat this behavior. We told her that she was not to flag the bus down at all; she was to stand stock still on the sidewalk with her hands at her sides, and the bus would stop. I said, furthermore, that she was not to ask random strangers when the bus would be coming because they had no more information than she did. We then asked the IA's son to report any other incidents. That problem was solved.

Taking the bus wasn't the only skill she needed to work on though. Anna didn't know how to manage money. Like many children of middle-class families, Anna had no idea where money came from or why it should be managed. But, for her the problem was deeper. While most parents have a foundation on which to build money-management skills since their children grow up shopping,

Anna lacked that foundation. She had never been comfortable in the retail environment. Clothing stores bombard customers with loud music and expect them to select their purchases from a chaotic abundance of colors, shapes and sizes. Grocery stores are somewhat less stimulating but the sheer number of choices can be numbing. Shopping had, therefore, always been very difficult for Anna, so, when she was younger, we could never get her to focus on what she wanted to buy or how much it cost. One day at the beginning of her junior year, I gave her $15 to spend at a local street fair for lunch and games. She is particular about her food and so bought herself a good, but expensive lunch. She then paid $9 for a little doll because the vendor suggested she buy it. When we asked how she was able to afford all that with only $15, it came out that she'd "borrowed" $14 from her friend. We didn't know whether she understood that she would have to pay her friend back.

At that point, we realized that we would have to teach money management skills explicitly. Dr. W. had a plan. She suggested a monthly budget that covered necessary, as well as optional, items. There would be money for Anna's bi-monthly haircut, her monthly bus pass, presents, savings, and charity donations, as well as pocket money for CDs, books, movies, junk food, and meals with friends. It involved a lot of money, but the inclusion of required items meant that Anna would have to seriously consider how she was spending it. Because the large sum could be difficult to manage, Dr. W. also suggested I buy a small folder with multiple pockets. Anna and I then clearly labeled each pocket with the spending category and the amount of money allocated to that category. We also tried to set up a reconciliation scheme using Excel, but that was too complicated and turned the monthly allowance payment into an ordeal. We hoped the arrangement would increase Anna's awareness of money matters. When she got tired of the campus food court in her senior year and ventured off campus to buy her own lunch, she was surprised at how quickly her money ran out and dismayed at having to settle for the campus food court again. Seeing more than one movie a month was out of the question, and new CDs appeared less frequently. We hoped she was learning to manage her allowance but we knew that a credit card was not in her immediate future.

Then we moved on to cosmetic issues. As a child, Anna had never been interested in clothing—except to take it off. She did have her share of twirly dresses, in which she gloried, but matching colors and developing a sense of style had been of no interest. Furthermore, even though she had been dressing herself since early in elementary school, she didn't know what teenagers were wearing. She wanted to wear dresses when everyone else was wearing pants, she saw nothing wrong with wearing the baggy T-shirts we had bought as part of elementary school fundraisers, and she didn't acknowledge dirt. Although I have little interest in fashion, I began to look closely at the tight, belly-button grazing camisoles, low-cut jeans, and flip-flops the girls were wearing. I was more conservative, but I did want to make sure that Anna's clothes did not mark her as different; well cut T-shirts, jeans and tennis shoes did the trick.

The one thing that didn't work was her hair. Adamantly holding onto it as a female marker, she wore it fairly long, with bangs, and refused the tied-back, sculptured look worn by all the girls because getting there was too uncomfortable. She always looked liked she'd just come in from a storm. Then, when she was eighteen, Tova, her thirteen-year-old cousin, came to visit. Tova loved styling hair and the two girls spent hours playing beauty parlor. Anna became a convert. She couldn't do her own hair smoothly, but every morning, I was ordered to create a very specific hairstyle. One day, it was braids. The next, a high pony-tail. Anna had finally begun to care about her hair.

But knowing how to use public transportation, manage money and dress appropriately are only three of the many skills Anna would need for independent living. Halfway through her junior year after a fruitless search for a summer class that would teach more of these skills, her friends' parents and I decided to start our own. We hired a facilitator and agreed on a four-week curriculum, which was divided into two two-week sessions and which included meal planning, shopping, cooking, budgeting, table manners, taking public transportation, group decision making, personal grooming, fashion, sex education and street safety. We weren't trying to create "girly girls," but the traditionally feminine skills did not come easily. During the four weeks of the program the girls planned some meals, did the necessary shopping, prepared the meals and cleaned up. They also played games intended to enhance their communications skills and engaged in a number of activities that were completely alien to them: they applied make-up, did each other's hair and nails, went clothes shopping, and made their own aprons. At the end of each session they held a party, which provided the opportunity to use their newly improved skills.[12]

Then, in Anna's senior and super-senior year, we made sure she used these skills. It was no longer enough to keep her bed made and her room clean. She began to do all the laundry, make dinner with support on weekends and take her turn at washing the dinner dishes. She was learning to take on some of the household responsibilities necessary for independence.

There was one more thing we had to do during Anna's last year in high school: explore options for the following year. Because of all her experience with medical professionals, Anna was determined to become one herself. So further education was necessary. Since she didn't want to go away to school, she and I visited every local college and talked to every disability counselor we could find. We finally settled on our local community college, where she would work towards the Associates degree, and we agreed that she'd do volunteer work on the side. We all hoped she was ready.

Passions/Obsessions

Anna comes from a long line of obsessive-compulsive personalities. Alan says he couldn't do everything he does professionally if he weren't so organized. I spent eighteen years as a professional administrator. Anna, with her high levels of anxiety, feels most comfortable ensconced in her routines and, once they're established, breaking out of them is difficult. She even creates her own verbal routines and can be still be somewhat perseverative. Her favorite shirt says it all:

I will not obsess.

I will not obsess.

I will not obsess.

Anna's biggest obsession was Children's Hospital. She had claimed to love the hospital throughout elementary and middle school. She felt she had to love it because she went there so often. As her hospitalizations decreased, Dr. W. convinced her that she didn't have to love the hospital even though it had saved her life many times. She had only to be grateful. The intensity of her obsession decreased, but it never disappeared entirely. Whenever we drove or took BART past the hospital, Anna would watch for its appearance. "I have to see my hospital," she'd exclaim. Whenever we had a doctor's appointment there, she wanted to go see the patients; whenever she knew someone who was hospitalized, she would insist upon visiting; and she was definitely going to work there when she grew up.

The obsession that has colored her whole life and will probably continue to do so is her focus on time. Focusing on time is one way to control the world, one way to know when things are going to happen, and one way to make sure that you don't miss anything important. Anna learned to tell time very early, moving fluently between analog and digital clocks. In elementary school, she'd start waiting for her friends' visits an hour before their expected arrival time. She'd begin to cry one minute after, and a girl who came an hour late destroyed the entire afternoon. She started to loosen up in middle school. By the time she got to high school, she would begin looking out the window only a few minutes early. But her friends still had to be on time, and the obsession remained. Every time Alan or I came home from a doctor's appointment, she asked the same questions:

"What time was your appointment?"

"When did they call you?"

"What time did the doctor come?"

She didn't ask about the outcome of the visit unless she had clear cause for concern.

An obsession with buses grew out of her obsession with time and her need for punctuality. She knew all the numbers and many of the routes. The drivers fascinated her, and she wondered out loud about their hairstyles, living situations and vacation schedules. Wherever we went, she would take note of the bus numbers, and she would stop whatever she was doing when a bus came by. "What a cute driver," she'd intone, peering hard inside the bus. Since she wasn't interested in driving, we joked that she would probably marry a bus driver or become a dispatcher.

Body piercing, which was all the rage as she was growing up, fascinated her almost as much. In elementary school, almost every other girl had pierced ears. As Anna got older, the girls began to pierce their belly buttons, their eyebrows, their noses and even their tongues. Boys got into the act too. But Anna wasn't having any of it. Perhaps it was because I was one of the few mothers who saw no reason to pierce her ears. Perhaps it was because she thought she already had enough holes in her body. Perhaps it was a fairly rational fear of infection. Or perhaps she just didn't want to be poked unnecessarily. She swore that she would never do that to herself, wondered how other people could and, on meeting new acquaintances, would always ask: "How many pierces do you have?" and "How old were you when you got your ears pierced?"

Music was still a big part of her life. She loved jazz and developed an interest in typical teenage music only in her junior year. She hoarded CDs, memorizing the name of every cut and its length, and she would write out a list of the cuts at every opportunity. The summer before her junior year we took her to see Dee Dee Bridgewater. It was a dream fulfilled. Then, two weeks later, we happened upon Bridgewater once more at the Tivoli Jazz Festival in Copenhagen. Anna couldn't believe her good luck and stood there entranced as Bridgewater sang all her old favorites. This girl who always had to be in bed at 9:00 sharp, the girl with no night-time drive, stood on her feet listening and laughing at Bridgewater's antics for two and a half hours - until 11:30 PM. Then we took her to see the musical "Chicago." This was a revelation for she had never seen a musical before. She sat intently, leaning forward in her seat, eyes glued to the stage, her entire body absorbing the music. Gone were the days when she would fall asleep because a performance was just too overwhelming. Gone were the days when I would sit through a performance anxiously monitoring her reaction.

Now, I could enjoy watching her as much as I enjoyed watching the performance.

But then, like most teenagers, she switched allegiance. Although she still enjoyed jazz, she entered the world of teenage pop, and she fixated on the Spice Girls long after the group had disbanded. She'd had a brief flirtation with them in middle school, but with the increased pressures of her first senior year, obsession flourished. Spice girl music, movies and websites dominated her free time, and she could spend hours dancing around her room singing Spice Girl songs. When asked, she could even do a mean Spice Girl imitation complete with English accent.

During her sophomore year, Anna's main obsession was *Little Women*. One day, I negotiated her into seeing the 1994 version of the movie. She had wanted to see "Freaky Friday" for the second time, and I agreed to watch it on condition that "Little Women" be next. When it came time to rent the video though, she was reluctant because she'd never heard of it before, but she kept her word. The movie touched her so deeply that she clamored to read the novel. She had never done that before. Seeing an opportunity to engage her in reading and eager to share my own love of the book, I got out my forty-year-old copy. She blanched when she saw how long it was. Then, after carefully examining it and recognizing the difficulty of the language, she asked me to read it aloud. She sat spellbound through all 537 pages.

Little Women is about four sisters living with their mother during the Civil War. The third sister, Beth, is the good girl who always puts everyone else's needs before her own and eventually dies from scarlet fever. Anna, with her own need to follow all the rules and her history of chronic illness, identified with her closely and found the chapter depicting Beth's illness intensely moving. She had feared reading it. She didn't want Beth to die, and at first, tried to deny how deeply she had been touched, saying, "That wasn't so bad, was it?" But I couldn't agree. "Yes, it was," I answered. "Beth was so sick she almost died, Marmie wasn't there, and everyone in the book was crying." That affected Anna profoundly. It evoked deeply buried memories of the hospital and made her truly sad, both for Beth and for herself. She didn't scream, she cried, as she had never cried before, for ten full minutes. She was feeling an empathy for Beth that she had never felt for any other literary character.

Once she identified with Beth, Anna began to think more deeply about the text. She asked questions about the social relationships and cultural issues it described. In one scene at a party, a rich society girl snidely says, "I heard your father's school was closed because he admitted a little dark girl" and Anna asked whether the comment was intended as an insult. Although the remark was phrased as a simple statement, Anna heard the snide tone, understood the racist implications, and felt the girl's motivation.

Once we finished *Little Women*, Anna wanted more, so we read the next two books in the series together – *Little Men* and *Jo's Boys*. But that wasn't enough: she wanted me to read *Little Women* to her again. Well, I wasn't going to do that. If she wanted it again, I told her, she'd have to read it herself. And so she did; she read *Little Women, Little Men* and *Jo's Boys* all by herself (and silently), stopping only right before the end of *Jo's Boys* because she didn't want to lose the characters who had meant so much to her. Alan and I loved seeing her sprawled out on the couch absorbed in a book. We welcomed her into the world of books, our world, and we hoped that she had finally become a reader. We were wrong.

Anna carried on her obsession long after finishing the books. She focused on Beth but was satisfied with anything involving *Little Women*. And just as she made lists of things that were important to her like hospital patients or cuts on a CD, she made lists of the chapters in each one of Alcott's books. She could even provide the name of a chapter when given the number. One day, she started a project: she would ask us for a number between one and forty-seven and then draw a picture illustrating the chapter of that number. She didn't stop until she had worked her way through the entire book. Although one chapter's illustration was not substantially different from another's, her figures had definitely improved from the minimally endowed stick figures she had always drawn, and the geometric patterns with which she decorated the girls' dresses grew more and more creative. Anna's focus on Beth became more intense; she would write her name everywhere and talk about her constantly. It pleased her immensely when her fellow students began to call her Beth.

And then, she wrote her first completely independent story. Attaching an article to a noun ("the Beth," "do the play") is one of her standard jokes.

Beth has Much Altered Again

Chapter 1

Boom! Boom! and BOOM went Amy, Meg, and Jo together because they wanted back the Beth. Suddenly, there was Beth but she looked very skinny.

Chapter 2

Marmie said "We'll have to give her food like ten pieces of chicken liver." Jo, Meg and Amy gave her the liver, but she wasn't getting any fatter.

Chapter 3

They called in a doctor who said to give Beth some junk food. But she can't eat junk food if she has just died and been sick.

Chapter 4

"This will be done MY way," said the doctor. He hooked up the famous Beth to an I.V. He poured a lot of junk food in to the I.V.

Chapter 5

"Yay!" said Amy, Jo, and Meg "our beloved Beth is coming back!" They were so happy they cried.

Chapter 6

"You may not, I mean NOT dance with this Beth because she is very weak and fragile." They were all shocked because they didn't know how long it would take her to get strong again.

Chapter 7 (4 years later)

"Our beloved Beth has recovered!" " Now we can play with her and do whatever we were doing with her!"

Chapter 8

And so it was, the Beth had grown healthy after the doctor let her rest and gave her (through an I.V.) a lot of junk food.

Chapter 9

They decided to celebrate Beth by inviting everyone and they surprised her with a piano.

Chapter 10

Beth played on the piano all of her favorite songs. Everybody joined in and started to sing because they were so happy to hear Beth do the play.

Chapter 11

They were so happy that they showered Beth with gifts and Beth was very pleased to have them.

Chapter 12

Now when Beth is sick, they put her on the I.V. and give her junk food and she will never be sick again.

This is the end of "Beth the mess."

Growing Up

Anna had no surgery at all in high school. She was consequently free to grow and develop. One of the ways we helped her grow was by maintaining the routines that made her feel secure. Although our lives were busy, we always had dinner together and each of us, in turn, would describe how we'd spent the day. After dinner, one of us would help her finish her homework or, if it was already finished, read aloud, listen to her read aloud or play a game. When she went to bed, which was usually at nine o'clock sharp, Alan and I would come in individually to say goodnight. Alan would call every night that he was out of town so that we could telephonically share our days and wish each other a good night. Our weekend breakfast ritual also remained in place; Alan and Anna continued to dazzle my taste buds with their culinary inventions. And every year, we celebrated the same holidays with the same good friends, a repetition which enriched rather than constrained our lives.

Anna's braces were removed the summer after her sophomore year, and she acquired two sparkly retainers. Removing the braces left a gritty glue residue, which had to come off. This girl, who used to scream at the sight of a needle and who never was able to sleep in her pre-surgical back brace, sat there quietly with her mouth wide open, her whole body vibrating, as the orthodontist ground the residue off her teeth. She was as thrilled to get the retainers as she had been to get the braces. But the retainers were another story. She thought she was supposed to love them, and she tried her best, but she finally realized it was impossible. They were uncomfortable, and they made her lisp. But she wore them almost without complaint - twenty-four hours a day for a month and then all night for many years.

Anna was very reliable in other respects as well. If we told her to come home at 4:00 PM, she would arrive precisely at 4:00 PM, and, if it was getting late, she would run. When she got her cell phone and started taking the bus home from school, she would always call if the bus was even a few minutes late. One of the reasons for this excessive reliability was her dependence on structure and rules. Rules could never be broken. We didn't worry about sex or drugs because she had rules against them, and rule breaking terrified her. One day, when a wire came off her braces, she was afraid that she had broken a rule and that the orthodontist would be angry. Another day, when a supermarket saleswoman convinced her to buy a cake and I made her take it back, she was afraid she'd broken another and that she would seriously disappoint the saleswoman. School rules were especially important and although she tried various means of minimizing her workload, she would never cut classes or fail to turn in an assignment.

Then, in her sophomore year, we had a breakthrough. She started to lie. It wasn't much, but it indicated that she wasn't quite as rule-bound as she had been, that she finally realized we weren't omniscient, and that she was becoming more independent. She told me she had finished her reading assignment in school, all seventy pages of it, and she insisted that I write the summary we always wrote together. Now I knew she couldn't have read all seventy pages in school. When her IA confirmed my suspicions, Anna was out having ice cream with her former second grade teacher. I called the teacher and asked her to prepare the ground for the discussion we needed to have. When they got home, she sat Anna down, insisted that she apologize for lying, and made her promise to do the work. That was very difficult for Anna. You could see the struggle in her face, but she did what she was told and learned an important lesson. The lying didn't stop though: it continued in other, small, typical teenage ways. If she didn't like a particular kind of food, she'd feed it to the dog or throw it out. She wouldn't tell us about events, like school dances, in which she didn't want to participate, she'd "forget" to tell us about tests she'd failed, and she'd sneak junk food whenever she could. She was becoming more "normal."

She was resourceful and always accomplished what she needed to, even if she did so in somewhat unusual ways. One day in her super-senior year, she was supposed to take BART from school directly to an appointment. But she realized at the last minute that she didn't have a BART ticket. Instead of getting upset and calling me, she convinced a fellow student to come with her to the BART station, lend her the money for a ticket, and show her how to make the purchase.

She was also becoming somewhat more flexible. One day, after I had helped her with a writing assignment and she had gone to bed, I found a description of the requirements, which I hadn't seen before. It was clear I'd led her off in the entirely wrong direction. What to do? I expected a tantrum. In the morning, I sat down with her and laid out the options. "We have a problem," I said, "and we have to figure out how to solve it." I told her I'd found the assignment, that the material we'd added the day before was inappropriate, and that we had a choice: she could hand it in the way it was or make changes. She asked me what I would do, but I refused to tell her. Then she asked whether I'd be willing to do the typing if she made the changes. I agreed. She removed the changes we had made the day before and wrote a paper that really fit the assignment.

She was more willing to try new things. Her high school opened a food court toward the end of her sophomore year. She had always brought her lunch, so this was a good opportunity. But she refused to try it until Suzanne said that she'd read about it in the newspaper. Anna took that as a suggestion and, the very next time that her friends were otherwise occupied, went over on her own to try it. She ended up having lunch with some of her classmates, thus expanding her social network, and we never packed lunch again. When she got tired of the food court, she began to do what most of the other high school students did at lunch: go into downtown Berkeley for pizza or some other cheap treat. So strong was the junk-food motivation that she needed no suggestion from us, and we found out only after the fact.

She was making a heroic effort to control her impatience. We went to Europe the summer before her junior year. Although a good traveler and very well behaved in airports, she was always anxious about being on time for our scheduled flights. One day, when we tried to check out of a hotel to leave for the airport, the credit card Alan wanted to use didn't work. It was two hours before takeoff, but Alan was determined to use that card. He talked to the hotel manager, fought with the credit card company, and talked to the hotel manager again. All we could do was wait. As time passed, Anna grew increasingly anxious. She talked non-stop, she paced, she yelled out loud enough to make heads turn, and she began to cry. But then, she made a grand effort: she took a deep breath and regained control. And her effort was rewarded: the hotel manager called us a cab to make sure we got there on time. When we arrived at the airport, we ran up against yet another obstacle. We were selected for an additional security check, and we were led to a separate room where a white-gloved security guard slowly, painstakingly unpacked and repacked every single one of our bags. Alan was fit to be tied and muttered curses while smiling obsequiously, but Anna showed no sign of impatience because we had vividly described the cost of inappropriate airport behavior. She was working on controlling her impatience in her everyday life as well. Waiting for doctors' appointments got easier and, during her super-senior year, she barely complained when we had errands to do on the way home from school. That was a big change.

By the time she was a junior, she was becoming more aware of her inappropriate behaviors. She would report on herself when her requests for attention forced a cashier to tell her he was still serving someone else, when a teacher told her she didn't like to be grabbed, and when her IA had to explain that she shouldn't show her a paper by shoving it in her face. She was realizing the offensiveness of these behaviors and the need to act in a more socially acceptable way. Her self-control was improving. One day, during her senior year, she had a massive tantrum because she'd lost an expensive calculator and we wouldn't let her use her money to order a CD until she either found the calculator or replaced it. The tantrum was so violent that I was afraid she'd revert to her old ways and hit me, but she didn't. So I congratulated her on her restraint. "I was afraid you were going to hit me," I remarked expecting only a weak demurral. But I was overwhelmed by her response: "I would never do that," she replied.

She was also starting to see herself as others saw her, to understand that her own perspective was not everyone else's. In her super-senior year, she became self-conscious about her age. She was born in January, a month after the cut-off date for starting elementary school. So she would have been one of the older students in her classes even if she'd started elementary school at the expected time. But she'd also spent one extra year in both preschool and high school. That meant she was a full three years older than some of her peers; she was twenty when she graduated. That age difference had never really bothered her because she hadn't realized how unusual it was. By the time she got to her super-senior year though, she knew she was different and it bothered her.

She was becoming more independent as well. Although we were still driving her to and from school during her freshman year, she would often hang out on the local main street eating junk food with her friends, she would walk to the store by herself, and she'd spend her entire allowance on junk food. She began to make her own plans and would stop only to ask me for permission or a ride. She would stay home alone (and sneak junk food) on school holidays when Alan and I had to work and during our occasional evening outings. She would come home to an empty house when necessary and walk over to appointments by herself. During her sophomore year, she began to walk to her swimming lessons directly from school, and, during her senior year, she started to take BART to her Feldenkrais sessions. She was even willing to stay after school for math tutoring sessions, to have her yearbook picture taken, and, to meet with her college counselor. During her super-senior year, we had a number of very complicated days, which she handled very well. On one of those days, she ate dinner by herself, cleaned up, walked the dog, and went to a therapist appointment on her own as Alan and I were heading out to a restaurant.

And she was learning to advocate for herself. The full-inclusion teacher always required her students to attend their IEP meetings, and Anna was extremely resistant during most of her high-school career. It made her uncomfortable to be the focus of so much attention. She attended her first meeting in ninth grade but wandered around the room and refused to participate. By the time she was a senior, she was sitting at the table with everyone else and listening intently to what they had to say. Her super-senior IEP meeting was the best of all. She was well prepared, led it effectively, listened to what we all had to say, and did an excellent job of articulating her goals.

As Anna grew more independent, her relationship with us was changing. There were control issues. She had never been through the two-year-old's "no stage," and sometimes we felt she was going through it in high school. The summer before her junior year, she began to take charge, frequently announcing, "I'm the boss here" in stentorian tones. When we were in London, she wanted to ride The Eye, the big wheel that rotates over the Thames, takes over a half hour to make a full circle, and costs an unreasonable amount of money. She was determined, but Alan was dead set against it and a shouting match ensued. We soon learned the value of discussion, negotiation, and compromise. She began to take a more active planning role and liked nothing better than to make restaurant reservations or to help plan trips. When we went out to eat, she would order from the menu, participate in the conversation, and sit quietly when she wasn't participating. No longer did she flit around the dining room, stopping at every table to inquire about the occupants' family or living arrangements. Alan's frequent business trips became much easier. She would help with the housework because she realized I couldn't do it all myself, and we would chat over the vegetarian meals that Alan scorned, complaining good-humoredly about how much he worked and traveled. But this was only when she had no other options. Like a typical adolescent, she preferred her friends' company to ours and didn't hesitate to show it. In December of her freshman year, when she was almost 16, we were all invited to a bris next door. As always, she was in a rush to get there. She went on ahead, and when we arrived, she let her displeasure show. "Not you!" she welcomed us. "Why'd you have to come?" And she was proud of her intolerance. For the next few months, she told this story wherever she went to whoever would listen. She even wrote about it in her English class journal that January. The question was "Do you treat your family nicely? Why or why not?"

> I am nice to my family but my mom says I am never nice to her. The reason for that is because when I get home I am always in a hurry to do my homework. The reason for that is that I want to get my homework over with. My mom should know that I want to get my homework done right away. She should not do Spunky's trick and shouldn't do what she needs to do. One time I left her out of friendship circle. I also wouldn't let her come to the bris or the chocolate factory.

During the summer before her junior year, she took a big step. She'd been wanting to volunteer at Children's Hospital for years. Most of her surgical procedures had been performed there, she felt at home, and it was there that she wanted to work when she grew up. We went to the orientation together and she listened intently, taking copious notes. Since volunteers were required to have had two TB tests within the past year, she called her doctor as soon as we got home to make the appointments. This was a first. When she was younger she'd always fended off shots, flailing and crying; she'd been a very "hard stick" as the hospital staff had put it. But she was eager to have these shots because they were part of becoming a volunteer; she sat in the car without complaint, waited patiently in the doctor's office, and stoically extended her arm when the time came. She would have done anything to be a hospital volunteer. Then came the interview. After speaking with her for a few minutes, the volunteer coordinator announced her decision. Anna would be an ambassador, escorting outpatients from the front desk to clinics on the first and second floor. She would not work with hospitalized patients because the coordinator felt that she wouldn't be able to handle the unpredictability of the patients' behavior or their medical conditions. The coordinator then handed Anna a volunteer uniform, a voluminous blue jacket whose sleeves hung down almost to Anna's knees. Anna didn't mind its size. She danced down the hospital hallways as we went to get her badge and then, once she had it hanging around her neck, used it to open every door that patients always found closed. Her eyes widened as she opened the ICU door, she exclaimed as she got into the inter-building bridge, and when she made her way into the anteroom of the surgical suite she positively beamed. The volunteer coordinator was pleased at her joy but took care to give her the explicit instructions I had suggested. She told her to make eye contact, to walk slowly, to be patient and to avoid pointing or interrupting, and she spent extra time showing her the location of all the clinics.

Anna learned the routes quickly and was happy to do whatever was needed. She would wait patiently by the front desk for clients and sit down only when the lobby was empty. She didn't overwhelm the security guards with chatter and even reported a spill that she'd seen in the elevator because she knew that spills were the province of the custodial staff. Then, late one afternoon, after she had spent three mornings at the hospital, the phone rang. It was the volunteer coordinator calling to say that Anna had to leave the program. She had received an email note from a staff member reporting behavior that he considered inappropriate. He said that Anna had asked an in-patient whether he was in the hospital and that upon hearing an affirmative reply, she had bubbled over with glee. "I'm not. I'm not!" she had chanted as she danced around the corridor. The coordinator was willing to investigate further because Anna denied the accusation. But I knew better; this behavior was typical of Anna. She was so thrilled to be *working,* instead of *being,* in the hospital that she could not contain herself, and since the behavior was purely impulsive, she didn't remember it. After much discussion, she began to understand what she had done, but it was too late. The coordinator refused to give her another chance no matter how many promises she made, and Anna was devastated. Her dream had been shattered. She could never work at Children's Hospital, she hated the coordinator, and she was even afraid to go to her medical appointments because she might see her. Several months later, a few weeks after her junior year had begun, she was still stewing about it. She was starting to feel that no one liked her and went around school asking everyone if they "wanted" her. The volunteer coordinator had taught her a bitter, but necessary lesson: the world is not always a friendly place.

Although this experience scarred her for a number of years and she subsequently worried about being fired from every job she had, she learned a number of things. She learned that she had to work harder to control her impulses, and, shortly thereafter at a friend's elegant retirement party, her behavior couldn't have been more appropriate: she welcomed the guests, asked them to sign in, served food and helped clean up, with nary a misstep. She did a great job, even making eye contact as she asked people whether they wanted milk and sugar in their coffee. People were enchanted, but of course this wasn't the hospital and the guests weren't patients.

Anna also learned to rely less on me and more on herself. Losing the hospital job lightened her summer schedule, so she signed herself up for a cooking class – all I had to do was pay the bill – and she called all the libraries and museums to which she could take the bus to find out about their volunteer programs. First to bite was the local library. There she spent many summer mornings and many Saturday mornings throughout her junior year doing whatever was needed – shelving books, cutting out pictures, copying documents – and she was greatly appreciated.

But she hadn't quite learned to control her negative impulses. Two years later, still brooding over losing the job of her dreams, she went to the cafeteria at Children's Hospital while I was talking to her cardiologist and told everyone who would listen that she hated the coordinator. Needless to say, the coordinator called me that evening.

When Anna was a junior, she learned another hard lesson: people aren't always honest. One day, she left her wallet on the counter at the school's food court. By the time she realized what she'd done, it was gone. She didn't have much money, but she did have a bus pass, a student ID, a YMCA card, a library card, and a Medic Alert card, and all these cards had to be replaced. She got right to work. She bought herself a new bus pass with her own money. She went to the school office, got a temporary ID, and went back three separate times before she could get the permanent card. She told the YMCA clerk and the librarian what had happened and was immediately issued replacements, and she called Medic Alert to request a replacement card. I could never have done all that in high school.

She learned about racism too. Because of her inability to see social cues, she had never experienced racism when she was younger. Throughout elementary school, she saw every child, including herself, as brown-skinned; in first grade, she referred to a very dark Eritrean girl as her sister and they visited each other regularly until fourth grade. In middle school, our queries about her classmates' ethnicity were met with blank stares. In high school, she didn't categorize her classmates and would hang out with anyone who seemed receptive. To her, racism was merely an academic concept that had been drummed into her head by the unrelenting liberalism of the Berkeley school district curriculum. But that changed the summer before her junior year in high school. She was reading *Little House on the Prairie* and came to a section in which two Indians invade the family's house. It included a large illustration of two tall, muscular, half-naked Indians dominating the author's kitchen. She brought me the picture in dismay, but she didn't connect the abstract discussions of racism she'd had at school with her discomfort. This was a learning opportunity. She finally understood how difference can promote racism. She began noticing racial differences and asking why people in certain job categories were predominantly African American. Although she had learned about racism in school, the knowledge didn't make a real impact until she was ready to absorb it.

The one thing she refused to learn about was physical violence. While many of her peers revel in violent movies and video games, the slightest cinematic violence was too much. Fistfights, shoot-outs, cataclysms, and any attendant blood were never stylized enough for her comfort and she would cover her eyes or leave the room when she knew they were coming. Even the dancing in "West Side Story" with its choreographed rumbles was enough to throw her off. Coming out of social group one day, we chanced upon a couple in the parking lot practicing a martial art that involved dueling with two very long sticks. Anna stopped short and grabbed my arm. She was afraid to move. "What are they doing?" she hissed. I had to drag her around them to the car, uttering reassurances as we went.

The Social Butterfly

Anna was blooming socially. Her relationship with Erika had become much more equitable. No longer was she testing Erika's tolerance by making fun of the way she spoke or cutting her hair. Their visits were becoming more interactive, while remaining somewhat ritualized. Anna would help Erika out in small ways when asked, and people would comment on her solicitousness as she untangled Erika's sweatshirt, ordered for her in restaurants, and helped her when she stumbled.

But Anna needed more than one friend. To expand her social network, Dr. W. suggested that I set up a girls group, which would provide a structure for day trips, shopping or simply hanging out. The full inclusion specialist thought that Soraya, another one of her students, would be interested and I arranged a meeting, which seemed to go well. After a round of typical teenage phone conversations, Soraya took the initiative and invited Anna and Erika to the movies. Such excitement! Anna couldn't sit down or focus on anything else for the entire morning before the event. I then had Anna invite the two girls to the zoo, and I let them wander around by themselves. Of course, they were nervous being on their own like that, and of course, Anna asked everyone she saw for directions to our prearranged meeting place. But they had a great time. Then, the full-inclusion specialist suggested one more girl for the group. This girl wasn't sure if she wanted to join, but she finally acquiesced and the group took off. Approximately once a month, one family would take the girls someplace and let them go. Lunch and movies worked well; science museums were manageable; but my trip to the Oakland Museum was a disaster. Erika was out of town. Since it was family art day, I left the three girls in the art room and went to look at the exhibits. When I returned to see how they were doing, I found Anna wandering aimlessly around the art room while the two other girls worked intently on separate projects. All I could do was take Anna to visit the galleries. This was the problem with having only three girls. If Erika had been there, she and Anna would have visited the galleries together and the opportunity for socialization would not have been lost. But despite the rocky start, group spirit was developing. Anna's phone rang more and more, and the girls began to make their own plans, leaving their parents out.

Anna was having fun, but she was also realizing some concrete benefits from these interactions and using what she was learning with the communications therapist. She was becoming much more responsive to other people's needs, her conversations were growing more natural, and her responses were becoming more appropriate. One day, while talking on the phone with the most recent addition to the group, she mentioned that she was going to get some cupcakes. The girl asked if she could come and a typical teenage visit ensued. They hung out together all afternoon, got Chinese take-out for dinner, and had a great time talking, listening to music, playing games, and giggling like only teenaged girls can. When a local festival that Anna had always loved conflicted with a family symphony performance in a series she enjoys, she opted for the social scene. She and her three friends spent the day strolling up and down the avenue with the crowds. What a change this was.

Anna was enjoying her social circle and feeling confident about her friendships. She started to branch out, socializing with more of her classmates. In elementary school, the more mature girls had helped her to calm down when she grew agitated by sitting with her, patting her shoulder and holding her hand. In high school, they "adopted" her. In the second half of her freshman year, she focused on a group of three senior girls. The journal entries below show how much these relationships meant and how carefully Anna had to monitor her behavior within them.

Journal 2/5/04

When I go to social group I will tell Toby that I made a new one. She will wonder what the heck I mean. I will tell Toby that I made a new friend. She will be glad to know that. I think that the other girls from social group would be glad to know that I made another friend. I have been friends with these seniors since the beginning of the year. I just made a new one. For the first time yesterday, I high-fived two of them. They understood and high-fived me back. I will not do it too often because then they will get bored with it. I can do it to my other friends but not all the time.

Journal 2/20/04

I saw all three of my friends today and one of them twice. I expected not to see any of them. One of them was in the P.E. locker room and I think I saw her from far away. The other one was inside of my teacher's room and she shocked me. The other was on my way from the drug store. I saw one twice. The second time I saw her was on the way out of my teacher's classroom.

But these girls were not good friends who would call her just because they felt like it, and Anna began to learn about degrees of friendship. While she saw almost every girl as her friend in middle school, she was now beginning to distinguish between her closest friends and friendly classmates. She was beginning to see the finer points in relationships: she could distinguish among the kids with whom she generally had lunch, the kids with whom she could have lunch, and the kids with whom she'd never have lunch. She was developing a more nuanced view of the world, a view in which dislike could replace hatred and politeness, friendship. She was beginning to understand that there was an emotional spectrum rather than merely two opposing emotional poles. She was also becoming more sensitive to other people's needs. One day, she told me she'd had a very sad conversation with another girl. Since the girl had bemoaned her lack of friends, Anna felt impelled to be nice and made a movie date. When I took them both to the zoo, Anna, who couldn't tell a Corvette from a Suburban, listened closely to an extended discourse on cars. She made all the necessary listening noises like "cool" and "uh huh" while the girl rattled on, and she walked with the girl, rather than rushing ahead. Even on the merry-go-round where they sat on adjacent horses, she leaned toward the girl so as to hear everything the girl was saying. I had never seen her so responsive. But I also realized the limits of that responsiveness. The girl's conversation consisted mostly of monologues and her ability to engage in interactive conversation was limited. Anna appeared responsive only because the conversational demands were not high; she could not yet maintain a truly interactive conversation.

She was, however, making strides in that direction. She was learning to express her emotions verbally. In her social skills group, she would talk about feelings of sadness, which she had often denied, and feelings of fear. She was also becoming more aware of the emotional signals sent by other people. Another journal entry from the second half of her freshman year shows that she had learned to interpret the signs of her teacher's anger.

Journal 2/3/04

I think that what some people did angered Mr. A. I know because he was going to give an explanation on something and people were too loud and Mr. A. gave up and said that he will not give an explanation. I could tell that Mr. A. got mad because he raised his voice and he said that he didn't want to give an explanation period. Even though Mr. A. didn't announce that he was angry he sounded like it and I wish the people that ruined it would apologize to him now!

As her awareness increased, she began to notice differences in others. When she encountered a girl with an autistic spectrum disorder, she remarked on the girl's tendency to soliloquize, her inability to tolerate interruption, her failure to make eye contact, and the pitch and volume of her voice. We hoped that this new awareness would motivate her to moderate these tendencies in herself.

Near the end of Anna's freshman year, the students in her small school organized an overnight, community-building retreat. I went along as a chaperone. When we arrived, the teachers sent groups of students off on their own to explore the area. I was concerned because I felt that Anna wasn't ready for that degree of independence. Although she would undoubtedly do her best to stick with the group, I was afraid that the group wouldn't stick with her.

I could see her hooking up with a friendly stranger and then being left behind when the group moved on. So I shadowed her – staying within shouting distance but managing to remain unobtrusive. I watched as she did what the others were doing; she left her shoes and her uneaten lunch in the middle of the sand, rolled up her pants, jumped in and out of the water, scrambled up and down the rocks, got completely soaked and squealed happily. Although she kept to the periphery of the group, she did not hang back, and she didn't hesitate to join a new group when her group took off. Later, when everyone had returned to the hostel and was sitting around chatting, Anna happily forced her way into several groups and seemed to enjoy every minute. She was part of their community. The next morning, she woke up before anyone else. She had never been known to sleep in and was certainly not going to do so now. Throwing her clothes on, she ran downstairs to the living room where the program director was sleeping, plunked herself down on the couch opposite, drew her knees up to her chest, and sat silent – her eyes fixed on his face – until he was awakened by the intensity of her gaze. He rallied quickly and invited her to help him cook breakfast. And so she did, cleanly cracking at least a hundred eggs.

But Anna was not really making friends with her neurologically typical peers. Her classmates were nice to her and a few of them made special efforts to include her. They would tease her affectionately – never for being different because she had a quality that deflected meanness, that invited tolerance and even protectiveness. They would cater to her obsessions, telling her they'd met someone named Beth, asking how Beth was doing, and making elaborately decorated nameplates inscribed with the name Beth. But she was not really part of their circle, mostly because of the difficulty she still had initiating and maintaining conversations. She couldn't tell when other people weren't interested in what she was saying and would forge blindly ahead. She didn't listen actively to what her peers were saying and made contributions that were frequently irrelevant or just plain silly. She violated personal space, pointed at people, asked questions to which she knew the answers, and directed inquiries to people other than the subject of the inquiry. "What's his name?" she would ask or "Does she still feel lousy?" In her innocence, she sometimes made inappropriate statements or asked inappropriate questions. One night, when we were driving home from an evening theater performance with another married couple, she announced in her usual fashion that she was tired and "wanted bed." She then asked the woman whether she wanted her bed and whether her husband would be in it. I had to tell her never to use the word "bed" in public again.

Anna has always been most comfortable with adults. Late in her freshman year, Anna learned that her tutor Suzanne was getting married. We had hired Suzanne earlier in the year, and Anna adored her. Starting with our friend Sally who had met Anna even before she left the hospital, moving on to her second-grade teacher Wendy who had helped her hold the brain tumor at bay, continuing with Annamarie who had introduced her to photography, sporadically advancing with Allie who often made Anna the focus of her attention, Anna had built a "stable" of adored and adoring women. Suzanne became number one. At first, Anna was jealous when she found out that Suzanne was getting married, but her jealousy evaporated in the excitement of the event. She was ecstatic when she was asked to help plan a shower. Since making it a surprise was part of the fun, she controlled her impulses and kept the secret for over a month. The first order of business was to make sure that Suzanne would come to our house for "tutoring" at the specified time. I held my breath as I described our schedule, and Anna stood quietly by. She was her usual self as we agreed upon the date and time, but we all exploded the minute the door closed. We had done it! Suzanne was coming and she had no idea why. Then Anna got to work. She made the invitations, went food shopping with the woman who had suggested the shower, decorated the house, and welcomed all the guests. All was quiet when Suzanne knocked. We opened the door, Suzanne saw the guests, and she turned around and walked out. She was floored. But Anna wasn't. She was ready with a speech and a bouquet.

> For those of you who don't know me, my name is Anna and Suzanne's my tutor. I want to give her these flowers because I love Suzanne. I love Kevin too. And I'm so glad they're getting married! Give it up for Suzanne and Kevin!

She never could have withstood all the cheers and applause that followed when she was younger. At the wedding itself, her behavior was entirely appropriate. She understood that Suzanne was not going to pay that much attention to her. So she turned her attention to people who would: the little children. The wedding was held in Monterey, and we were there for three nights. Every morning she would run over to the breakfast room as soon as it opened and find a small child to play with. At each of the events associated with the wedding she rounded up all the little children she could find and they trailed behind her like ducklings.

But then, her eyes began to open. She took a couple of cooking classes and complained because all the kids were much younger than she. That sort of thing had never bothered her before. She was beginning to understand the extent to which she didn't fit in, and she became less willing to force acceptance – to barge right in and make herself a part of the group – as she had done in the past. Her summer day camp experience deteriorated. She had loved camp so much before high school that we kept her there the summer before tenth grade even though her peers had moved on. That was a mistake. These were not the kids with whom she'd spent the previous nine summers; she was not part of this group. Her isolation increased when she chose to work with the five-year-olds instead of participating in the camping trip that crowned the session. Family night at the end of the session was a disaster; she didn't leave our side and we went home early. Her junior-year school retreat didn't go well either. When the other kids went off to explore on their own, she insisted on going hiking with me. She bridled at the community-building activities and refused to go on the senior retreat. She was more comfortable at school because of the routines that had been previously established and because she could have lunch with her group of friends, but by the time she reached her senior year the girls in this group had all graduated. She had no one to eat with. That didn't stop her though. She cheerfully trundled downtown, bought her lunch and went back to wait for her next class. She never admitted how much it bothered her, and she never invited anyone to join her because, as she said, "it's just too hard." Anna was starting to deal with some of the difficult social issues that plague all American teenagers.

She wasn't learning much about boys though – only that they weren't as bad as she had thought in middle school. One day, she remarked, without any clear evidence, that she thought one of her male classmates had a crush on her; she, of course, denied any interest in him. She insisted that another boy liked her when it was her friend he was calling and hanging out with, and she got giddy with excitement when a boy actually came to our house. But she did not understand the social guidelines. One day when a boy and a girl were visiting, I agreed that the girl could spend the night. But five minutes later, I realized I had to be more explicit and told her privately that the boy was not included. She asked why not, in surprise, and I could only answer that it was not appropriate for a boy to sleep over at a girl's house. A journal entry from the last third of her sophomore year demonstrates her level of understanding and her refusal to deal with infatuation on a personal level.

Journal 3/1/04

Prompt: Do you think everyone is searching for love why or why or why not?

Yes! I think teenagers have a lot of crushes. But not moi! I have seen a lot of kids with boys and I think that they love them. If I ask them if they love them they say that they do. If they do then I love it. If not that is fine too! Some people say that the names of their friends are private.

She focused instead on her female teachers. She was asked to write a biography and naturally chose her favorite teacher.

Do you know a teacher who is funny, helpful, and cares at the same time? I do. She was my 9th grade Identity and Ethnic Studies teacher. This teacher is named Hasmig M.

She can be very funny. One day, she sat next to me and said, "I'm Eleanor." I thought that was funny because Eleanor is my aide and Hasmig doesn't look anything like her. I started laughing. Other times, she started to sing before class. I always cracked up because I thought it was funny.

Also, she is helpful. One time, at a school picnic, Eleanor told me that if I did anything rude, I would go to the end of the line. Two seconds later, I said "No food for you," to Eleanor I said it because I was hungry and I wanted to be first. I went to end of the line and of course I raised a fuss. Everybody wanted to know what the fuss was about. Eleanor got Hasmig to calm me down and I was fine after that. Another time, I had been complaining about two students that monopolize Hasmig. One day I went up to her room and told her that they talked too much. She talked to me and gave me some suggestions to help me with this problem.

Another example is that she cares. For example, my parents met with her a few days after school had started and asked if I could have extra time on some assignments. She said "Absolutely." My dad announced to Eleanor the day after that he was very impressed with her. "I was very impressed with Ms. M.," said he. On the last day of school, Hasmig started to cry because she was reading the letter of appreciation. She had been laid off and would miss us next year.

Hasmig has been very helpful to me. She cares about me and always tries to make me laugh. She got rehired at the end of the summer. Maybe some people that are going into high school will have her.

Throughout all this, Anna was trying very hard to understand social dynamics. She would ask questions about behavior we hadn't seen and, therefore, couldn't answer. She would watch movies like "The Brady Bunch" and pommel us with questions. "Why was the man who wanted to buy their house so mean?" she'd ask. "Why were all the children trying to make money?" "Why was the middle sister so mad at her big sister?" She would also try to figure out the movie's place in the real world and ask questions designed to sort out reality from fiction: "Is he really her brother?" "Is that really her mom?" She had difficulty following the plots, but as she watched the movies she built on her understanding of social situations and she began to see how relationships move the world. But this was only a beginning.

To really understand social dynamics, you have to know that other people may have different perspectives and you need some insight into what they are thinking. Anna's tutor Suzanne tried to help her learn about other people's feelings in the literature they read together. But then, she came up with a project that could really make some inroads. Since she knew that Anna loved the day camp she was attending at UC Berkeley as a Camper in Leadership Training or CILT, she worked with Anna to develop a handbook for new CILTs. Here's an excerpt.

As a New CILT, You May Feel...

Nervous

You have never worked at Blue Camp before. Everything is new to you, and you may feel nervous because you don't know what to expect. You won't know exactly what will happen in your day. Don't worry. All the other new people at Blue Camp feel nervous, too. The nice staff will be very helpful to you. They will explain your schedule to you and tell you where different activities are located. If you don't know where something is, you can always take a buddy with you. If you get lost, you can always ask any staff member for directions, and they will be happy to help you.

Confused

There may be problems you have to solve as a CILT. For example, you may want to help a kid doing an art project. If you don't understand what to do, it will be hard to explain it to the kid. Don't worry. You can ask the instructor or group leader to help you so that you can help the kids. You may also see problems between the campers. If two campers are arguing over a ball, you may want to stop the argument. Don't worry again. You can ask the instructor, group leader, or CIT for help. They will understand that you are feeling confused and may not have experience working with kids. You should watch how they deal with problems, and you will get ideas for next time.

Overwhelmed

There are lots of little kids and many new adults to meet at Blue Camp. You may be overwhelmed by a lot of questions you would like to have answered, how many names you need to learn, your new schedule, and all the new places at the camp. You may even have a lot of kids asking you questions and wanting to get all of your attention. Don't worry. You can always ask counselors, group leaders, or instructors for help. You can also talk about how you are feeling in H2, when you get together with the other CILTs to talk about your camp day.

Excited

This might be your first time working with kids. You may be thinking about how much fun it will be to meet the kids in your group. You may also feel very excited about the different activities you'll be able to do as a CILT. You may be very happy about meeting the other CILTs. Blue Camp is glad you're here. You should share this excitement with the kids. You should have fun doing the activities. Enjoy being a CILT!

Happy

As you participate in the activities with your group, you will probably help campers do some things that they couldn't do on their own. You may also learn how to solve conflicts between campers. When you do activities with the other CILTs, you may feel happy because you learn something new or begin to understand how to work with the younger campers better. Blue Camp is glad you're here and would love to see you again next year. You should feel proud of yourself and all the work you are doing. Congratulations!

Once the handbook was finished, we insisted that Anna give a copy to the camp's program director. The director was so impressed that she passed it on to her group leaders to use in training their new CILTs. Anna was proud, and so were we.

By the time Anna finished high school, she had learned a great deal about social dynamics, but, to her, niceness was still paramount. She would always ask if someone I'd just met was nice, even if we'd merely said "hello." Her first question about any professional encounter was the same. A firm teacher was mean, as was a store clerk who resisted her friendly overtures. She still had a lot to learn.

Academics

Anna worked very hard throughout high school. She wanted to do well, and she wanted to please her teachers. Although she couldn't work late into the night like many other students because she lacked their stamina, she could and often did spend the whole weekend doing schoolwork. Her focus was impeccable, but she needed a great deal of support. In her freshman video class, she had to learn technical skills and make many choices. One day, she came home saying she had to choose a piece of music for her video. This was too much, despite her enormous jazz collection, and she refused to do the assignment. Decisions were difficult, but most of her anxiety in this case stemmed from her uncertainty about the project: since she didn't know how to import the music, its selection became an insurmountable obstacle. Refusing to do something when she didn't understand how to do it became her modus operandi. Then, when she understood and things clicked into place, she would realize that the anxiety was unwarranted. "Is that all it is?" she would ask, and she would happily do the assignment.

Despite her overwhelming anxiety, she was gradually becoming more independent. One day in eleventh grade, when I didn't have time to help her, I suggested she review her chemistry and do the problems on her own. And so she did. Then she decided to type up her vocabulary words and their definitions, even though she'd already written them out, because she felt that the typing would help her remember. When she left for school, she was carrying the typed definitions in her hand so that she could study them on the bus. That was a first! Other days, I came home to find her finishing up a French or an English assignment.

She was beginning to do more things on her own, but only if she knew exactly what she was doing and how to do it. Otherwise, she was so unsure that she was afraid to even try. Meanwhile, her teachers were trying hard to help her become more independent. In her junior year, her IA stopped going to Spanish with her. Foreign languages were Anna's forte; she had a good ear and an intuitive grasp of language structure. In her senior year, her IA stayed out of Spanish and P.E. And when her IA was ill, her full inclusion specialist didn't call in a substitute; Anna had no need for a babysitter who rapped his way across campus or who objected to the tenor of class discussions. Anna navigated those days entirely on her own and sometimes without prior notice. In her super-senior year, her IA came to only one class.

In her senior year, we had a breakthrough. Anna was taking second year algebra. Although she'd had serious problems in geometry because of her spatial deficits, she'd done very well in first year algebra. She began the year constantly asking for help. Perhaps it was hard for her to get her math brain back in gear after a year's hiatus; perhaps she was used to needing help in chemistry; perhaps she was just being sociable. But we knew she could do algebra by herself, and after we all reassured her, that's what she did. Whenever she sat down to do her math homework, she would chase everyone away. We were not to check her answers. We were not to even come near. We worried that she was taking this too far, but we didn't want to undermine her growing independence. So we asked the teacher to monitor her progress and let us know if she saw declines in either her class work or homework. Then we sat back.

Anna was maturing cognitively too. In her sophomore year, she was asked to write a letter from the perspective of the governor of India. This would have been impossible in her freshman year because she wasn't well enough anchored to write from a perspective other than her own. Changing perspective was still difficult, and she couldn't quite transform herself into the governor. But she could take the somewhat less drastic step of becoming the governor's wife. She was also starting to separate fact from fiction. I was a bit concerned when we rented "The Terminal" because we fly frequently and I didn't want her to think she could actually get stuck in an airport terminal, so I took care to tell her it wouldn't happen before we started to watch the movie. "I know," she replied calmly. "It's only a movie." This was a grand leap forward. She was also starting to use context to figure out meaning. When I remarked that her tutor's appointments weren't "carved in stone," she agreed, even though she was unfamiliar with the phrase, and added that the only appointment "carved in stone" that week was the one with Dr. W. Her ability to make inferences in social situations was also improving. When I asked Suzanne, who was a graduate student, how long her dissertation would take, Anna stopped me cold. She had inferred that we were talking about the length of Suzanne's stay in the Bay Area and she wasn't having any of it. But her thinking was still very concrete, and terms like socialism and democracy, which are basic to a high school social studies curriculum, were very difficult for her to understand.

Anna still needed a lot of academic support and she got it. Not only did Suzanne, Alan and I work with her at home, but she had the support of several IAs at school. And she never hesitated to ask her teachers or fellow students for help. Working with her over an extended period could be disorienting. Sometimes, she really knew what was going on and just zipped along. But sometimes, although she looked focused, her brain just wasn't there and she couldn't do even the easiest things. We called it brain fizz. Dr. W. attributed these fizzes to distractibility, anxiety, stress, fatigue and the time of the month. Whatever the cause, pushing on through was not the solution. During a full-blown fizz, she couldn't answer the simplest question correctly. Three times three could become twelve, even though she knew her math facts cold. She had to stop, take a break, and do something entirely different like listen to music and dance. Once the allotted break-time was up, she could frequently sail through the assignment.

But the work was getting harder, even in her favorite subject – French. Although her ear was excellent and she sounded more French than many of her classmates, she was beginning to have trouble with the written exercises. She could conjugate verbs easily, but choosing between verb tenses to complete a paragraph requires sophisticated language processing skills. Students need a clear picture of what each sentence is trying to communicate, an understanding of the ways the actions described are chronologically related. Anna sometimes resorted to random answers. The class was also starting to read literary selections. This added to her already heavy reading load and, in her junior year, precipitated a switch to Spanish.

For Anna, the best academic experiences of her high school career were those based in the real world and those that she was able to select herself. Because they were also larger projects, she spent more time with them and could reflect upon them much more deeply than she did upon other projects. The major project of her freshman year was to create a magazine dealing with an important social issue. Its components included a personal statement welcoming the readers, a research-based article, creative pieces like poetry and artwork, an editorial, previously published articles taken from periodicals, contributions from three classmates and an interview. Since the assignment required that different components be submitted at different times during the school year and then combined into the magazine, it dominated the students' freshman experience. Anna chose to write about AIDS. Her fellow students were horrified, but she was fascinated; illness and hospitals were her thing. This is Anna's personal statement.

Personal Statement

This magazine is about women and children with AIDS. I chose this topic because I am interested in hospitals and health care. I have had eleven surgeries and have spent a total of seventeen weeks in the hospital. I am fine now and I like hospitals because they took such good care of me when I was there. I want you to understand how many women and children have AIDS, how AIDS is spread, how AIDS is treated, the effect of AIDS on everyone, and what people are doing to find a cure. I want you to think about how to help people with AIDS.

This paragraph starts with Anna's usual hospital preoccupation, but it goes beyond that. It moves from the egocentrism of her preoccupation to an other-centered perspective, which is part of growing up.

Anna's best experience with the magazine was the interview. At my suggestion, and with a script from me,

Anna called the communications department of Children's Hospital and explained the assignment. She got an appointment with the head of the Pediatric AIDS Program. She then prepared a series of questions, which the doctor answered patiently, at the right level, and speaking slowly enough for Anna to take notes. Anna also recorded the interview. She had seen plenty of sick children during her hospital stays, but she had never gone beyond the individuals she had seen. This interview expanded her perspective and forever changed the picture she had of "her hospital." It enabled her to be at the hospital in a non-patient role, which in itself was significant. Because the doctor teared up while talking about some of her patients, it helped Anna understand that doctors are real people with real emotions. And it gave her some indication of the amount of work required to run the programs that serve these children.

The doctor then invited us to meet a patient who was HIV Positive but did not have AIDS. She wouldn't tell us the patient's name of course, so Anna used an old trick of Dr. W's: she called her "Notcha," as in "it's notcha (not your) business." Meeting Notcha grounded the interview in a concrete, individual reality. It brought Anna's two worlds together by helping her understand how individual patients fit into the larger world of the hospital. Also, because, unlike Anna, Notcha refused to tell people about her illness, it enabled Anna to see that there could be perspectives other than her own. Some people, she realized, are more discreet.

The other project that was most meaningful for Anna took place during her first senior year. Each student in her small school is required to do an internship involving community service and to write a paper analyzing related issues. This too was an extended, real-world experience of Anna's choice. Anna loves children and chose to work in the after-school program at a local elementary school. Once a week, she supervised kindergartners and first graders as they played, helped them with their homework, read stories aloud to them, and taught them computer games. The children adored her, running to meet her when she arrived and giving her big hugs. She was their "fwenny" (friendie), and they didn't seem to notice the differences that isolated her in school. Anna loved working with them. She learned a great deal too; she stopped "freaking out" at the slightest sign of conflict, her self-confidence increased, and she started to take charge when necessary. One thing that troubled her as she worked was the large number of conflicts she saw. She wondered about the best way to handle them and consequently decided to focus her senior essay on child development, friendships, and conflict resolution in the schools. It was an interesting choice for someone whose development was anomalous, who has difficulty making friends, and who obsessively fears violence. It's another example of Anna's leanings towards top-down learning. Just as a required paper on Louis Armstrong initiated a fascination with jazz and a chapter in *Little House on the Prairie* crystallized her understanding of racism, she used a school assignment to better understand the social mechanisms that often eluded her.

Reading and Writing

Anna still wasn't a reader. She didn't finish many of the books she started and rarely picked up a book without encouragement from someone. She didn't even read labels; she would bring home snacks she hated like spicy chips or peanut M & M's and end up throwing them away. And she would never read anything left lying around, even if it had her name on it. One day during her junior year she brought home an essay topic proposal she'd given to her history teacher. She wanted to do a historical analysis of rock and roll, and the teacher had scrawled a response suggesting that she focus on one musician or singer. As soon as she got home, she thrust the proposal in my face crying "Does this mean I can't do it?" "Just read his comment!" I replied in frustration. "Oh," she said. "I did a duh."

The summer was a great time for working on reading. Although we were busy, Anna worked with Suzanne for at least six hours a week. Freed from the pressure of reading her assignments for school, Anna's reading skill blossomed. The summer before her sophomore year, she read short assignments in Jacqueline Wilson's *The Lottie Project* and *Bad Girls* independently and discussed them with Suzanne. Although she could generally follow the plot line, she often missed major elements because of her social naïveté. In one book, for example, a girl was horrified to find out that the sweater her mother had just bought her at a thrift shop (an embarrassment in itself) had belonged to a classmate's grandmother. Anna didn't understand the reason for either the girl's dismay or her snobbish classmate's glee. The summer before her junior year, she and her friend Erika were looking at books and Anna picked up *Little House on the Prairie*. I had tried to read that to her when she was in elementary school, but she had refused to listen after the protagonist took sick. Illness was too scary, just as the "damage" (this was Anna's term) inflicted on the letters in *Chicka Chicka Boom Boom* had been. But now, illness had become an intriguing fact of life. She examined *Little House* thoroughly, memorizing all the chapter titles, announced she was going to read it, and read two hundred pages in just two days. Sprawled out on the couch, she looked like the print-obsessed teenagers that both Alan and I had been. We were ecstatic. The summer before Anna's senior year we went on vacation with a short list of easy books. Anna read them all, but mostly because Suzanne had assigned them; she wanted to please Suzanne more than anything else. That summer, I also decided she was ready for the books that everyone reads in middle school: *The Diary of Anne Frank, The Miracle Worker,* and *To Kill a Mockingbird.* And so she was. Suzanne divided up the books into short assignments, which Anna read independently and silently. They met three times a week to discuss what Anna had read and to work on writing short essays about the books. It was a relief to see Anna working independently and at a level appropriate for her skills and sophistication especially since she was struggling to work way above that level during the school year.

Part of the problem was that her teachers expected the students to have a fairly good knowledge base and that, except when it came to hospitals and medical procedures, Anna's was much less extensive than that of her classmates. When she was a toddler she hadn't explored the world as thoroughly as other children; she hadn't played with her peers as much when she was older and she had serious social skills deficits. This meant that she really didn't understand how the world worked. She didn't read as she was growing up – although we did read to her – she didn't watch television, and she didn't go to many movies. When she did engage in these activities, her engagement and her learning were limited by deficits in language processing and abstraction. Because she usually saw stories as collections of data bits rather than as whole entities to which the data bits contributed, she had trouble understanding how plot details contributed to a story. In the movie "Finding Nemo," for example, she didn't understand that the fish fouled their tank intentionally so that the owner would clean it and give them the opportunity to escape.

As she got older and made her way through high school, English and history concepts became more abstract. A journal entry she wrote in response to a prompt from her sophomore English teacher shows that her thinking was, however, still very concrete.

Journal 1/16/04

Prompt: If God exists and you could talk to him or her what would you say?

I don't know. I would tell him/her to tell teachers to stop giving too many tests. Right now my friend is now finishing up a test. I think that the test is way too long and I am wondering if she will finish the test and if she doesn't will she stay after school. I also wonder if I will meet her on the way to history if she is done with the test.

The school reading assignments were difficult, and the teachers were beginning to require more abstract reasoning. Students were also expected to connect their reading assignments with previously learned material, to draw their own conclusions, and to form and defend opinions. Anna wasn't ready.

Writing essays, especially literary analyses, was also difficult, partly because Anna's expressive language was still somewhat anomalous. She confused "bought" and "brought." She would occasionally reverse subjects or adjectives, saying the opposite of what she meant: "I'm not big enough for that dress" would emerge instead of "That dress is too small;" "Margretha wanted me to pick you up around noon" meant "Margretha wanted you to pick me up;" and "Angela, dad said I know her brother" was directed at her dad, not at Angela. She would also sometimes misuse conjunctions as in "I wanted poached eggs because I asked for them. " But these anomalies gradually disappeared as she made her way through high school.

More enduring were Anna's inability to construct effective descriptions, which made her writing repetitive and uninteresting; her focus on data bits and the difficulty she had in seeing the whole picture, which made it hard for her to develop cohesive written arguments; and the concreteness of her thinking, which trivialized discussions of abstract concepts. Suzanne and I tried to start at Anna's level by using concrete data bits to help her understand the abstract concepts she was required to write about. Descriptions were the easiest to deal with. Giving her lists of adjectives from which to choose made her descriptions more complex. Other kinds of word lists were also helpful. Providing terms like "plot," "setting," "characters," and "problem resolution" helped structure a literary discussion and enabled her to see the ways in which each of these elements supported her thesis. Brainstorming and formulating thesis statements using the concrete examples she had found helped her see the relationship between the abstract and the concrete. As she moved through high school, she became adept at organizing her thoughts and could produce relatively well organized, but rather thin, five-paragraph essays using concrete evidence.

One change that helped improve her writing to a surprising extent was the purchase of an Alphasmart, which is a simple, lightweight word processor with eight files whose contents can be uploaded into a computer or printer. A laptop computer would have been too heavy for her to carry and too complicated to use, but the Alphasmart was just right. She carried it to school, used it to take notes, and often composed essays on it while sitting on the couch at home. Once the essay was printed out, rather than scrawled on paper, it was much easier for her to improve its organizational structure. In addition, because the Alphasmart eliminated the physical work of writing, Anna's spelling and punctuation improved.

Her best essays were those for which she had a strong knowledge base. The AIDS magazine she put together in her freshmen year is a good example. This is the editorial she wrote for the magazine.

We Need Money for AIDS Education

AIDS education is important. If they had good education, then people with AIDS would be treated better. People would understand what the person with AIDS is going through. They would also understand how you get AIDS and that you can't get it just from being with a kid who has AIDS. AIDS education could help prevent AIDS by teaching you not to have unprotected sex and not to share needles. You need money for AIDS education. People should give money to support AIDS education.

In the 1980s, Ryan White was a 13-year-old boy with hemophilia, which is a disease where you can't stop bleeding. Ryan got AIDS from a blood transfusion that he had to have for his disease. At the time, they didn't know that you could get AIDS from a blood transfusion. They thought that you could get AIDS from just being with a kid with AIDS. The public school system tried to keep Ryan out of school. The people in the community were mean to him. The public school system finally allowed him to go back to school. He got separate eating utensils and a separate bathroom. He couldn't go to the gym or the swimming pool. They had to disinfect the building every night. Even with all these precautions, parents kept their kids home from school. If they had a better education, then they would have understood how you can get AIDS and they wouldn't have done all these things to Ryan.

In 1986, the Ray family lived in Florida. They had three sons and the sons were all HIV positive. The family was told not to go to school. In 1987, they moved to Alabama and were told they couldn't go to school. People were making threats against the Rays. They burned the house up with gasoline. If people had better education about AIDS, then they might not have treated the Rays that way.

In 1988, John and Sharon Boyce wanted to adopt a child. They were afraid that the kid would have AIDS especially since you can't tell if they have the virus until they are 24-26 months old. They found out about Brianna when she was three years old and they knew she had AIDS. But they adopted Brianna anyway because they were educated about AIDS and less afraid to adopt children with AIDS and take them home. They really loved Brianna and treated her very well until she died. They treated her better than people treated Ryan because they were nicer and because they had a better education and a better understanding of the disease.

The people who treated Ryan White and the Rays so badly had a lot of misconceptions about AIDS. For example, people thought you had to be a homosexual to get AIDS. People thought you could get AIDS easily so they were afraid to work with or talk to people with AIDS. So many people were getting AIDS that they got hysterical. In 1987, President Reagan gave a speech that focused on increasing routine and compulsory AIDS testing. People protested against what Reagan said. They were arrested by policemen wearing yellow, arm length gloves. When the people saws this on TV that gave them the idea that it was dangerous to touch people who had AIDS.

People may not understand how AIDS is transmitted. If you don't understand how AIDS is transmitted, then you could get it. You need teaching programs for kids in schools so they won't have unprotected sex or share needles. You need programs for mothers with AIDS to teach them about drugs that will prevent the baby from getting AIDS and that they shouldn't breast feed so the babies don't get AIDS. All people need to know how to prevent AIDS. There is a global AIDS epidemic. The only way to stop it is good educational programs for everyone in every country. You need to have a lot of money for good educational programs. It's up to the federal and state governments to provide the money. So we must all write letters to convince the president, the senators, the representatives and the governor, the state senators, and the assembly persons to give money to the AIDS educational programs.

This essay tells a great deal about Anna herself. It is well organized with a clear introduction and conclusion because, just as Anna requires structure in her daily life, she understands the importance of structure in her writing. The essay reflects her level of understanding in its concreteness and its focus on specific examples, and its choppiness indicates her continuing difficulty with expressive language.

In her junior year she wrote a long paper on jazz and in her senior year, she focused first on healthcare. Then, there was the paper she wrote while doing her internship during her first senior year. It was a long paper about conflicts among school-age children, and it consisted of five parts:

1. Anna's background in the subject

2. A reflection on the paper-writing process

3. An interview

4. The research narrative

5. A list of works cited

Here is her reflection on the paper-writing process.

> When I first heard that I would be doing an I-Search related to my internship, I thought, "Yuck," because I hate research papers; they are too hard. I like working with little kids so I didn't mind going to Thousand Oaks school each week to help with the after school program. I knew that I was going have to do the I-Search, so I decided to research why children have conflicts so that I do a better job

working with kids. I immediately had to begin dealing with conflicts at Thousand Oaks, but I often needed to get a grown-up to help out because I freak out because I don't know what to do. The grown-up helps me understand and get closer to solving the problem. I observe these adults so I can learn, but researching why children have conflicts and what can be done gave me more information and strategies for approaching conflicts in my internship.

At the beginning of this project, I went to the Berkeley Public Library to get some books on why children have conflicts. I used the computer to locate call numbers to find books. Many of the books that I checked out were in the same area because they were all written for teachers and were education books. I also talked to people who have had experience teaching so that they could provide some book recommendations for me. I talked to my tutor about the Vivian Paley book because she used to be a teacher. Because of talking to Sally in my interview, I was introduced to the Second Step program, and my second grade teacher lent me the videos because Sally knew that Mrs. F. had them.

I read the Paley book out loud and marked important passages. I put dashes where someone said what they thought about the new rule. I also read parts of other books out loud. I took notes by typing reasons for conflicts and good ways to solve them in my own words. I did this so I could avoid plagiarism. Then I watched some videos on the Second Step program and took notes to include in my paper, too.

At first I thought that I would interview Ms. Dee Dee, the teacher that I work with in the Thousand

Oaks after school program. As time passed, I was running out of time to get an interview scheduled and I couldn't get the courage to ask her. I was afraid she might say. "No." My mom suggested that I interview Sally G. because she is a retired elementary school teacher. Since she is someone I have known for my whole life, I am comfortable with her. But this doesn't mean that the interview was easy. Sally pushed me to explain myself and give definitions of what I am talking about. I think this helped me write the paper.

I wanted my research paper to have an interesting beginning so I thought about my own experience. I described it vividly to hook the reader's attention. Then I planned a mock-up of my paper. I thought about what the paragraphs should be and how I should organize them. Then I looked through my notes, putting them into categories to write the paper. As I was putting the ideas together, I had a hard time. This was because some of the ideas were hard and some of the language in the books was challenging, too. It was really difficult to imagine all the different ways of dealing with conflicts and to pick the best one. Instead, I tried to find portions that I understood well that could be combined. I tried thinking of ways to apply what I learned to solve problems in my internship and over the summer at camp.

Four years had passed between the two essays, and the changes are enormous. With Suzanne's help, Anna had become more reflective, her style more natural, and her language more flexible. But her difficulties with reading and writing were far from resolved. She and Suzanne would have to put in many long, hard hours before Anna would be ready for post-secondary education.

Mathematics and Science

Anna had done very well in the first year of algebra despite a tendency to make copying errors such as substituting a plus for a minus, and visual-motor deficits which made it difficult for her to line up the digits in complicated arithmetical problems. We joked that she'd gotten the math gene from her father, the mathematician. But she faced geometry in tenth grade, and we worried about her ability to reproduce or even understand geometrical figures. Drawing a piano, for example, was very difficult for her, even though she knew what pianos looked like. When she asked an articulate, visually oriented friend of ours how to draw one, she was told, "You start with a rectangle. Then you divide the rectangle into keys, putting black keys between the white ones." This is what Anna drew:

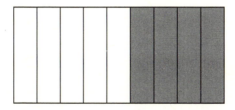

Identifying corresponding parts of two similar figures was very hard for her. She couldn't always see that side AC corresponded to side DF.

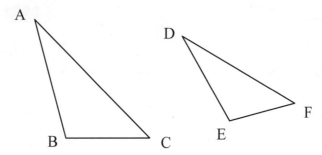

Given a circle, she couldn't tell which angle belonged to which arc.

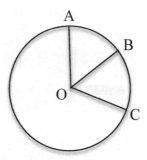

She couldn't see that AB was the arc for AOB and BC was the arc for BOC. Alan compared it to an ice cream cone, but that didn't seem to help. The only thing that did help was having her trace the whole angle, putting her fingers on the points where the angle intersected the circle, and then having her trace the arc.

Even though she knew what parallel lines were and understood their effect on a figure, she couldn't use this information to make inferences about the figure. So, for example, it was very difficult for her to see that in this figure AB = FE + DC – that is, since AB = 6 and FE = 4, then DC = 2.

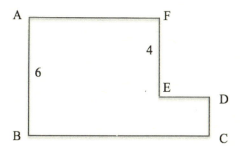

Similarly, it was also very difficult for her to see that in the figure below the length of the slanted side can be found by drawing a right triangle with the slanted side as the hypotenuse, inferring the length of the two legs and using the Pythagorean Theorem.

That is:

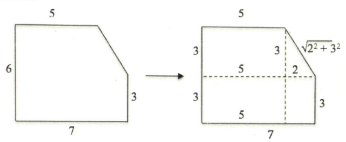

We would break each problem down step by step to make sure she understood the logical connections and have her trace figures with her fingers to mitigate her perceptual difficulties.

Anna took chemistry in eleventh grade, and the homework was long and difficult. Alan usually had to explain it, to reinforce the class discussions. But once he did, Anna was off and running. Monitoring was still necessary, since she tended to copy numbers, signs, and figures inaccurately, but she really did know what she was doing. Forging through her chemistry assignments also helped her to develop more complex attitudes towards work. She would complain the class was hard while simultaneously admitting that she actually liked the material. She had never liked such a difficult class before. The class taught her to be more adaptable. The assignments were long and the teacher fairly flexible about due dates. Anna was beginning to accept that she didn't have to finish all of her work the minute it was assigned. Her attitude toward schoolwork was improving. Although she had an enormous amount of work, as is typical for the junior year, she was handling it well. She would spend most of her free time working, and one Saturday, as she sat with her head buried in books, she remarked, "I've stayed home all day, but I like it!" No longer was she crying and moaning simply because she had work to do.

Anxiety

Anna's anxiety increased during the first two years of high school. Work was hard, teachers' requirements confusing, and social situations mystifying. Even when the work was easy, she craved reassurance and would seek help from anyone – her IA, a friend's teacher or a random adult walking down the hall.

Anxiety ruled. It crystallized whenever she had to wait in line; to make the line move faster, she would yell out "my turn" or "skip them" and sometimes she would push the people ahead of her. It focused on pleasing teachers; her hand would shoot into the air before the teachers had finished their questions. It intensified her fear of being late; she would pack up ten minutes before the bell rang so as to arrive at the next class on time. And it drove her to exhaustion; she always insisted on going home the minute she was dismissed. On the first day of standardized testing in her freshman year, she picked her lip so much that it bled. I had to cut out of a conference call, call the doctor to get a prescription for antibiotics, take BART to my car, drive to the pharmacy and take the antibiotics to the school. I didn't really think she'd get endocartitis (infection of the heart wall) from picking her lip, but we had to be careful.

The transition between home and school was difficult. Alan drove her in most days during her freshman year. She considered him a "dawdler" and felt responsible for making sure they left on time. The ritual would start at least half an hour before they were to leave: "Take your shower," she'd bellow. "Put on your shoes." Her voice would get louder, her tone stentorian: "No pee! It's time to go." He wouldn't stand for it and risked hysteria by putting her in her room for five minutes. When I picked her up in the afternoon, she pushed me to get her home as fast as possible. "Go!" she would cry, while I waited for cars to pass before pulling out into traffic. "Don't stop!" she would yell when I stopped for a pedestrian. Doing errands on the way home was out of the question.

Once we got home it was time for homework; she insisted on doing it the minute we walked in the door. The sessions went well if the assignment was clear and she felt she could handle it. But since the work assigned during her sophomore year was long and difficult, she couldn't always finish up on time. One day she refused to go to school. She made her point, as usual, by crying and screaming loud enough to be heard on the other side of town. But now she could also verbalize her concern; she knew that she wouldn't be able to finish her history packet by the day it was due. When we reminded her that her IEP allows extra time for assignments but that she'd have to warn the teacher, her screams grew louder. The teacher had made it very clear that no extensions would be given, and Anna's reasoning didn't brook exceptions. She calmed down and went off to school only after Alan wrote her teacher a letter requesting more time and noting that this accommodation was specified in her IEP.

Anna's anxiety didn't let up even after homework was done. She was having trouble sleeping and would lie awake in bed for hours. She worried when guests didn't arrive exactly on time. "Where are they?" she'd yell. She worried even more when Alan was a few minutes late coming home from one of his frequent business trips. "Where is he?" she'd whine. "Is he dead?" She'd watch our aging dog closely as he slept, anticipating his death, and get up in the middle of the night to check on him. And phone calls had become traumatic once more; she would jump up from whatever she was doing and, cursing at the top of her lungs, run to answer. She was also picking at her fingers and at her face.

Outings had to be carefully planned: we had to specify what we were going to do, when we were going to do it, and how long it would take. Whenever we suggested something she had never done before, her response was "just plain no" - "NO!" to a ranger presentation at a national park, "NO!" to the Cirque du Soleil. But we ignored her screams, reassured her, dragged her grumbling to the performance, and were always rewarded with smiles, laughter, and sometimes wide-eyed rapture. One day, a classmate invited her and Erika home to watch a video. Anna didn't want to go because this was a new experience with new people. She didn't even tell us about it until Erika called to give her the address. Then it was tantrum time: she screamed; she yelled. But I had promised to drive, so she let herself be loaded into the car. We picked up Erika and headed over, but we couldn't find the house. After I made two carefully calculated right turns expecting to see it, all we saw was a grocery store. Something was not right. It was getting later and, horror of horrors, we were not going to be on time. Anna started screaming "we're late" and trying to persuade herself that it didn't matter. "They won't give a darn," she insisted. Erika couldn't stand it and started yelling "shut up." I made a U-Turn thinking that the house was on the other side of the street and found the numbers were much higher. Then I went back to the grocery store; it was still a grocery store and the numbers were too low. So I called the girl they were visiting and found out that Erika had given me the wrong address. But the circus continued:

"Please read the addresses," I asked Erika. Anna was screaming.

"2320," yelled Anna, "we're here."

"Stop lying," said Erika.

"OK, I'll stop. It's not right. Keep driving."

"2320," yelled Erika.

"Are you sure?" I asked.

"Yes, we're here," she replied. We got out of the car, locked it up and discovered we were at 2220.

"I'm not getting back in the car," yelled Anna.

So we walked – two long blocks in the dark. I tried to be friendly when we arrived and laughingly described our adventure, but it was too much for Anna; I had served my purpose. "Leave!" she screamed. "I'm going!" I screamed back, sighing and rolling my eyes at the mother of the house. Another pleasant evening with Anna, Erika and Anna's anxiety.

Any plans we made were set in concrete. Changes were out because they implied that anything could happen, and dissolved Anna's fragile sense of control. One day, we decided to take Anna and her friends on a tour of a chocolate factory. To help her organize the outing, I drew her a matrix with four possible dates on the top and her friends' names on the side. I had her call each of the girls to find out their availability and, once she found a date that worked, call the factory to make the reservation. Unfortunately, I neglected to tell her to call her friends with the date she'd selected and the inevitable confusion arose: Erika left a voice mail suggesting a different outing for the same date. Anna was devastated. She tried to control her tears because Suzanne was coming. She had to get it together and focus on her work. But it was hopeless. She had worked so hard to set up the tour that she couldn't consider alternative dates or even gear herself up to explain to Erika that she'd already made the reservation. I had to do the explaining. Another time, a movie Anna and her friends were planning to see left the theater. Even though she'd never heard of the movie that had been originally suggested, she refused to consider another. She preferred to do nothing at all.

Anna's impatience was legendary. She couldn't wait in line. She wouldn't buy discounted BART tickets or order a yearbook because it meant waiting in line, and she wouldn't wait for a restaurant table. One day, we decided to go to a Chinese restaurant, which was, unfortunately, much too popular: the line was almost a block long. Anna surprised us. She gathered her forces together and waited, listening to our friend's stories about her students. Then, Alan went in to see how much longer we'd have to wait. Big mistake. His momentary disappearance set her off: the fussing began, then the crying. She just couldn't stand it anymore. "Let's go!" she yelled. Alan came out and she was off – back to the car – in the wrong direction. Alan tried to stop her by grabbing her hand, but the physical contact was more than she could bear: she lashed out and punched him in the stomach. By the time we got to the car, she had completely forgotten what she'd done. But she had not forgotten how angry she was and she soothed her spirits muttering "f-u-c-k-y-o-u" all the way home. She wouldn't actually say the words. Another day, we arrived at a dim sum restaurant in San Francisco only to discover a long waiting list. We resigned ourselves, but she couldn't. She started muttering, "Not them. It's our turn." She moved on to forceful hand gestures: pointing to herself, making faces, and shaking her head like a very strict teacher reprimanding a particularly obstreperous pupil. I tried to ignore it, knowing that any intervention would increase the volume of her protest, but it was too much for Alan, and the shouting match began.

Anna's behavior got worse and worse. One morning, she was slated to go bowling with a school club. New experiences like this made her very anxious. She exploded and jabbed me in the ribs when I told her she'd have to empty her lunch box before I gave her the money she needed. Then she grabbed the money. She couldn't understand why I took it back because she didn't know what she'd done. She had been blinded by her anxiety.

Anna hated this kind of behavior, she really did. But she couldn't control it because the anxiety at its base was too overwhelming. We tried punishing her, and when that didn't work, punishing her some more. But punishments work only when a child is reflective enough to predict her behavior. Since anxiety precludes reflection, it was the anxiety we had to deal with. We turned to the psychiatrist. He advised us to increase the Buspar she was already taking and suggested Inderal, which many performers use to alleviate stage fright, for test taking and other high anxiety situations. We gave Anna her first dose of Inderal for the Passover seder we held in the spring of her sophomore year. She had been singing the four questions beautifully in Hebrew since the age of ten, but now she was becoming more self-conscious. She no longer wanted to be the center of everyone's attention and, in her freshman year, had sung the questions with her back turned to our guests. This time, she sat through the entire ceremonial dinner without hounding us, and when it came time to sing, she sang out clearly, looking straight at her audience. Her teachers also reported that she was much calmer. It seemed that the increased dose of Buspar and the addition of Inderal were really helping.

Once we reduced the anxiety to more manageable levels, it was time to tackle the unacceptable behaviors. We had to tighten the screws. Anna would often take the bus home with Erika during the second semester of her sophomore year. She couldn't stand what she called Erika's "dawdling," which consisted of talking to the teachers and moving slowly, and she tried to speed things up by kicking Erika and covering her mouth so she couldn't talk. Their teacher put a stop to that behavior by threatening to call Security. When Anna lost the thread of a teacher's lecture and couldn't get back on track, she'd put her fingers in her ears and yelled, "shut up." Going to On-Campus Suspension took care of that one. After all, she really did want to be a "good girl" and please her teachers. Her behavior slowly grew more appropriate.

At the end of Anna's sophomore year, we had her IEP meeting. This meeting is held every year to establish the goals, objectives, procedures, and accommodations for the following year. All staff members providing services, including at least one general education teacher are expected to attend, along with the parents and (now that Anna was in high school) the student. Anna had been present during her freshman IEP meeting, but only in body; she had wandered around the room, refusing to participate and hadn't appeared to be listening. This year, she acted like most kids would act: she insisted the meeting was boring and that she didn't like being the center of attention, but she sat in a chair, listened, and responded when addressed. We wondered if the increased dose of Buspar was responsible for the change. During the meeting, everyone lauded the social gains she had made. We noted that she was starting to hang out with one or two "neurotypicals" – typically developing students. We also noted her frustration at the level of discussion in her English and history classes; it was often over her head, although, determined to participate, she held on. But the biggest problem, one that even her first grade teacher had complained about, was that she rushed through everything. She was in such a hurry to finish her assignments and tests that she couldn't show what she actually knew. The full inclusion specialist noted that her entire caseload of special education kids, except Anna, took advantage of the extra time they were allowed; they would take six hours to do a three-hour test, but Anna would finish any test in less than one hour. And never mind proofreading or checking. Anna heard these comments and she listened. Before the meeting, she had already taken most of that year's state standardized tests, but there was one left, social science, and she actually slowed down when she took it. We wondered if the Inderal was helping.

Anna's junior year started out very badly. Although her IEP clearly stated our intention to alternate science and math, she had somehow been scheduled for both and had to drop her algebra class. She obsessed, she fussed, and she whined. Then one day she threw up. She didn't tell us though. She told only her tutor Suzanne, blithely assuring her that the shunt was not failing and that she was merely stressed out. Tension grew as the homework assignments started to ramp up, and any suggestion that she edit her work was greeted with red-faced screaming.

But then, she began to calm down. She was comfortably ensconced at Berkeley High, she had friends, and it had been a full three years since her last surgery. When her Spanish teacher asked the students to ignore the bell signaling the end of class and keep their books open until she said "adios," Anna forced herself to sit quietly. This was a major change. She was also beginning to realize that she couldn't always be first and stopped protesting when teachers called on other students before her. Her attitude towards work was improving. The work was hard, the workload was heavy, she would sometimes spend a full weekend working, and she needed a tremendous amount of support, but she would usually forge ahead without screaming. She was even becoming more willing to edit.

Home life was getting easier too. For one, Anna was loosening her stranglehold on the phone. We could make calls whenever we wanted, as long as we let her know whom we were calling. One night, Jerry, her nemesis, called just after she'd gotten into bed. A few years ago, that would have been a catastrophe. But times had changed. "There's no point in getting all riled up just because Jerry called," I said, as I'd said many times before. There was no screaming. Anna merely looked at me, nodded, closed her eyes, and went to sleep, while Alan talked on the phone.

Her attitude towards illness was becoming more realistic. She woke up on her seventeenth birthday with a bad cold. The timing was particularly unfortunate since birthdays, with their hoopla and associated fears of growing up, had always made her anxious and since her shunt had failed on her fifteenth birthday. On her sixteenth birthday, she had expected her shunt to fail and was astonished when it didn't. But now, she just had a cold, and she was determined to carry on. So she did – through a tutoring session, some visitors and her planned birthday celebration with three of her friends. But that was just Anna, the survivor, the unstoppable. What had changed was her ability to admit that she was sick and her realization that colds do not generally land you in the hospital. When we ran into Dr. W. during the birthday celebration, Anna proudly introduced her friends and announced that she was sick. She knew that her illness was only a cold.

She was even getting better at waiting for doctors' appointments. One day, when we went to see Dr. W., we found a woman sitting in the waiting room. Her son was with the doctor. The woman, who appeared to have had considerable experience dealing with children like Anna, carefully explained that she was going to spend a few minutes talking to the doctor after her son came out. Anna was not happy, but she controlled herself, chatting first with the mother and then with the son, for twenty-five full minutes. A first-time achievement that would be repeated with increasing frequency as she matured.

But the sailing was far from smooth. Anna's anxiety began to increase once again in the spring of her junior year, along with the number of tests she had to take. She would pick her lips until they bled, and she had trouble sleeping. She would watch the mail obsessively when progress reports were due, even though she usually knew her grades in advance, and she would scream when she saw the report on the table. Seeing the report upset her so much, in fact, that I took to telling her the grades before letting her see them.

Afternoons were hard. Anna would come home from school wanting to relax, loosening the tight grip she'd kept on herself throughout the day, but knowing she had enormous amounts of difficult work to do. She wanted to start immediately, allowed no time for a snack, and wouldn't change her clothes no matter how uncomfortable she was. She demanded reassurance and I had to sit by her side. Sometimes, although she appeared to be focused, her anxiety would distract her so much that she couldn't function. It weakened her already shaky reading comprehension, especially if she thought plot details made no sense. When reading about a rebellion in Pakistan, for example, she couldn't understand why the rebels would be starting fires and insisted that "petrol" was actually being used to extinguish them. A complex math problem, which she really did know how to solve, would become impossible when anxiety clogged her brain. A problem asking how much fertilizer was needed in a garden plot, for example, would generate so much anxiety that she could not perceive and execute the necessary problem-solving steps.

Anna always insisted on getting right to work when Suzanne came for tutoring. A few minutes of socializing, the usual exchange of pleasantries, could produce nasty comments and gestures, and any serious discussion an explosion. Although I tried to prepare her for Suzanne's visits, making sure she understood that we had to plan the session, she couldn't stand the delay. One day, after trying hard to maintain control, she started yelling and flinging her arms out in a "cut" gesture. Since her behavior was just as intolerable at the end of the session, I informed her that Suzanne would leave without working with her if this behavior continued. But the threat worked only that one time. A more effective means of helping her maintain control was to prepare her for the visit, set the timer for the amount of time needed for pre-session discussion, and make sure not to exceed the time limit. With Anna, structure was paramount.

Anna's anxiety would come to a head when she was faced with MRIs. Although she coped with the MRIs themselves fairly well, other stresses – academic work in particular – could precipitate tantrums. A few days before her April, 2004 MRI, Anna told us she had read part of an assigned novel on her own. It was a lie. "Write me a summary," she begged. "But your teacher wants you to read the whole book, not just a summary," I countered. Then Suzanne tried to convince her to start reading. Anna hit the ceiling: crying, screaming, yelling that she hated school. She threw a toy at her bedroom wall, making a huge dent, and I feared I might be next. "I want to hurt someone," she sobbed. "Go hit your pillow," I said, and she did. Alan thought changing focus would help and tried to get her to do math. Of course, it was no go. She couldn't focus and tempers rose. It was 7:00 PM. I sought refuge in the kitchen, shaking as I sliced beans, seething as I sautéed fish. At first, Anna was too worn out to eat. It was only as we returned to our routine, asking her how her day had gone and listening to her stories, that she got hungry. After dinner, she and I worked painfully through the math and she went to bed without doing any of the reading.

Anna's anxiety had many sources: the difficulty of her schoolwork, the frustration caused by her learning differences and, most important, the fear that she could end up in the hospital having surgery at any moment. Her difficult behavior stemmed from that anxiety, so we tried to be sensitive to its origins. We tried to remain calm when she yelled at us because screaming back would only exacerbate the situation. We learned to avoid physical restraint because she would lash out physically in return, and we didn't want anyone to get hurt. Each situation required a different response.

Sometimes we had to accept her behavior, inappropriate as it was, and steer into it, as you would into a skid. We knew we were in for it when we had to wait our turn in a restaurant, at a theater, or at a doctor's office. "Skip them!" she would bellow when the family ahead of us got their table. "It's our turn!" she would self-righteously exclaim when another patient was called to the examining room, and once in the hospital she cheerily responded "I'm here!" to the other patients' delight when the name "John" was called. Alan tried to clamp down on this behavior, but it rarely worked and such efforts usually degenerated into shouting matches. One day, we unexpectedly encountered a line at a local restaurant. Anna managed to wait fairly calmly for a few minutes, though her anxiety was mounting. I carefully kept my distance, watching from afar, noticing how well she was doing and how fragile was her control. I knew that any contact with her would break the bubble with which she'd surrounded herself. I said nothing, but the friend we were with felt impelled to comment. "You see," he said, "waiting's not so bad." The bubble burst. Our friend's comment crystallized the anxiety that Anna was trying so hard to control, and she hit me. Hoping to save the situation, I did not clamp down but instead, gave her a "don't hit me" look and continued to keep my distance. She regained control. Five minutes later, when our table was ready, I praised her for good waiting, but I also told her I would not tolerate hitting. She didn't even remember that she'd hit me, agreed not to do it again, and hasn't ever.

Sometimes – usually only at home – we had to clamp down on the behavior, yell loud enough so that she could hear us over her screaming, or just leave the room. One day, she and I were working on a particularly difficult homework assignment. "You make me work too hard," she cried. "Not me," I replied. "I'm only trying to help. It's your teacher who makes you work hard." "Well, I'm going to slap you," she yelled. That was too much. I sent her to her room, but she wouldn't go, and I wasn't going to get into a shoving match. So I took the newspaper and went into my own room for ten minutes. She was calm, repentant, and willing to work when I came out.

Sometimes we had to eliminate, as much as possible, the anxiety causing situation. One day, Anna came home with a long chemistry assignment that covered material the teacher hadn't taught yet and some other, less difficult homework. It was too much. She wanted to do it all because she always does. But she couldn't possibly, and the screaming began. It continued for half an hour despite my attempts to let it play itself out. Then I tried suggesting she take deep breaths, but that didn't work either. Finally, I had to take charge. I told her that she wasn't going to finish it, that I would write a note to the teacher, and that we were going to walk the dog and get a pizza. The only way to calm her down was to forget about the homework that day.

Sometimes, we had to give her another focus, something she could do instead of submitting to her anxiety. One day, while I was trying to talk with her pediatrician after her physical exam, Anna started muttering. The muttering escalated into screaming and threats of bodily harm: "No more talking," she yelled; she wanted to go home "NOW," and I was a "bitch" because I wanted to talk to the doctor. I had to give her something else to do, a structure, so I told her to walk up and down the hall five times and that I'd be ready to leave when she had finished. She did and I was.

Anna's anxiety still ruled our lives. She had been on Buspar for some time, but finally, her prescription had run out, and her psychiatrist would not renew it without seeing her. So we trucked over to his office. There she sat as if frozen, rooted to the chair, her arms tightly folded, the intense effort she was making to control her anxiety painfully obvious. The psychiatrist suggested we try a small dose of Zoloft. He hoped it would dampen her anxiety and reduce some of her obsessional behaviors. He had been unwilling to use SSRIs previously because of her heart, but now her heart was in good shape. We had been unwilling because we just didn't like pills, but we knew that something had to be done now—for all of us. Anna took the high school exit exam a few days after we started the small dose, and for the first time, without prompting, she took six hours to finish a three-hour test, she read both tests aloud, and she made a real effort to do her best. She was finally willing to use the accommodations specified by her IEP, and, as a result, she passed the math portion of the test. She was also becoming more willing to put off work when necessary and to stop work when tired. As her junior year went on, she began to take full advantage of all her accommodations. She took extra time on all tests and requested extra time for many assignments. Her teachers remarked that she seemed calmer and more in control. I noticed that she was better able to assimilate her history assignments, and I attributed this to the reduction in her anxiety. Suzanne said that even her smile looked different.

We had another appointment with the psychiatrist three months later, and Anna was entirely different from the child he had seen before. She sat and listened, saying little, as she had done before, but she was no longer as tightly wound. Then about halfway through the session, she began to squirm and slide off her chair. When I asked why, she replied that we were making her feel uncomfortable. Reduced anxiety had enabled her to become more reflective. The psychiatrist smiled, increased her dose slightly, and suggested we see him again in two months. It was shortly thereafter that she arrived home while I was talking on the phone. Before the Zoloft, that would have set her off, but now, she came in quietly, merely asked who I was talking to, opened her chemistry book and set to work. A big change. Two months later, she announced that the visit to the psychiatrist would be boring and decided to bring her new cell phone along. As she waited for the doctor, she played one of its games. When he called us in, she spoke to him very briefly at my request and then returned to her game, looking like a typical, bored teenager. Again, the doctor smiled and increased her dosage slightly.

One of the first things that happened when Anna started the Zoloft was that her sleeping habits changed: she began sleeping later on weekends, remembering her dreams and reporting them. The dreams, which would often take place in hospitals or relate to medical procedures, served as outlets for her anxiety. In one, she was having some sort of medical test, which required the placement of "stickies" (electrodes) all over her body and which consisted of violent shaking induced by the "stickies." In another, she was taking an academic test with a friend and had to go to her pediatrician to pick it up. This made us wonder whether her acute test anxiety stemmed from her extensive experience with higher stakes medical testing. Right before an MRI, she dreamed that she had to have chemo and that she lost all her hair as a result. Then she had a dream that she reported in somewhat more detail.

> I was in the hospital. I had been there for 3 days. Not doing very well. Then Ms. A. [her full inclusion specialist] came and took me out in a wheelchair to the garden. She said I was doing well. Then I had to have an X-ray on the 5th floor. Someone was on the X-ray bed. I had to swim to it. I couldn't wait till he was done. So I started complaining. But I had to wait. I waited for what seemed like a long time.

This dream links three of her major anxiety sources: hospitals, school and waiting. It shows how they are entangled in her anxiety and indicates how difficult it would be to disentangle them. It also shows how hollow people's assurances may seem: Ms. A. says Anna's doing well when Anna knows she isn't.

Although anxiety continued to plague Anna, especially when her workload became overwhelming or she had a test, the Zoloft made a huge difference. She became more flexible and more and more tolerant of changes in plans. One day, when we had left the house for a birthday party leaving the present on the kitchen table, she suggested doing something she'd never been willing to do before—going back to get it. Another day, we were heading to a symphony performance in the city when I discovered the Chinese New Year Parade was scheduled nearby for later in the day. She was eager to stay for the parade and, when storm clouds appeared, accepted the possibility that we might have to leave. When her friend invited her to graduation on the day she was scheduled for a camp interview and I was scheduled to help at the graduation, she sailed through several plan changes, negotiated an increasingly complex day, and handled the interview well.

There were many other changes after Anna started the Zoloft. In school, she took full advantage of all the accommodations she was eligible for. Spending four hours on a two-hour test became the norm, and she would periodically ask for extra time on assignments. She developed a more realistic perspective on the workload, which enabled her to work more independently, to stop work when she knew she couldn't finish and to keep herself from becoming overwhelmed most of the time: as she put it, "I'll do this one nibble at a time." She matured emotionally, became more reflective and became more willing to discuss some of her fears. And she started to enjoy her birthdays without expecting the shunt failure that dominated her fifteenth or worrying so much about the implications of growing older.

She began to do a better job of controlling her impatience. The summer before her senior year, she took public transportation with her independent living skills group. Some of the girls didn't move as quickly as she would have liked, and she was afraid they'd miss the bus. "Let's go," she'd cry, pushing and pulling in her urgency. We took a closer look when her teachers reported that she seemed irritable. She had finally gained enough weight to look like a real teenager, so the Zoloft dose was becoming less effective. We increased it, with the psychiatrist's permission, and even waiting in line became easier. In her senior year, she stood in line to buy BART tickets and to order a yearbook, and she overcame one of her long-standing phobias. There is a restaurant in Berkeley, which is known both for excellent Japanese food and extremely long lines; customers generally arrive half an hour before it opens at 5:30 and stand in line outside. Anna was never able to forget the pain of waiting one day when she was about eight years old and had adamantly refused to try it ever again. Until we increased her Zoloft. Although she was not pleased about waiting in the line, there were no meltdowns and she truly appreciated the quality of the food.

Graduation

High school was hard for Anna. The work was hard and the social situations harder still. But she's always been a survivor, and in high school she did much more than simply survive. She completed all the graduation requirements, including the more rigorous university eligibility requirements, with excellent grades. In California, though, there was one more requirement, one that could have prevented her from getting the high school diploma she so richly deserved: the California High School Exit Exam (CAHSEE). The CAHSEE, which tests competency in English reading comprehension and writing and in mathematics, first became a requirement for graduation in 2006. That year, because of a court case, special-education students were exempted from the requirement. But Anna was to graduate in 2007. She took both tests for the first time in 2004.

Anna's reading comprehension is fair. She can answer questions about what she has read and write a passable essay, and she has a good head for math. But she cannot take standardized tests. I've seen her try. Tests are handed out, her anxiety level rises, she begins to shake and the multiple-choice options run together. Even when she manages to control her anxiety, the very format of the exam becomes an obstacle. In the reading comprehension portion of the test, she had to analyze four decontextualized statements and determine the relative extent to which each one answered the question. Each statement presented its own difficulties – unfamiliar words, idiomatic expressions, and figurative language for example. But none of the statements provided the contextual clues that she was used to seeing in her everyday reading. In the math test, the multiple-choice answers played into her perceptual difficulties: pluses became minuses, decimal points floated, and numbers mutated. Anna decided that the CAHSEE was a stupid test and that she didn't care about it.

Despite that Anna tried her best. After zipping through the tests in March, 2004, failing them both and starting on the Zoloft, she retook them in November, spent six hours on each one, and passed the math portion. It took her three more tries to pass the English portion, and in May 2006, we were finally able to celebrate. But passing these tests, especially the English portion, was no easy task; it required enormous amounts of work, in addition to her usual academic load. After her first attempt in 2004, Suzanne, Anna, and I spent the summer going over the sample test questions that had been released by the state. I did the math and Suzanne, the English. Anna passed the math portion that November, but failed the English portion by ten points even though her score had increased astronomically. The next test was given in May 2005, but Anna's workload precluded much studying, and she failed—this time, by only four points. Although we were getting desperate, we had other fish to fry that summer. Anna and Suzanne were reading some real literature, they spent only some time preparing for the test, and Anna failed again by only four points. The school year went on. This time, as the March 2006 test date approached, I shouldered the full responsibility for helping Anna with her class work, while Suzanne handled the CAHSEE preparation. I also took another look at the test accommodations. Special-education students are allowed to have accommodations such as extra time and a quiet place to take the exam. The state provides a long list of acceptable accommodations that don't change the nature of the test and that, unlike the more substantive modifications, do not require any special procedures. After reviewing the list, we added two more accommodations to Anna's IEP. Now that she was spending approximately six hours on most standardized tests and fatigue was undoubtedly affecting her score, we suggested administering the test over two days. We also asked that she be allowed to use a word processor without a spell or grammar checker – that is, her Alphasmart. Since we knew that using the Alphasmart improved her spelling, punctuation and organization, we hoped that it would also improve her score on the essay. We were right. These extra accommodations and Anna's intensive study sessions with Suzanne did the trick. Anna passed the CAHSEE in March 2006 with nine points to spare. Interestingly enough, her short answer scores had not improved, but she scored proficient on the essay. Organized writing, at least in the form required by the CAHSEE, had become a relative strength. In the process, however, Suzanne, Anna, and I had spent enormous amounts of time on test preparation, when we could have been engaged in more fruitful endeavors. We would have preferred to devote more of that time to school work, to serious reading and writing development, or to the development of Anna's social skills, and Anna would have learned a whole lot more.

Anna would now be eligible to receive a high school diploma in June 2007 after taking biology, the one requirement we had saved for her "super senior" year. But most of the students with whom she'd spent the past four years were going to graduate in 2006. They would have two graduation ceremonies – the school-wide ceremony in which approximately 800 students walk the stage in front of several thousand people and the smaller CAS ceremony. Anna joined in the CAS ceremony at the insistence of her "CASmates."

When the day came, Anna could barely contain herself. She had a beautiful new dress, her four best friends and some of her adult friends were invited, and a barbecue was planned for later. Luckily, she was number ten, first in the second row of graduates, but waiting was still hard and she danced around the stage. When her turn came, a photograph Alan had taken appeared huge on the screen, the song she had chosen, Ella Fitzgerald's "Ding Dong the Witch is Dead," began to play, and the cheers of the CAS community resounded. Anna strode onto the stage and stood smiling, composed as the entire assembly heard what her English teacher had to say.

> Anna is one of the great community builders in CAS. She's always there to greet someone new when they come in, and she's always concerned that the class focus and that we do meaningful work in the class. She keeps me honest. She doesn't let the day slip without something new being developed and brought up. And she's just a fantastic community builder every day in class.

Then, it was Anna's turn. She looked straight at the audience and gave what was one of the most coherent and the most heartfelt speeches of the afternoon.

> I would like to thank Suzanne, my tutor, my parents, all my teachers, Eleanor [her IA], and all my friends for helping me make it through Berkeley High for the past four years. I've enjoyed being in CAS and getting to know all of you. I loved it when we did the dance at the talent show. [Loud cheers.] I really liked the internship because I learned how to deal

with kids. I learned so much and will continue to do it. I will never forget everything I've done in CAS and I certainly will never forget you guys.

She had completed almost all the course requirements for graduation, passed the exit exam, and demonstrated that she was an important part of the CAS community.

But unlike her CASmates, Anna was not finished with high school. She had one more year. It was filled with her classes, her Workability job, her volunteer work and our visits to the small number of local community colleges. She wanted to stay in school, to get the education needed for a medical career of some sort. But since we feared that the community colleges would not provide all the support she needed, we spent a lot of time exploring the options, and the year went quickly.

In May, Anna brought home some exciting news: she'd been chosen for Senior Spotlight. The yearbook staff highlights a small number of individual students for academic, artistic, musical, or athletic achievement. They also choose two students for "Special Achievement." Anna was one of them. She had a half-page picture in the yearbook with a whole paragraph describing her accomplishments, and she was invited to participate in the Senior Awards Ceremony. While most of the kids slouched through the ceremony, she marched up proudly when her name was called and, when the ceremony ended, she actually leaped into Alan's arms.

Then it was on to the real graduation – June 15, 2007. About 7,000 people sat in the blazing sun on the hard concrete bleachers of UC Berkeley's Greek Theater. There were songs, dances, skits and speeches. Then there was Anna. She had decided she was going to speak at the ceremony, and so she'd auditioned, been accepted and participated in the rehearsal just like everyone else. Now, she was standing in front of all those people with a grin as broad as the stage. She looked directly at the audience and gave this speech in her strong, clear voice.

When I first came to high school, I needed a lot of help. I had an aide with me in every class and it was hard for me to make friends. But now I am mostly going around on my own and I deal with other people much better. I get A's and B's in my classes. I also work in the Cafeteria. I'm even giving this speech!

After school I tutor first and second graders at Thousand Oaks School. I started this job as part of my CAS community service, but I liked it so much I continued working at Thousand Oaks even though I don't have to.

I am also a counselor at a summer camp for little kids at U.C. Berkeley. With the help of my tutor I wrote a book to help new counselors learn about the camp.

I like Berkeley High and I'm very proud of what I've accomplished here. I would like to thank all my Berkeley High School teachers, counselors, and aides, all my doctors at Children's hospital, my tutor Suzanne and my parents for helping me get to where I am today.

I'm going to start college in the fall. I'm going to Berkeley City College and I will start taking courses that I hope will enable me to be become a nurse. I want to be a nurse because I want to do as much as possible to help children get the kind of wonderful medical care I got at Children's hospital. I know I can do it, and I appreciate all the help I've gotten at Berkeley High.

The theater exploded in cheers; air horns blared. And she was famous. A store clerk said he'd been there for his sister's graduation and complimented her on her performance. People stopped her as she walked the dog around the neighborhood saying it was the most coherent and moving speech of the evening. Anna was ready for the next challenge.

What Next?

Anna is now twenty-seven years old. She's doing well medically. Her heart is strong, the size of its ventricles relatively normal, and her ventricular pressures good. The remaining brain tumor is small, it doesn't appear to be growing, and she hasn't had a shunt failure in twelve years. Her kidney lesions are very small and, so far, she doesn't appear to have signs of the lung problems frequently associated with tuberous sclerosis. Her back is fairly straight, though growth following the surgery has caused some crankshafting.

When I wrote this book, seven years ago, Anna wasn't ready to move out of the house. But that's exactly what she did four years ago when she joined a program that is teaching her to live independently. She's moving through the program and now lives in an apartment and is honing her independent living skills. She works at a non-profit organization that provides work training, work opportunities, and job placement services for adults with disabilities. Although she started out as a typical employee assembling products, she has moved into the helper position in which she coordinates and prioritizes the supply needs of thirty people. She loves working with people who have more disabilities than she and her supervisors know it. Calling her unofficially an "assistant foreman," they praise the intuition and directness with which she relates to the employees. Perhaps some day, she'll leave this safe environment for a more challenging job, but working with people who have disabilities is her calling.

Lessons Learned

Each time Anna was diagnosed with life-threatening conditions, Alan and I accepted those conditions and entered into partnership against them with Anna's doctors. Once the immediate threat was deflected, however, we did our best to treat her like a "normal" child. We wanted her to lead a "normal" life with "normal" aspirations. Since other children are the best teachers, we enrolled her in regular schools and surrounded her with typically developing children. We didn't see her as "disabled," and she didn't either. When Erika persuaded her to join Best Buddies, a high-school club dedicated to pairing typically developing adolescents with their developmentally disabled peers, she labeled herself non-disabled on the application form.

But there's a downside to refusing to see yourself as disabled. Accommodations and services are available only to people with disabilities. Anna needed to accept the label in college so that she could receive the accommodations she needed. There, she began learning how to advocate for herself – to describe her differences, explain their origin, determine what special assistance she needed, and request that assistance – without feeling disabled. And she's still learning.

In many respects, raising a child with one or more chronic health conditions is like raising any other child. Our goals were the same: we wanted Anna to have a fulfilling life and to grow up to be a happy, productive adult. To give her a good shot at these goals, we treated her, as much as possible, as if she were leading a normal life. This is not to say that we denied reality. Anna had eleven major surgeries. She knows that most other young people haven't had even one and she considers herself something of a record holder. She's almost disappointed when she meets someone who's had more. She has frequent medical tests and doctors' visits, which, though sometimes unpleasant, are just a fact of life.

Alan and I have tried to be equally matter of fact. I stopped attending a support group for parents of cardiac kids because hand wringing was not my style. I couldn't stand it when one of the participants said that she and her seven-year-old daughter had spent the previous night crying because the daughter's heart condition would probably prevent her from bearing children. What made her think she could predict the state of her daughter's heart in twenty years? Didn't she know how quickly medical technology was changing? And what about adoption? When I found that email support groups also had their share of sob stories, I gave them up too.

We try to relax until there's a crisis, and when there is a crisis, we put our heads down and barrel through. Then, when it's over, we collapse – usually one at a time. But crises are not always what they seem. The greatest obstacles to maintaining a normal life are simple viruses and environmentally induced gastroenteritis. Since Anna has a VP shunt in her brain and shunt failure, a life-threatening complication, looks like gastroenteritis, it's hard not to go into overdrive when she develops a headache and starts throwing up. It's hard not to scream shunt failure at five thousand feet when it's just altitude sickness or on a boat in the middle of the ocean when seasickness is to blame, but we do our best to avoid over-protectiveness. That is crucial because over-protectiveness stunts growth, and children with chronic health conditions must become self-reliant and strong – even more so than children without these conditions. But that's not the only lesson we learned. Here are some of the others.

1. Enjoy your child.

It was hard when we were rushing back and forth to the hospital. It was hard even when we weren't because Anna's development was substantially delayed, because she wasn't having an easy time in school, because her impatience and impulsivity often made life difficult, and because she lacked many of the social skills necessary for maintaining relationships. But each child is unique, and experiencing that uniqueness is part of the fun.

Anna has her own wacky sense of humor, an enthusiastic commitment to whatever she's doing, an intense desire to please, and the strength to be what she is. When, as a five year old, she pushed us away, we could appreciate these qualities from afar. Then, when Dr. W. had convinced her that we had not abandoned her to medical maniacs and when she had convinced us that Anna was not going to die after all, we could move closer. Then, Anna settled in for the long haul, and, unlike most teenagers, she felt most comfortable at home. She had no interest in alcohol, drugs or sex and a great deal of interest in just being with her family. Although she preferred to see her friends, she was happy to hang out with us, to see our friends (usually), to go out with us and to travel with us. Now, that's she's making her own life, hanging out and traveling with us is no longer top priority. But we know she's a part of us, and she knows it too.

2. Don't apologize for your child.

We tried to avoid feeling that we had to explain Anna's behavior to strangers – even when she was lying on the floor in the supermarket screaming. It wasn't their business, and any advice would have been offered in ignorance. Anna is different, but everyone is different deep down.

For many years, Anna couldn't handle a local supermarket. It was crowded, the fruit and vegetables displayed were overwhelming, the lines were long, and the cash registers made noises disconcertingly similar to hospital noises. We had to understand all these things before we could begin to acclimatize her to the environment, before we could teach her that it wasn't so bad. Then when it was time, a good friend took up the gauntlet, carrying Anna screaming around the store. Other shoppers were appalled, but Anna was learning an important lesson.

3. Don't underestimate your child and don't let anybody else do it either.

When, at the age of five, Anna was first assessed by a school psychologist, the resulting report put her in a box and glued on the label. It described her performance on the Wechsler Preschool and Primary Scale of Intelligence as follows:

> Anna worked diligently to complete all tasks asked of her. Her performance on this test varied considerably. A significant discrepancy between her Performance I.Q. and her Verbal I.Q. exists. This significant difference between Anna's obtained I.Q. scores suggests that her higher Verbal I.Q. may better represent her "true ability." Therefore, Anna's cognitive functioning appears to be in the Low Average range. Anna's distractibility during the testing may have interfered with her performance.

> Thus, these scores must be considered cautiously and viewed as approximates of her "true" ability.[13]

Dr. W., Alan and I felt that the test had been used predictively, rather than merely as a description of Anna's then current skills. We objected specifically to the words "true ability," "therefore" and "viewed as approximates of her 'true' ability," and we asked that the paragraph be rewritten as follows. Deletions are crossed out and additions italicized.

> Anna worked diligently to complete all tasks asked of her. Her performance on this test varied considerably. A significant discrepancy between her Performance I.Q. and her Verbal I.Q. exists. This significant difference between Anna's obtained I.Q. scores suggests that her higher Verbal I.Q. may better represent her ~~"true ability."~~ *performance at this point.* ~~Therefore,~~ *Currently,* Anna's cognitive functioning appears to be in the Low Average range. Anna's distractibility during the testing may have interfered with her performance. Thus, these scores must be considered cautiously ~~and viewed as approximates of her "true" ability.~~ *Given her current trajectory, there is a chance of significant improvement if her health remains good.*

Although psychologists can formulate prognoses based on their professional experience, these prognoses don't always play out. And prognoses can do more harm than good – they may create unnecessary obstacles for the children, limit their options, and destroy their self-esteem. Anna is a prime example. Dr. W. has told us that when she first started seeing Anna, she could never have predicted that Anna would make it through high school.

Not only did Anna make her way through high school, but she did well.

Instead of focusing on prognosis, we worked with the professionals to make sure we had a realistic understanding of Anna's current strengths and weaknesses. We were then able to collaborate with Anna's teachers to build on these strengths and compensate for – or perhaps even help overcome – the weaknesses. If we hadn't, prognosis would have become self-fulfilling prophecy.

4. Understand your child's anxiety and its sources.

Anxiety, which is typical for children with chronic health conditions, especially if they have a family history of anxiety, is one of the hardest problems we've had to handle. It hobbled Anna's academic performance and could rock the house. She feared medical crises and losing a parent or her dog. She feared tests of all sorts and long, difficult homework assignments. She feared buses would never come, and she feared being late.

To help her handle these fears, we had to understand their source and the ways in which they affected her behavior. We had to assess the inappropriate behavior they caused, analyze each situation, and determine how to proceed. If the situation was predictable we would set up a structure to minimize the expected anxiety. Seeing the northbound bus from our kitchen window, for example, assured her that the bus she'd be taking south would be on time because it was the same bus; using a timer to limit working time to an hour made schoolwork less onerous; and having her write down what she was doing every sixty seconds while she waited in line structured her waiting time. We had to deal with unexpected or unavoidable anxiety-causing situations as they came up. Sometimes, we had to sit back and let the anxiety play itself out and sometimes, if possible, we clamped down on the resulting inappropriate behaviors. Each situation had to be separately assessed.

When the anxiety was too debilitating, we turned to medication. Anna would never have made it through high school without the Buspar she started taking in sixth grade and the Zoloft she began in eleventh. Although, initially, we had been reluctant to put her on psychotropic drugs because of her medical conditions and our own, probably irrational, dislike of pills, the resulting reduction in her anxiety made her more reflective and facilitated her maturation. Now, at the age of twenty-seven, Anna has made great strides in learning to manage her own anxiety and control her impulses.

5. Make your lives as structured as possible. Anxiety cannot tolerate unpredictability.

Anna depends on her routines. When she was still at home, she got up everyday at 6:30, got ready for school and walked the dog. She would forget to pack her afternoon Buspar until packing Buspar became part of her routine. After school she would do her homework and attend previously scheduled therapy sessions until dinner. She would never drop everything to hang out with friends because it would have disrupted her routine. Dinnertime was, for us, the most important part of the day, and she participated fully. And, even at the age of twenty-seven, her bedtime routine is still intact.

As Anna got older, she became more flexible, but her routines were still the basis of her home life. Some of them – like dinner, bedtime, and special holiday dinners –

became rituals. As such, they helped shape her world, they helped ensure a level of comfort that enabled her to be productive and happy, and they enriched our lives.

6. Read, read, read!

Many children with chronic health conditions have difficulty learning to read. Reading enriches children's lives and makes it easier for them to meet future goals. Reading to children helps them develop a feeling for narrative, which is essential for academic success. It embeds reading in the family, gives it warm associations, makes it a more social activity, and may motivate them to read on their own.

We read to Anna from the time she was only a few months old. Now, at the age of twenty-seven, she loves being read to and enjoys reading to others, but she will read silently only if absolutely necessary and the book is relatively easy. I don't know if she'll ever become an avid reader or be able to read college-level texts without support, but our persistence, our focus on making reading a social activity, and Suzanne's investment in her reading brought her to the point where she was able to read and analyze such books as *The Diary of Ann Frank* pretty much on her own.

7. Try to surround your child with typically developing children because her peers are the best role models.

Children learn more from their peers than they ever learn from their teachers, and they'll be better equipped to function in the real world when they grow up.

We made play dates with children whose parents were sensitive to Anna's needs. These dates had to be well structured, since Anna was not particularly interactive.

But when they were thoughtfully structured, the kids came back. We also enrolled her in regular schools and, and, because repeated failures would have devastated her self-esteem, we made sure that she had the support necessary to succeed both academically and socially. If a regular school or class had been out of the question, we would have made sure the school had a well-developed plan for making the transition to a regular school or class and frequent opportunities for contact with typically developing children. We also sought out opportunities for such contact in community programs such as the Girl Scouts, youth groups and summer camps. Nowadays, neurologically atypical children who are not overly disruptive will be welcome in many groups, as long as their parents do their share of the work. When Anna's social sphere seemed more limited than it should have been, we started our own group. I asked Anna's teachers for the names and phone numbers of possible candidates, called their parents, and took the kids on excursions. This group was the source of some lasting friendships.

8. Make sure that you have good relations with the schools.

We participated actively in the school community by providing some of the volunteer labor on which schools depend. Joining committees, helping plan and set up events, and even sending Anna to school with treats and classroom supplies raised our family's visibility in the school community. Even though we both worked and were often overwhelmed by Anna's needs, we felt it essential to make positive contributions to the school community. These contributions helped Anna fit into the community and ensured that serious efforts were made to meet her special needs.

9. Communicate with your child's teachers, and make sure they understand her strengths as well as her weaknesses.

We wrote a letter to each of Anna's teachers at the beginning of each school year. The letter described Anna, as well as our concerns, and included a health description. It also included an offer to meet with them. Here is a copy of the letter we sent to Anna's seventh-grade teachers. The scoliosis and the second shunt failure are not mentioned because they took place the following year.

> We are writing to you as school starts because we thought you might find it useful to have some information about our daughter Anna.
>
> Anna has a very complex health history, which is described in the attached letter. As a result of that history, which includes nine major surgical operations, she is an unusual child.
>
> She has many strengths including an excellent memory, good vocabulary and spelling skills, and a reasonably good grasp of math facts. She also has a number of surprising deficits. Her fine motor skills are poor; her reading comprehension is shaky, though reading aloud helps enormously; she rarely picks up on social cues; and she has difficulty with problem solving and conceptualization.
>
> Anna can also be very anxious. That anxiety manifests itself in repeated questions, the need to be first, a tendency to interrupt, occasional tantrums, and a tendency to act out when she doesn't understand an assignment. Despite this, Anna has made tremendous progress over the years. Her

differences have decreased and she generally fits in with her classmates.

As you can imagine, Anna is not always easy to deal with. She is, however, basically a very good (and naïve) kid who wants to please. The best way to make sure that happens and that the 7th grade experience is productive, as Anna's sixth grade math/science teacher Rebecca B. will attest, is to ensure that Anna has a clear understanding of classroom rules and teacher expectations. If she understands, she will not act out. She will, instead, work productively and as effectively as she can.

We have been very pleased with the education Anna has received at both Jefferson and King. We have always worked closely with Anna's teachers and hope to continue doing so this year. We would, in fact, very much like to meet with each of you, either individually or as a group. We hope that can be arranged as soon as possible. Please call us at (phone number) to arrange a time.

Health Description

Anna is healthy now, but her health history is complex.

She was born with several serious heart defects, known as Tetralogy of Fallot and Pulmonary Atresia. Most of these defects were corrected in the course of four major operations at the ages of 2 days, 1 month, 15 months, and 3.5 years. Part of the repair involved implanting a conduit to replace the missing portion of her pulmonary artery. This conduit was replaced last summer because she had outgrown it. The extreme narrowness of her left pulmonary artery could not be corrected, and her left lung is consequently not functional. This is not necessarily a problem as many people have lived well into old age on just one lung.

On June 28, 1996, Anna was diagnosed with a brain tumor. Eighty percent of the tumor was removed, and a few days later a VP (ventricular-peritoneal) shunt was implanted to drain excess cerebrospinal fluid. The shunt failed during the 1996 winter break and had to be repaired, necessitating another short hospitalization. The tumor continued to grow. On April 21, 1998, Anna underwent another operation in which 90% of the remaining tumor was removed and the shunt adjusted. On September 2, 1998, she had an unprovoked seizure. The neurologist says that since this was her first seizure since birth (11+ years), she may not have another; but there is no guarantee.

Several things should be kept in mind because of her history:

Although Anna has no physical limitations, she cannot run as quickly or as far as other children, and has less stamina. She can participate actively in all games but should be encouraged to do so rather than pushed.

Shunts are very strong and cannot be easily broken. They do, however, sometimes fail. Symptoms of shunt failure are clear: they include lassitude, relentless headache and vomiting. Her parents should, therefore, be immediately notified if any of these symptoms occurs.

If Anna has another seizure and does not hurt herself, 911 should NOT be called. Instead, she should be allowed to rest and her parents called to pick her up. If she hurts herself badly or the seizure continues for more than 10 minutes, 911 should be called and she should be transported to Children's Hospital, Oakland.

If Anna is cut inside the mouth, her parents should also be notified immediately. A cut in the mouth can lead to infection of the heart wall since the mouth contains more bacteria than any other part of the body. This type of infection is easily prevented by prompt administration of antibiotics. If Anna cuts the inside of her mouth, her parents will quickly provide the necessary antibiotics.

If Anna is hurt and a trip to the emergency room is necessary, she should be taken to Children's Hospital in Oakland because they know her history.

All important phone numbers are listed below.

Parents

(Parents' names and phone numbers)

Doctors

(A list of Anna's doctors)

Communicating with Anna's teachers on an ongoing basis was harder, especially in high school, but email was an excellent way to keep in touch. We always made sure, though, that our email notes were as carefully written as our letters.

10. Be your child's advocate and teach her to become her own.

Effective advocacy is rooted in communication. It means clearly describing your child's strengths, weaknesses, and the kinds of support services she needs. That was the purpose of the letters we sent to each one of Anna's teachers. It means listening to what the professionals have to say, reflecting on it, and responding calmly and thoughtfully. That's why we had to reply to the school psychologist's assessment described in item 3. It means entering into partnerships with your child's teachers and meeting your child's needs as a team. Most of our IEP meetings addressed everyone's concerns in sociable but well documented conversations. But it also means doing your own research and being prepared. I was the one who found out that breaking a one-day state exit exam into two days and using a word processor without a spell checker were accommodations allowed under state law, and I was the one who called an additional IEP meeting to add these accommodations to Anna's IEP. And it means being vigilant enough to make sure your child is getting the services to which she's entitled. Anna went without speech therapy for several months in high school, and a therapist wasn't assigned until I started calling the school district's office of special education every other day.

Teaching a child to become her own advocate is more complex. It's a gradual process that requires frequent exposure to opportunities for self-advocacy. Anna did not attend her IEP meetings in elementary or middle school. She was, however, required to attend in high school and although she was uncomfortable, she slowly began to participate. Her IEPs included self-advocacy as a goal;

she was gently urged to speak up for herself when necessary; and we all praised her efforts.

11. Get other people involved because raising a child – especially one with chronic health conditions – really does take a village.

In spite of our dedication, we could never have provided all the support Anna needed. Some special services – like speech, occupational therapy, physical therapy, adapted P.E. and tutoring – are available at school. But these services weren't sufficient. A neuropsychologist specializing in children with chronic health conditions was essential. Anna's neuropsychologist assessed her in greater depth and with greater understanding than many of the school psychologists we encountered and helped pry additional services out of the school district. She also suggested activities that helped Anna grow, such as additional services, social-skills groups and community groups that welcomed atypically developing kids. As Anna's schoolwork got harder, we needed tutors. Even though we could handle high-school work, the workload was tremendous, our patience was more limited that that of professional tutors, and Anna was more willing to work with other people. For all that, we needed money. Although our health insurance was good and covered every single one of Anna's medical procedures completely, it did not cover any of these supplementary services, and they are not cheap.

12. Take care of yourself.

Everyone always says this, but it's true. You can't take good care of your child if you don't meet your own needs.

During Anna's hospitalizations, one of us usually spent the night with her. We would go home together only if she was heavily sedated. If she was not, we would alternate bedside duty: Alan would stay one night and I would stay the next. Since neither of us slept much at the hospital, a night at home was essential. Sometimes, after surgery, our bodies forced vacations on us: Alan and I both developed serious respiratory infections after one, and after another I got a sty so big that it seriously (though temporarily) impaired my vision. I worked part time for most of Anna's childhood, partly because it gave me another focus, but I couldn't have worked any more than that.

GLOSSARY
Cardiology Terms

The normal heart has four chambers, two atria and two ventricles. Oxygen-poor blood is pumped from the right side of the heart, through the pulmonary artery, to the lungs. Once the blood is oxygenated in the lungs, it is pumped into the left side of the heart and through the aorta to the rest of the body.[14]

- o Aorta: the largest blood vessel in the heart. It sends oxygenated blood to the rest of the body.
- o Atrium: one of the four chambers of the heart
- o Balloon angioplasty: a medical procedure used to widen a narrow artery
- o Cardiac catheterization or cath for short: a medical procedure in which a tube is inserted through a blood vessel often in the groin and used to diagnose and sometimes treat heart problems
- o Conduit: in Anna's case, a tube inserted to replace the missing part of a pulmonary artery. The tube can be either synthetic or sterilized donor tissue.
- o Ductus arteriosus: the blood vessel which is used to bypass the lungs in the fetal circulatory system and which is supposed to close after birth
- o Echocardiogram or echo for short: an ultrasound scan which enables the doctor to see heart motion and calculate chamber pressures
- o Hypo-Oxygenation: a condition in which the patient is not receiving adequate oxygen

- Lung perfusion scan: a medical procedure used to determine how much blood is going to the lungs
- Oxygen saturation levels or sats for short: the amount of oxygen in the blood expressed in percentages
- Pulmonary atresia: a medical condition in which part of the pulmonary artery has not developed properly
- Pulmonary artery: the blood vessel that carries deoxygenated blood to the lungs so that the blood can take up oxygen
- Pulmonary artery stenosis: a narrowing of the pulmonary artery
- Septum: in cardiology, the wall between two cavities of the heart, either the ventricular or atrial septum.
- Tetralogy of Fallot: a condition in which the circulatory system has four defects. Details vary, but in Anna's case, pulmonary artery stenosis, transposition of the major arteries, a ventricular septal defect, and enlargement of the right ventricle.
- Transposition of the major arteries: a heart defect in which the aorta and the pulmonary artery are in abnormal positions
- Transeptal catheritization: a more invasive form of catheterization in which a tube is threaded through both atria by puncturing a hole in the atrial septum
- Ventricle: one of the four chambers of the heart

- Ventricular septal defect: a hole in the wall between the two ventricles

Tuberous Sclerosis Terms

Tuberous sclerosis is a genetic disorder that causes tumors to grow in the major organs. Although these tumors are not cancerous, they can impair function and cause many of the symptoms that are described below.[15]

- Autism spectrum disorders: developmental disorders characterized by social skills deficits, communication difficulties and repetitive behaviors[16]
- Cerebrospinal fluid: fluid that circulates in the brain and around the spinal cord. It provides nourishment to the nervous system and cleans up waste products.
- Electroencephalography (EEG): a medical test in which electrodes are attached to the head to produce a graphic representation of brain waves. EEGs are used to determine whether a patient is prone to seizures.
- Facial angiofibromas: small benign tumors that generally appear on the cheeks and that can be confused with acne
- Hydrocephalus: a medical condition that prevents cerebrospinal fluid from draining properly and that can consequently increase intra-cranial pressure
- Hypocoloration: lighter color than the surrounding tissues
- Intra-cranial pressure: pressure exerted on the brain usually by an excess of cerebrospinal fluid

- Renal angiomyolipomas: kidney lesions composed of blood vessels, muscle and fat
- Sub-Ependymal Giant Cell Astrocytoma (SEGA): tumor typically found in patients with tuberous sclerosis usually located in one of the ventricles of the brain
- Tonic-clonic seizure: seizure that affects the entire brain and is characterized by loss of consciousness and intense muscle contractions. There are many different kinds of seizures.
- Tumor resection: partial or full surgical removal of a tumor
- Ventricle: one of the four fluid filled cavities of the brain
- Ventriculoperitoneal (VP) shunt: a plastic catheter that runs from the brain into the abdomen and that is used to drain excess cerebrospinal fluid

General Medical Terms
- Apgar score: a scale used to rate the physical condition of a newborn. It is based on heart rate, respiratory effort, muscle tone, response to stimuli, and skin color. One is very poor and ten is excellent.
- Arthroscopical: a minimally invasive way of performing surgery which leaves only a small scar
- Catheter: a plastic tube that can be inserted into the body to drain fluids like urine or for diagnostic purposes
- Computerized tomography (CT or CAT) scan: a non-invasive medical test, which uses radiation to

show pictures of tissue slices and which then reconstructs these pictures into an image of the organ being viewed.
- DC'd: discontinued; used when medical instruments or support are removed from a patient
- Intravenous (IV) pole: a pole holding a bag of nutrients or medication that is being infused through a catheter and needle into a vein in a patient's body; used when a patient cannot take in the nutrients or medication orally
- Magnetic resonance imaging (MRI): a non-invasive medical test, which uses a large circular magnet and radio waves to visualize anatomical structures. MRIs are particularly useful for showing tissue composition and distinguishing tumors from normal tissue.
- Phlebotomist: a technician responsible for drawing the blood used for testing

Education Terms[17]
- General education: the educational curriculum followed by average students
- Full inclusion: An educational placement in which the student spends most of his/her time in the general education classroom
- Individualized Education Program (IEP): a program designed to meet the needs of a student with special needs. In the United States, an IEP is required for many students with special needs by the Individuals with Disabilities Education Act (IDEA). The IEP usually includes information

about academic placement, accommodations and additional services such as speech therapy.[18]
- IEP meeting: a meeting held to develop a student's IEP. It may include the student and usually includes parents, teachers, service providers like speech therapists, and anyone else the parents consider important.
- Neuropsychologist: a clinical psychologist with a Ph.D. who specializes in the "assessment, diagnosis, treatment, and or rehabilitation of patients…with neurological, medical, neurodevelopmental and psychiatric conditions, as well as other cognitive and learning disorders."[19]
- Occupational therapy: occupational therapy in schools tends to focus on helping students improve their fine motor skills so that they can be more successful in academic work.
- Special education: the educational curriculum followed by students with special needs
- Special needs: the individual educational requirements of students with disabilities

NOTES

[1] Brad D. Berman, M.D. and Caroline B. Johnson, Ph.D. Child Development Center Comprehensive Evaluation. Children's Hospital, Oakland, July 9, 1991.

[2] Ann Edelman, Kay Sims, Lois Stokes. Berkeley Unified School District. Psycho-Educational Evaluation. May 27, 1992.

[3] Margaret Zawadski. Berkeley Unified School District. Educational Assessment. February 24, 1995.

[4] Ann Korchin. Berkeley Unified School District. Psycho-Educational Evaluation. April 20, 1996.

[5] Shari Curtis. Berkeley Unified School District. Occupational Therapy Evaluation. February 1, 1993.

[6] Deirdre McCann. Berkeley Unified School District. Occupational Therapy Evaluation. April 2, 1996, pp. 1-2.

[7] For more information, see http://tsalliance.easy.cgi.com/pages.aspx?content=2

[8] A copy of the letter can be found in "Lessons Learned."

[9] For more information, see http://www.upledger.com/therapies/cst.htm

[10] Preceding sections of this book were organized chronologically because they revolved around Anna's eleven surgeries. Since Anna had no surgery in high school, this section focuses on the ways in which her past surgeries and the resulting delays in development dominated and shaped her growth. It is organized thematically rather than chronologically.

[11] Sharon Shapiro, OD. Binocular Vision Evaluation and Perceptual Skills Report. University of California, Berkeley, December 30, 2003.

[12] For more information about the summer independent living skills class, see Schoenfeld, Jane. "Independent Living Skills Can Be Fun. *Exceptional Parent*, March, 2006, pp. 44-47.

[13] Ann Edelman, Kay Sims, Lois Stokes. Berkeley Unified School District. Psycho-Educational Evaluation. May 27, 1992.

[14] For more information, see http://www.heart.org/HEARTORG/Conditions/CongenitalHeartDefects/AboutCongenitalHeartDefects/About-Congenital-Heart-Defects_UCM_001217_Article.jsp

[15] For more information, see http://www.tsalliance.org/

[16] For more information, see http://www.autismspeaks.org/what-autism

[17] For more information, see http://www2.ed.gov/about/offices/list/osers/osep/index.html?src=mr

[18] For more information, see http://dredf.org/special-education/special-education-resources/the-iep-cycle/

[19] http://en.wikipedia.org/wiki/Clinical_neuropsychology